KNIVES AND SCABBARDS

DEDICATION

This work is dedicated to the memory of
Caroline Rochester, 1957–1984,
who worked as an illustrator in the DUA during 1982–3
and drew several of the scabbards included here.

FRONT COVER

The drawing on the front cover by Nick Griffiths,
Museum of London, is based on the original illustration
CUTLER TULDNER, 1425, taken from '*Das Hausbuch der
Mendelschen Zwölfbrüderstiftung zu Nürnberg*', folio 12v.
  The original book is held by Stadtbibliothek
Nürnberg.

MUSEUM OF LONDON

MEDIEVAL FINDS FROM EXCAVATIONS IN LONDON:1

KNIVES AND SCABBARDS

J. Cowgill, M. de Neergaard and N. Griffiths

with contributions by
F. O. Grew, A. G. Vince, T. Wilmott and P. Wilthew

THE BOYDELL PRESS

First published 1987
Her Majesty's Stationery Office

New edition 2000
The Boydell Press, Woodbridge

ISBN 0 85115 805 6

A Museum of London Publication
Museum of London, London Wall,
London EC2Y 5HN
www.museumoflondon.org.uk

The Boydell Press is an imprint of Boydell & Brewer Ltd
PO Box 9, Woodbridge, Suffolk IP12 3DF, UK
and of Boydell & Brewer Inc.
PO Box 41026, Rochester, NY 14604-4126, USA
www.boydell.co.uk

A catalogue record for this book is available
from the British Library

Library of Congress Catalog Card Number: 00-044497

This publication is printed on acid-free paper

Printed in Great Britain by
St Edmundsbury Press Limited, Bury St Edmunds, Suffolk

Contents

Acknowledgments

This monograph is largely the work of Jane Cowgill, Margrethe de Neergaard and Nick Griffiths, although a number of other people have been involved in its preparation. It is impossible to name the many archaeologists who dug the sites which produced the bulk of the finds considered here, nor those whose work behind the scenes, processing and accessioning the finds, allowed this work to take place. Nevertheless, we offer thanks to them all and also to the members of the Society of Thames Mudlarks and Antiquarians for their help at Swan Lane and with the Billingsgate Watching Brief.

The authors would like to thank their colleagues in other departments of the Museum of London, John Clark, Jean Macdonald, Brian Spencer, Kate Starling, Peter Stott, and Rosemary Weinstein. Help and advice have also been given by Dr Ian Stead and John Cherry, both of the British Museum, Mrs Victoria Gabbitas, Keeper of the Northampton Museum of Leathercraft, Dr Sarah Bevan, David Blackmore and Mr A V B Norman of the Royal Armouries, Tower of London, and Dr Ian Goodall of the RCHM. Finally, Margrethe de Neergaard acknowledges her debt to Mr David Watson, without whom her work would never have been completed.

The photographs are the work of Jon Bailey. Leather was identified by Glynis Edwards of the Ancient Monuments Laboratory. Unless otherwise stated the illustrations are the work of Nick Griffiths. Other illustrations are by Sue Mitford (SM), John Pearson (JP), Caroline Rochester (CR) and Despina Savva (DS). Figs. 14, 20, 23 and 32 appear by permission of the Bibliothèque Nationale, Paris, Figs. 15–19, 21–2, 26–7, 31, 34, and 36–8 appear by permission of the British Library, Figs. 25 and 29 appear by permission of the Bodleian Library, Oxford, Fig. 28 appears by permission of the Dean and Chapter of Hereford Cathedral, Fig. 30 appears by permission of the Master and Fellows of Trinity College Cambridge, Fig. 33 appears by permission of the Dean and Chapter of Durham.

A Vince
May 1986

Foreword

This volume, originally published in 1987, marked the first stage of an important series of publications describing and interpreting medieval finds from excavations in the City of London. Previously the only catalogue had been the London Museum's pioneering *Medieval catalogue* of 1940, which had been used by excavators all over Britain and much of Europe.

The programme of intensive archaeological excavation in the City which began in 1973, with the formation of the Department of Urban Archaeology of the Guildhall Museum (from 1975, part of the new Museum of London), resulted in a wealth of material, especially from the many waterfront sites. Here reclamation dumps which could be accurately dated by coins and dendrochronology produced thousands of medieval artefacts. A publication programme with the support of English Heritage began the mammoth task of publishing catalogues, and this volume on knives and scabbards was the first in 1987. Subsequent volumes have dealt with *Shoes and pattens* (1988), *Dress accessories* (1991), *Textiles and clothing* (1992), *The medieval household* (1998) and *Pilgrim souvenirs and secular badges* (1998). We hope that further volumes will appear in due course.

These catalogues are a fundamental work of reference for medieval artefacts and material culture, and should be appreciated throughout Europe. They are among many important publications from the excavations in the City of London in the 1970s and 1980s, under the publication programme directed by John Schofield, Alan Vince and Francis Grew. Other colleagues who have assisted in the production of this publication are noted in the Acknowledgements.

Dr Simon Thurley

Introduction to second edition

Geoff Egan

This new edition, almost fifteen years after this first volume of the Museum of London's series on medieval finds was originally published, provides an opportunity not only briefly to draw attention to further developments on the study of knives and scabbards, but also to take stock of this particular volume's impact and its place in the development of the subject.

It was not clear when the series was first embarked upon just how central it would prove to be to the study of everyday material culture in the medieval period in Britain. Although there are now other major publications of knives from the Middle Ages found at Winchester (Goodall 1990) and York (Ottaway 1992), this remains the largest corpus for the period *c*.1150-1450. While one has to look elsewhere for specific social and institutional contexts for medieval knives, the discovery of so many in London's riverside rubbish, with all the preservative qualities of those deposits, furnishes an apparently random sample from the capital as a whole. It is by no means certain that any comparable assemblage of well preserved, closely dated medieval cutlery will ever become available again.

Further information than that considered in the mid-1980s has, inevitably, altered a number of points of detail and some wider perspectives. The entire dated corpus should be viewed bearing in mind that while the broad dating framework presented here remains valid, there is a trend for some of the defining ceramics now to be assigned slightly earlier than they were at the time the text was in preparation. With hindsight, several of the more elaborate drawings (particularly the

ones of all-over, multiply-stamped scabbards) characterise an era of more fully endowed archaeological provision; these images now stand as monuments to the patience not only of the leatherworkers in the Middle Ages but also of the modern archaeological illustrators as well.

Knife No. 136 was in 1985 so unfamiliar in form that it came under suspicion of being an exotic, possibly intrusive item and was almost removed from the publication corpus altogether; it is perhaps ironic that the discovery in the year after publication of a pit group of the (?)14th century at a site at St Mary Axe and St Helen's Place (SAY88), consisting of large numbers of handle components in a striking variety of materials (bone scales with inlays of amber and jet, all held together by pierced sheaths of sheet copper alloy or iron), along with other, single discoveries, has made this now probably the most extensively represented form of all from the Middle Ages. Archaeology is constantly subject to this kind of unexpected supplementation of the accepted wisdom by some new perspective suddenly brought into the arena by accidents of preservation and recovery. From the early 16th century, at the very end of the medieval period (slightly later than the finds in this volume), a small number of unfinished knives unearthed at the Abbot's Lane site in Southwark (ABO92) have been recognised (Egan, in preparation). These appear to be tools that went wrong in different ways under the blacksmith's hammer while they were being shaped on the anvil – flaws in the metal for the blades are evident in some instances from the X-ray plates.

The number of maker's marks noted during the preparation of the volume can now be supplemented as a result of a subsequent check by conservators on a sample of 25 of the blades, which were fully cleaned to remove corrosion products. About a third of these proved to have significant features (marks, inlays etc) not evident from the X-ray images. In this and other aspects, like the profiles of iron versus carbon steel in blades, there is scope for plenty of further analytical work.

Scabbard No. 459 was republished by Pritchard in the volume in this series on dress accessories (1991) with an alternative identification as a needle case (No. 1781). A couple of further observations on the decoration of some of the scabbards should highlight phenomena not noted by the researchers in the 1980s. A small group may be defined of early/mid-14th- to early/mid-15th-century scabbards, which seem to feature strawberry decoration, some of the red colouring from

which survives; these must originally have appeared somewhat garish (Nos. 418, 479 & 487). If the site dating is accepted, scabbards (?not leatherwork in general) must by the early/mid-14th century have been almost the last category of everyday goods to continue the tradition of decorative interlace, which originated long before the Norman Conquest, and in other media was almost at an end by the late 12th century (see Nos. 405-11 & 413).

Historical studies, too, have advanced the subject. The significance of Thaxted in Essex in the production of knives and scabbards for medieval London has now been highlighted. It has been suggested that the arms corresponding with those of Fitzwalter (a fess between two chevrons) on some of scabbards (Fig. 12, No. 20) may relate to aristocracy in that part of the county, an alternative explanation to that offered by Wilmott in this volume (Keene 1995, 234-6).

EGAN, G & PRITCHARD, F, 1991 *Dress accessories: Medieval finds from excavations in London 3*, London

EGAN, G, in preparation, Finds from Bermondsey, London: mid-15th to 17th Centuries

GOODALL, I H, 1990 Knives, shears and scissors, in *Object and economy in medieval Winchester* (ed M Biddle) Winchester Studies 7.2ii, 835-63

KEENE, D, 1995 Small towns and the metropolis: The experience of medieval England, in *Peasants and townsmen in medieval Europe* (ed J M Duvosquel & E Thoen) Studies in Honour of Adriaan Verhulst – Centre Belgique d'Histoire Rurale 114, Ghent, 223-38

OTTAWAY, P, 1992 *Anglo-Scandinavian ironwork from Coppergate,* The Archaeology of York 17.6, York

Addenda & corrigenda

p. 36, Fig. 9: for 456 read 457

Bibliography – 'forthcoming' are now:

McDONNELL, J G, 1992 Analysis of knives: microfiche in Ottaway as above

PRITCHARD, F A, 1991 Small finds, in *Aspects of Saxon and Norman London, 2: Finds and environmental evidence* (ed A G Vince) London Middlesex Archaeol Soc Special Pap 12, 120-278

Introduction

F O Grew

Blades from knives or shears are among the most common and varied metalwork finds on medieval sites. This fact, together with the evident skill with which many were forged and hafted, reflects their importance as tools for work or in the home, while the elaborately decorated scabbards in which they were sometimes sheathed are of intrinsic fascination besides being indicators of the popular artistic tastes of the time. It is appropriate, therefore, that they should be the subject of the first fascicule in a series dealing with all medieval objects recovered from London sites by the Department of Urban Archaeology of the Museum of London during the past decade.

The catalogue contains nearly 500 items. It includes shears, scissors, knives and small scabbards of all kinds, but apart from two sheaths which are illustrated for comparison of their ornament it excludes daggers, swords and their fittings; in fact, very few of these have been found on recent sites, although there is a magnificent short sword from Billingsgate and several fragments, all of which will be published separately. The objects described here are mainly from six major excavations along the waterfront (Table 1), and they are mostly dated with unusual accuracy by the peculiar circumstances of their disposal, in vast tips of refuse thrown behind timber revetments at the time of construction. A collection of this size has the value of permitting some statistical analysis – of alloys or handle types, for example – although here the chronological patterns are obscured to some extent by the fact that almost half the finds belong to a period of just half a century (c.1350–1400). The preservation of both metal and organic parts is in general outstanding, and this has made it possible to identify the types of leather used and all the alloys used for decoration or as inlay in makers' marks. At the same time, since the collection is so well preserved and it must be the policy of a museum to preserve objects intact for future generations, destructive examination has been limited to no more than a dozen blades; and these, inevitably, cannot be representative of the whole range. Ironically, if the collection had consisted of corroded metalwork, incapable of conservation, there would have been no objection to the destructive analysis of every blade.

The first knives and scabbards in the catalogue belong to a time just before c.1140, the date of the first reclamation dump and revetment at Seal House; earlier finds, ranging from the 10th to the mid 12th centuries and mainly from rubbish pits in the central parts of the City, are published elsewhere, with the other Saxon objects recently recovered from London (Pritchard, forthcoming). As might be expected, several of the knives in the first Seal House group belong firmly to the Saxon tradition, with an angular 'hump' on the back of the blade and pattern-welding. This type did not persist long beyond mid century, however, and the knives of the later 12th and 13th centuries mainly have simple triangular blades. Yet it is with these rather plain knives of the early 13th century that we may associate a series of scabbards marvellously decorated with fantastic animal scenes – hares, hounds, boars and birds with elaborate, elongated tails – which it is tempting to see as part of the final flowering of early medieval zoomorphic art in England and which might be compared with marginal illustrations on manuscripts of the same period. In the later 13th and 14th centuries more sober designs, often a combination of debased heraldic motifs, were to become the fashion.

As is especially clear from the present collection, fundamental changes took place during the course of the 14th century. Before c.1300 all knives had solid handles fixed on a spiked 'whittle' tang, whereas after c.1360 over half had a composite handle consisting of plates riveted to a flat 'scale' tang. With this development went a tendency towards longer, more slender blades with more metal fittings – end caps and shoulder plates – which often provided striking decorative effects. At the same time, that is, in the years immediately after c.1300, makers' marks first

Table 1.

Date	Site	Knives	Folding Knives	Shears	Scissors	Scabbards
Late 12th	BIG	2				
	SH	2				
	SWA	6		1		1
Early–mid 13th	BIG	3		1		4
	LH					1
	SH	7		2		8
	SWA	4		1		1
Late 13th	BIG					2
	SWA	18	1	2		13
	TL					3
Early-mid 14th	BC	9		1		22
	BIS	1				
	CUS	7		1		13
	LH					1
	LUD					7
	PCD					3
	SWA	1				
	TL	9		4	1	1
Late 14th	BC	62		12	1	4
	BWB	100	1	21		1
	CUS	1				3
	DUK	1				1
	FLE	1				
	OPT	1				
	SH	2				
	SWA	3				
	TL	12		1		3
Early–mid 15th	BWB	1				
	SWA	13				
	TL	14		4		1
Unstratified	BC	2		1		5
	BIG	3				6
	BWB	2			1	3
	CUS	1				2
	LH					1
	POM	4				
	SH	2				1
	SWA	8		1		2
	TL	1		1		1
	TUD					1
	Total	303	2	54	3	115

became widespread, presumably reflecting the increased sophistication and self-consciousness of the craftsmen themselves – a self-consciousness that also found expression in the craft companies which developed at roughly the same time. And, finally, it seems that after *c.* 1350 fewer and fewer knives were carried in scabbards; whereas over twice as many early 14th-century scabbards as knives have been recovered, the figures for the end of the century are only 11 scabbards compared with 173 knives. As for the early 15th century, only one scabbard has been found, alongside 28 knives and a huge collection of other leatherwork, demonstrating that this change is not related to poorer preservation of leather in the later deposits. These late medieval knives must have been stored where they were needed – in some cases, perhaps, specifically for use at the table – not regularly carried by their owners. Such changes, themselves suggestive of corresponding changes in social organisation, look forward to the Tudor and later periods – stages which regrettably are not represented in the present collection, since the construction of a stone wall along at least part of the Thames bank in the mid 15th century brought to an end the process of steady reclamation with rubbish-laden deposits.

The present volume contains a comprehensively illustrated catalogue of the whole excavated collection. This is preceded by a discussion of the dating evidence, essays on technology and decoration, and on the types and functions of the various items. All the objects, together with detailed archival reports, are stored in the Museum of London, where they may be examined on request.

Dating

A G Vince

Almost all the knives, shears, scissors, folding knives and scabbards illustrated in this catalogue are from recent archaeological excavations and are mainly from stratified contexts (Table 2). Unstratified material, whether from the Museum of London's older collections or from sites excavated by the museum's Department of Urban Archaeology, is only illustrated where it helps to amplify a point arising from the study of stratified artefacts.

Much of the material included here comes from excavations along the Thames waterfront and was collected from the massive dumps of domestic rubbish used to make up the ground behind timber revetments. Revetment dumps are usually composed of black, highly organic refuse interleaved with recognisable tips of material such as building debris and oyster shells. Foreshore deposits on the other hand consist mainly of silts and gravels, also often highly organic. Unlike the dumps, which seem to contain rubbish brought from a wide area of the City, the foreshores can be expected to contain material discarded from the waterfront itself which may therefore reflect medieval riverside activities.

The size of the excavated assemblages and the methods of recovery vary from site to site and this limits the information which can be extracted from the data. This applies both to the relative quantities of artefacts between sites and the ratio of leather to metal finds within sites. Thus, any statement about preferred dumping points for artefacts along the waterfront based on our data is probably unjustified, as would be any attempt to compare the ratio of knives to scabbards through time if the pattern found were not repeated on different sites. There is no reason to suggest that either the knife or scabbard collections are biased, and, providing the assemblages are of sufficient size, they can be used as a representative sample of their date, gathered, one suspects, from a wide area of the City.

The dating of these deposits is based on a wide range of techniques. Where possible, dendrochronological analysis of the timber revetments themselves has been undertaken, but the most precise dating comes from coins, tokens and jettons. These finds are so numerous that they can be used to give a deposit a *terminus ante quem*, the date before which the group must have been deposited. The late 13th-century deposit from Swan Lane, for example, produced 43 coins and 94 lead tokens, and none of the coins would have been legal tender after *c.*1280. Some of the smaller deposits, and most of the finds from inland sites included here, are dated less precisely by the pottery assemblages found with them. Even when dated by pottery alone there are few items included in this publication which cannot be dated to within half a century. The methods used to date the sequence and a description of the major changes in the

Table 2. The objects according to deposition date.

Date	Knives		Folding Knives		Shears		Scissors		Scabbards	
	nos.	%	nos.	%	nos.	%	nos.	%	nos.	%
L12th C	10	3			1	2			1	1
E–M13th C	14	5			4	7			14	12
L13th C	18	6	1	50	2	4			18	16
E–M14th C	27	9			6	11	1	33	47	41
L14th C	183	60	1	50	34	62	1	33	12	10
E–M15th C	28	9			4	7			1	1
Unstrat.	23	8			3	5	1	33	22	19
Total	303		2		54		3		115	

pottery found is published elsewhere (Vince, 1985). Unless otherwise stated, the identification of the numismatic finds is by P Stott, of the Medieval Department, Museum of London, while dendrochronological analysis is by J Hillam and C Groves, of the Sheffield University Dendrochronological Laboratory.

The medieval waterfront sequence begins in the late 10th and ends in the mid 15th century. However, before *c.* 1150 most of the finds from the city come from occupation sites in the City, with all the problems of dating and interpretation which such sites present. This material is therefore being prepared for publication together with the excavations on which it was found. Similarly, the one Tudor waterfront assemblage of any size, from Baynard's Castle (the fill of the robber trench of the west wall of 'Baynard's Castle dock'), is not a city-wide rubbish deposit, as are the medieval groups, and the finds are best considered alongside those from pits, wells, cellar fills and other deposits from individual tenements excavated in the City. These groups span the early 16th to 19th centuries and will provide a wealth of information on the date and associations of Tudor and later post-medieval artefacts. For these reasons, only

finds dateable from the mid 12th to the mid 15th centuries are included here.

BC72: 'Baynards Castle Dock' (Fig. 1 No. 1).

Excavations in the area of Baynards Castle took place in 1972 (Webster and Cherry, 1973, 162–3). They produced two large medieval dump deposits, both related to a stone-walled dock, recently identified by T Dyson and C Taylor as the common or public East Watergate (pers. comm).

1   The location of excavations mentioned in the text.

  1   BC72: 'Baynard's Castle Dock'
  2   BIG82 and BWB83: Billingsgate Lorry Park
  3   BIS82: 76–80 Bishopsgate St
  4   CUS73: Custom House
  5   DUK77: 2–7 Dukes Place
  6   FLE82: 140–3 Fetter Lane
  7   LH74 and LUD82: Ludgate Hill
  8   OPT81: 2–3 Cross Keys Court
  9   POM79: General Post Office site, Newgate St
 10   PCD59: The Public Cleansing Depot (Dowgate)
 11   SH74: Seal House
 12   SWA81: Swan Lane
 13   TL74: Trig Lane
 14   TUD78: 5 Tudor St

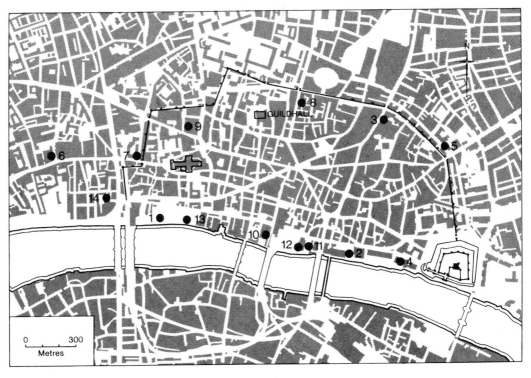

(i) The construction of the dock

The northern wall of the dock was formed by utilising an earlier timber waterfront, and the eastern wall was a pre-existing stone wall. The west wall, however, was formed by reclaiming an area of foreshore within a stone wall. The dump behind this wall can probably be dated by jettons to the 1330s or later. The difficulty in providing a precise *terminus post quem* is that the jettons are of a type, copying the sterling coinage of Edward I–II, which could conceivably be as early as *c.*1280. Other finds from the dump include a pewter *ampulla* of late 13th-century date and two lead tokens of Rigold's type D2–4 (Rigold 1980, 103–5). The large pottery assemblage from this dump has yet to be examined in detail but initial examination supports a mid 14th-century date. The group contained nine knives, a pair of shears and twenty-two scabbards.

(ii) The use and filling of the dock

A layer of silt within the dock contained a moderate-sized assemblage of pottery, and a post-sterling jetton. These suggest that it was in use in the mid to late 14th century. A vast assemblage was recovered from the back-fill of the dock, behind a further stone wall, which blocked the dock. Coins, pilgrim souvenirs and jettons suggest a deposition date in the last quarter of the 14th century. The group produced sixty-two knives, a pair of scissors, twelve pairs of shears but only four scabbards.

BIG 82 and BWB83: Billingsgate Lorry Park (Fig. 1 No. 2)

The Billingsgate Lorry Park excavation in 1982 examined a large area of late Saxon and medieval waterfront (Youngs, Clark and Barry, 1983, 191–2). The late Saxon deposits, however, were only exposed in a small area. Finds recovery on a scale unprecedented on a controlled excavation in London was undertaken using metal detectors and sieving. Despite this, datable artefacts were few until the late 12th century. The late Saxon to medieval sequence can nevertheless be dated accurately by a combination of coin-dating, estimates based on the structural sequences and pilgrim souvenirs.

(i) The later waterfronts

From the middle of the 12th century onwards, the sequence of reclamation at Billingsgate was similar to that discovered elsewhere. The junction of two properties with different reclamation sequences was recorded on the site. The interrelationships of these revetments, and the occupation deposits on top, allow a very long stratigraphic sequence to be constructed with groups deposited in some cases only 10 to 20 years apart.

The first major reclamation appears to be dated *c.*1160 by pottery and by its position in the sequence. This produced two knives. From *c.*1180 onwards these groups can be given an absolute date by the associated artefacts. The first such group is coin-dated to 1180 or later, and includes a pilgrim souvenir datable later than 1170. The next large dump can be coin-dated to the early years of the 13th century. These groups produced three knives, a pair of shears and four scabbards. The latest revetment found in the excavation is dated by a group of coins which were probably deposited soon after 1250 and contained two scabbards.

Following the excavation, in 1983 came a watching brief, and finds recovery also took place where the spoil was dumped. Although little of this material can be related to a single deposit, the analysis of the coins, pottery and other datable artefacts shows that the majority of these finds come from mid to late 14th-century revetment dumps to the south of the excavated structures. The scale of the discovery, and the emphasis on metal finds, can be judged by the fact that one hundred knives were recovered, twenty-one pairs of shears, a folding knife, but just one scabbard. A single knife was found with pottery of early 15th-century date, from the extreme south of the site.

BIS82: 76–80 Bishopsgate St (Fig. 1 No. 3)

Excavations in 1982 revealed a rubbish pit containing a small assemblage of late 13th to early 14th century pottery (Youngs, Clark and Barry, 1983, 192). The absence of large quantities of London-type baluster jugs suggest a date early within this bracket, perhaps the last quarter of the 13th century for the knife found in the pit.

CUS73: Custom House (Fig.1 No.4)

The Custom House excavations took place at the extreme eastern end of the City waterfront, just to the west of the Tower (Tatton-Brown, 1974, Tatton-Brown, 1975). A foreshore deposit overlying the remains of Roman timber quays contained a small quantity of early 13th-century pottery in its lower levels (group D2) and early to mid 14th-century pottery in its upper levels (Group D1). The majority of the usefully stratified medieval finds came from a revetment dump overlying this foreshore and from deposits stratified later than this dump.

(i) Group C2
The filling behind the group C2 timber revetment can be dated by pottery to the early 14th century or later. A tentative dendrochronological date for the revetment gives a *terminus post quem* of 1328 and there is documentary evidence for waterfront activity in the late 1330s, associated with defensive works at the start of the Hundred Years War. Material from the silting in front of the group C2 revetment (Group C1) can also be dated to the early to mid 14th century by the pottery. These deposits produced seven knives, a pair of shears and thirteen scabbards.

(ii) Group B
Material from the robbing of a structure in front of the timber revetment can be dated by pottery between *c*.1380 and *c*.1420 and included a knife and three scabbards.

DUK77: 2–7 Dukes Place (Fig.1 No.5)
Excavations at Dukes Place in 1977 disclosed a stone-lined cess-pit (Webster and Cherry 1978, 176). In the medieval period this pit would have been within the precinct of the priory of Holy Trinity Aldgate. The deposit was dated by pottery to the mid to late 14th century and produced glassware and textiles of high quality. A knife and a scabbard were also found.

FLE82: 140–3 Fetter Lane (Fig.1 No.6)

Excavations in 1982 revealed a rubbish pit containing a small medieval pottery assemblage (Youngs, Clark and Barry, 1983, 193). The pottery types

present include two types found in the late 14th century which are rare or absent in early 15th-century deposits, and one which came into use *c*.1400. If all three vessels were in contemporary use then a date in the first quarter of the 15th century would seem likely for this group, and therefore for the knife found with it.

LH74 and LUD82: Ludgate Hill (Fig.1 No.7)

Excavations of the city ditch at Ludgate Hill in 1982 showed that where it abutted the street at Ludgate Hill it contained a single-period dumped deposit (Youngs, Clark and Barry, 1983, 194). This was confirmed by the discovery of sherds from the same pottery vessel throughout the excavation. Dating evidence consists of a coin minted 1302–10 while documentary evidence shows that the area was occupied by houses by 1340 (T Dyson, pers. comm). The deposit produced seven scabbards. A previous excavation in the area in 1974 sampled what was probably the same deposit and produced two further scabbards (LH74).

Further north the 1982 excavation showed that the ditch here seems to have been partly filled in the mid 13th century. The 1974 excavation produced a scabbard from what may be the same deposit.

OPT81: 2–3 Cross Keys Court (Fig.1 No.8)

Excavations in 1981 at Cross Keys Court showed that there had been a substantial rise in ground level during the medieval period due to the dumping of refuse on the site (Youngs and Clark, 1982, 192). The pottery from these layers includes much 14th-century material, as well as a number of late 12th-century sherds. Later activity on the site, including metalworking, may be dated to the 15th century. The knife included in this publication was found in a layer containing pottery of all dates from the late 12th to the 15th centuries.

POM 79: General Post Office site, Newgate Street (Fig.1 No.9)

Excavations in 1979 on the site of the new British Telecom building revealed a stone-lined cess-pit of 14th-century date (Webster and Cherry, 1980, 253). The finds assemblage from the pit was small but composed largely of smashed pots. This assemblage probably dates to the early to mid 14th century, the probable date of the knife from the pit (No. 294).

PCD59: The Public Cleansing Depot (Dowgate) (Fig. 1 No. 10)

Assemblages dated by pottery to the middle of the 14th century and closely comparable in composition with those from other waterfront revetment dumps were recovered under salvage conditions in 1959 at Dowgate. The finds included three scabbards.

SH74: Seal House (Fig. 1 No. 11)

The excavation at Seal House produced a medieval sequence starting in the late 11th to early 12th century with a foreshore deposit overlying the timbers of a Roman quay (Schofield, 1975, 53–7; Morgan and Schofield, 1978, 223–38). Small groups of 12th century date were recovered from the succeeding revetment dumps together with large groups of the early and mid 13th century.

(i) Waterfront I
The earliest dump was associated with a collapsed and robbed revetment, waterfront I, from which a dendrochronological date of 1133 or later was obtained. One knife (No. 3), was found in the dump but there is the possibility of later 12th and early 13th century contamination, since sherds of this date were noted in the pottery assemblage.

(ii) Waterfront II
The second dump was found behind a timber revetment which was partially intact. A date of 1163–92 for the felling of the latest timber was obtained from the revetment. The pottery assemblage appears to be of one date, containing no obvious residual or intrusive sherds and the deposit produced one knife (No. 1).

(iii) Waterfront III
The third dump was found behind an *in situ* revetment. A date of 1193 or later was obtained for the felling of the latest timber in the revetment. The dump was cut through to insert a timber-lined drain from which a date of 1203 or later was obtained by dendrochronology. The deposit produced two knives, two pairs of shears and four scabbards. Five knives and four scabbards were found in building levels contemporary with the use of waterfront III (Nos. 16, 17, 19, 22, 23, 374, 375, 377, 380).

(iv) Waterfront IV
The latest excavated dumps at Seal House post-date the waterfront III revetment and were found on either side of a large mortared stone wall foundation, resting on the foreshore. Three groups were distinguished on stratigraphic evidence but are all probably of one date. Pottery is the only dating evidence and suggests a date of *c.* 1250 for the one scabbard, published as unstratified (No. 481).

SWA81: Swan Lane (Fig. 1 No. 12)

The 1981 excavation and watching brief at Swan Lane uncovered an almost complete sequence of activity on this site from the late Saxon period to the middle of the 15th century (Youngs and Clark, 1982, 193; Youngs, Clark and Barry, 1983, 194–5).

(i) The late 12th-century waterfronts
Immediately above a late 11th to early 12th-century foreshore deposit were revetment dumps containing late 12th-century pottery. These were observed both in the excavation and subsequent watching brief and had a wide extent. In virtually every instance the timber revetment itself had been destroyed to re-use the timbers, so that the distinction between one dump and the next was unclear. There is little sign from the associated finds of any distinction in date between these dumps. The latest dumps were found behind *in situ* revetment walls. Three coins from these dumps indicate a deposition date later than 1180. Dendrochronological analysis by J. Hillam and C. Groves has shown that timbers of mid 12th century or later date underlie the earliest dumps. The deposits, which produced six knives, a pair of shears and a scabbard, can be broadly dated to the second half of the 12th century.

(ii) The mid 13th-century waterfronts
In front of the late 12th-century revetments, and separated from them by a series dated to the early

13th century by pottery, were dumps datable to the mid 13th century, found behind *in situ* timber revetments. The finds include one short-cross penny and one long-cross penny, consistent with the evidence of the pottery for a mid 13th century deposition date. The dumps produced 4 knives, a pair of shears and a scabbard.

(iv) The late 13th-century waterfronts
The most productive dumps found at Swan Lane lay in front of the mid 13th-century revetments. A large series of coins and tokens was recovered, showing that the waterfront across the middle part of the site was reclaimed at a single period, if not as a single operation. Coin-dating alone suggests a date between *c.*1270 and *c.*1279 for the deposition of the dumps. The pilgrim souvenirs suggest a date after 1270, and possibly later than 1280. The dumps produced eighteen knives, two pairs of shears, a folding knife and thirteen scabbards.

(v) The early 15th-century waterfronts
In the extreme south-east corner of the site large groups of finds were recovered from either side of a timber revetment. Those behind the revetment date to the very end of the 14th century or to the beginning of the 15th century, recently confirmed by a dendrochronological date of 1394 or later for the base plate of the revetment. The dump produced three knives. The deposits in front of the revetment (which could be divided into those from the foreshore and those from the revetment dump above) produced thirteen knives and can be dated by coins to 1422 or later. The latest coin came from the foreshore but analysis of the lead tokens show that the dump contains a higher proportion of later types. It is likely that the foreshore contains material accumulated between *c.*1400 and *c.*1430, while the overlying dump contains mainly material dating closer to *c.*1430. The absence of coins of Henry VI is thought to preclude a later date for either deposit.

TL74: Trig Lane (Fig.1 No.13)

The Trig Lane waterfront sequence, excavated between 1974 and 1976, extends from *c.*1250 to *c.*1440 and provides large dated finds assemblages of late 13th-century, late 14th-century and mid 15th-century date (Milne and Milne, 1980).

(i) Groups 2 and 3
The earliest large groups of finds came from dumping behind the G2 revetment. Only the base-plate of this waterfront remained, the G3 superstructure having been rebuilt about 20 years later. The pottery from the dump associated with G3 is remarkably similar to that from G2, including some sherds from the same vessels. This suggests that the G3 finds are in fact derived from the G2 dump, which was dug out and then backfilled when the back-braces of the G3 waterfront were inserted. The deposit contained three scabbards, which probably date to *c.*1270, but may possibly date to *c.*1290.

(ii) Group 7
A substantial foreshore in front of the G3 revetment was sealed by the dump behind the G7 structure. There is no independent date for G7; the date of *c.*1340 given in the excavation report is based on a combination of pottery dating and an estimation of the time needed after *c.*1290 and before *c.*1360 for the foreshore to accumulate. The dump contained nine knives, four pairs of shears, a pair of scissors and a scabbard.

(iii) Group 10 and 12
A further advance of the waterfront was represented by the G10 revetment, which sealed a foreshore deposit. The G10 dump is dated by dendrochronology to *c.*1360 and contains three knives and three scabbards (Nos.82, 110, 128, 453–4, 459). It was repaired over part of its length in *c.*1430 (G12). Examination of the pottery from G12 shows that this dump is composed mainly of redeposited spoil from G10, although dendrochronology shows that it was a repair of the G10 waterfront dated *c.*1430. The knife from G12 could therefore date either to *c.*1360 or *c.*1430.

(iv) Group 11
A large group of finds comes from the dump behind the G11 revetment, dated *c.*1380 by dendrochronology, jettons and pilgrim souvenirs. Amongst the finds are five knives, (Nos.68, 253–5, 277).

(v) Group 15
The foreshore in front of the G11 revetment was examined over a wide area and is dated *c.*1380–*c.*1430 by jettons and pilgrim souvenirs. Eight

knives (Nos. 88, 104, 107, 149, 175, 250–2) were also found in this deposit. The dump above this foreshore was associated with a stone river wall, G15, resting on a timber base-plate, dated *c.* 1440 by dendrochronology. It produced eight knives, four pairs of shears and a scabbard.

TUD78: Tudor Street (Fig. 1 No. 14)

Excavations on the site of Bridewell Palace showed that the area had been under water until the early 15th century. The unstratified scabbard (No. 478) was probably deposited in river silt during the 14th century.

Manufacturing techniques

JANE COWGILL

There is no archaeological evidence from London for the production of any of these artefacts and knowledge of the manufacturing methods employed has therefore been gained primarily from an examination of the finished objects. This has been supplemented by a brief appraisal of medieval documentary records (pp. 32–34). For clarification, the terms used in the text are shown on Figures 2–4.

The Knives, Shears, Scissors and Folding Knives

All the metal objects were studied using radiography, and the resulting X-radiographs reveal many details of manufacture, for example traces of solder or scale rivets. Over two thirds of the makers' marks are not visible except by this means.

The non-ferrous metals (decoration, inlaid makers' marks and fittings) were qualitatively analysed by Paul Wilthew at the Ancient Monuments Laboratory, using energy dispersive x-ray fluorescence, which is non-destructive (Wilthew 1984a; for a simple description of the technique, see Tate 1984). To avoid contamination from corrosion, the areas to be analysed were cleaned, but low levels of copper, lead and, sometimes, zinc were often detected, even on ferrous areas. They are almost certainly the result of contamination during burial. Using this method an area of about one square centimetre on the surface of the object could be examined. This is too large an area for the composition of adjacent non-ferrous metals on the artefacts to be determined and for this reason solders and end plates composed of more than one copper alloy could only be given non-specific identifications (for example No. 261)

It was possible to examine a small sample of the iron tools, ten knives and five shears, to show both the exact method of construction and the quality of the materials used (Appendix 1). Blades were only considered suitable if the full length survived in good condition, so that several sections could be removed. Those selected were all as similar as possible in form, but from different periods, to emphasise any changes in technique through time. Nevertheless, both whittle- and scale-tang knives were chosen from the late 14th and 15th-century groups. The results show not only the precise methods of construction employed but also variations in the quality of the finished tools.

BLADES

I Forging

The blades were forged mainly from wrought iron, but as this was not hard enough to give a good cutting edge, an additional harder iron section was often built into them. Wrought iron cannot be hardened by heat treatment, whereas irons with a higher carbon content (carbon steels) can be tempered and hardened (Hodges 1964, 80). For simplicity wrought iron is here referred to as 'iron', and irons with a higher carbon content as 'steel'; for the exact terms see Appendix 1.

The carburisation of iron is a slow process and it was not economical for the individual smith to produce his own steel, which was expensive and sparingly used (Tylecote 1981, 45–6). It was usually imported from Sweden, Russia or Spain, since native ores were generally unsuitable for conversion during the medieval period (ibid, 44).

The blade and tang of a knife, and the arms and blades of shears, were forged from a single piece of iron to which the steel cutting edge was welded before shaping. The metals were cooled rapidly, or 'quenched', to increase the hardness of the steel. This made the steel brittle, and therefore it was sometimes gently heated, or 'tempered', to increase resilience. (For further details see Hodges 1964, 84–5.) Metallography has revealed many different ways of combining iron and steel within a knife blade, summarised by Tylecote (1981, 47). Five combinations were recorded within the analysed sample, as well as tools made

a) WHITTLE TANG

b) SCALE TANG

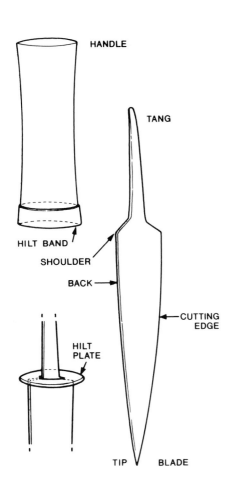

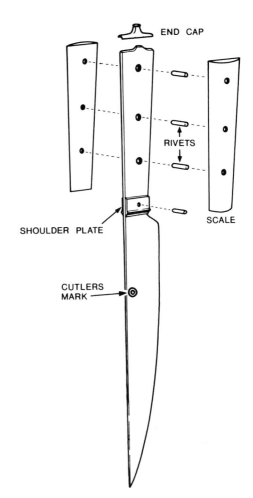

HANDLE

TANG

HILT BAND

SHOULDER

BACK

CUTTING EDGE

HILT PLATE

TIP BLADE

END CAP

RIVETS

SCALE

SHOULDER PLATE

CUTLERS MARK

2 The main components of a medieval knife:
(a) with whittle tang,
(b) with scale tang.

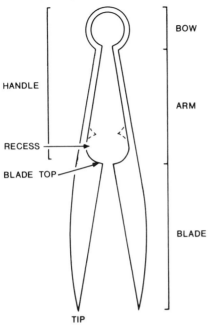

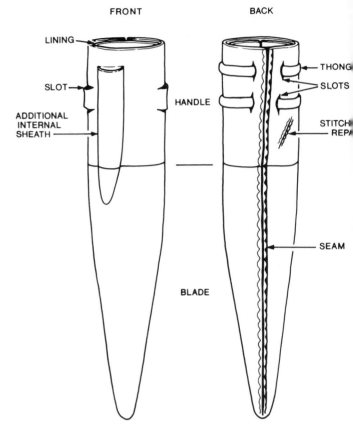

3 The terminology used to describe medieval shears.

4 The terminology used to describe medieval scabbards.

5 Methods of combining iron and steel in edged tools.

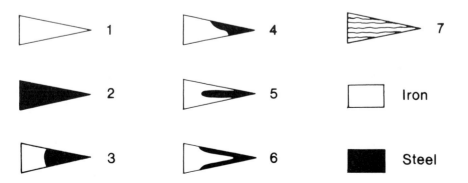

from a single piece of metal (Fig. 5). The methods are listed below. In addition some knife blades were identified through x-radiographs as being pattern welded (see below, p. 16):

(1) a single strip of wrought iron
(2) a single strip of steel
(3) a steel cutting edge butt welded to a wrought iron back
(4) a steel cutting edge scarf welded to a wrought iron back
(5) a steel cutting edge with a wrought iron back wrapped around it
(6) an iron core with a steel cutting edge wrapped around it
(7) wrought iron strips welded together

No examples of Tylecote's type C – alternating layers of steel and iron to produce a piled material – were identified. Given the small size of our samples this may be unremarkable but at the 10th-century and later city of Novgorod, USSR, where 304 knives were analysed (Thompson 1967, 73–4), it was found that before the 13th century knives were usually manufactured by this method whereas the later blades often had a steel strip welded along the cutting edge (method 3 above). The single 12th-century knife analysed was constructed using method 5, while knives and shears made by method 4 were in use early in the 13th century (Table 3).

On fragmentary or corroded blades, where no analysis was attempted, multi-piece construction may be suspected from the way the blade has corroded. The cutting edge usually appears to be in much better condition than the back, suggesting that methods 4, 5 or 6 were used (Pl. 1). This is clearly visible on knives and shears of all dates and has been noted in the illustrations (for example knives Nos. 27 and 106, and shears No. 337). The existence of two or more metals can also sometimes be seen on x-radiographs, when some sections of the blade appear denser than the rest (Pl 2).

The metallurgical analysis of the shears shows a greater degree of standardisation in manufacture with method 4 predominating (Table 3). The arms and bow were probably made from the same piece of iron as the blade. A number of characteristics of shear blades remain unchanged throughout the medieval period, the most notable being that the left blade always overlaps the right. The cutting surface had to be flat, the reverse is usually slightly rounded with a chamfer at the cutting edge.

The three pairs of scissors (Nos. 369, 370 and 371) were considered too rare to be destructively analysed but they were probably manufactured in a similar manner to the shears. The production of a pair of scissors requires considerable skill. If two flat blades were simply pivoted together they would not work properly because the material they are trying to cut will force them apart. The blades must therefore be made to curve or twist inwards from pivot to point, so that in use they only touch at the cutting point where the pressure is concentrated. The bows may have been formed from the same piece of metal as the arms or as a separate section, as suggested by the x-radiograph of the circular bows on No. 370.

The two folding knives in this assemblage were also not analysed. The thumb rest on the complete knife (No. 309) was forged as an extension of the blade back. Both the scissors and folding knives used iron pivots, in the case of the complete pairs of scissors combined with a copper alloy washer (Nos. 370 and 371).

The final stage in the manufacture of shear and knife blades was the filing of all surfaces to remove traces of working and to create a smooth finish.

Table 3. **Summary of the metallurgical analysis.**

KNIVES

Cat. no.	Date	Tang type	Quality	Type
2	L12th C	Whittle	Quite good	5
12	M13th C	Whittle	Excellent	4
16	E13th C	Whittle	Very poor	1?
26	L13th C	Whittle	Good	3
44	M14th C	Whittle	Poor	6
63	M14th C	Scale	Excellent	6
84	L14th C	Whittle	Very poor	1
121	L14th C	Scale	Very poor	7
258	M15th C	Whittle	Poor	7
266	M15th C	Scale	Good	6

SHEARS

Cat. no.	Date	Quality	Type
313	E13th C	Good	4
320	M14th C	Quite good	1
325	L14th C	Poor	2
359	M15th C	Excellent	4
364	Unstrat.	Good	4

PLATE 1
Differential corrosion on knives and shears
caused by variation in metal composition.
(a) Knife No. 27
(b) Knife No. 31
(c) Shear blade No. 311

a

b   c

PLATE 2
Evidence for construction revealed by x-radiography.
(a) The different density of areas on blade No. 233
(b) Slag lines on Blade No.54.

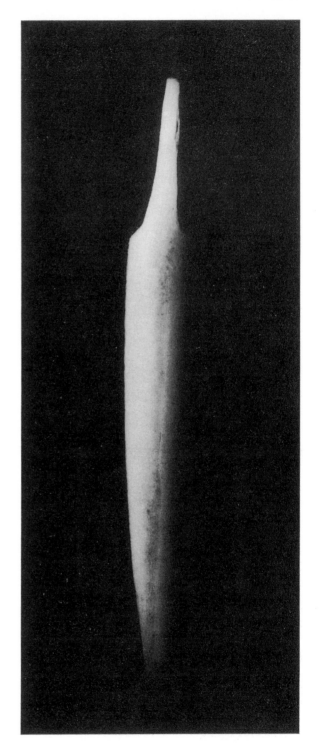

a

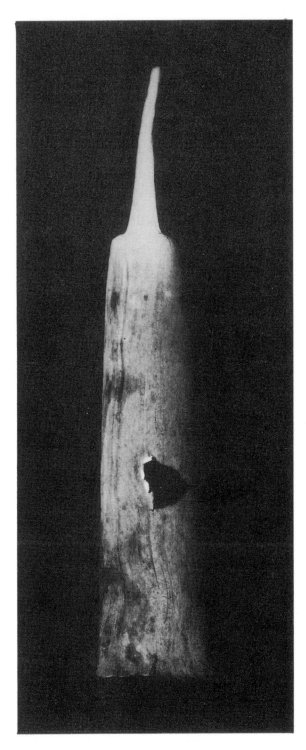

b

Possible filing lines, running in all directions across the blades, the backs and the angles between the blades and backs, are visible on the better preserved objects. Some of the lines may be due to re-sharpening, but they sometimes continue onto the back and it seems more likely that they are the original file marks.

II Decoration

Five main methods of edge-tool decoration were used (Table 4). They are discussed below in approximately chronological order. The earliest, pattern welding, was both a manufacturing technique and a method of decoration. Strips of iron and steel were twisted together and beaten flat to produce a blade decorated with marbling. The steel cutting edge was then welded on. Pattern welding is known from the late Roman period onwards in sword manufacture but seems to have had a shorter life, from the 10th to 12th centuries, for knives. The use of non-ferrous metals on knives and shears in this collection began in the mid to late 13th century with blades decorated with silver. This technique is not found later. Another late 13th-century blade is decorated with a series of inset brass discs (No.36). 14th- and 15th-century blades are more often decorated, but using simple techniques; usually a groove, which sometimes contains an inlay. Inlaid stamped designs are less frequent.

Until the end of the 13th century both sides of the blades were decorated but from then on, coinciding with the first appearance of makers' marks, only the marked side was decorated. The choice of non-ferrous metals also changed with time. Silver and brass were used during the 13th century while gunmetal (copper-zinc-tin alloys), brass and tin occur after *c.*1300. The metals for the inlays were probably bought in a refined state, perhaps already prepared as sheet metal or wire. With one possible exception (below, p. 17) the alloys do not seem to have been reused, unless they were well refined before their secondary use.

The majority of the techniques described below apply only to knives. Only four pairs of shears have decorated blades, two with overlaid decoration, and two with grooves. The fact that so few shears are decorated, a task no more difficult than ornamenting a knife blade, may simply be because of the small size of the sample, rather than any

Table 4. **The methods of decorating blades by date.**

Method	L12th C	E–M13th C	L13th C	E–M14th C	L14th C	E–M15th C
Pattern welding	3	1			1	
Overlaid wire		1	2 + 2*			
Inset discs			1			
Groove		1		1	17 + 2*	1?
Groove with decorated back				2	1	
Inlaid					3 + 1?	

* shears

manufacturing problems. The arms of the shears are more commonly decorated but only in two instances with a non-ferrous metal (see below p.00, Nos.316 and 317). Usually the decoration was formed from the arm iron and is a simple design (Nos.314, 332, 334, 336, 345, and 359). The complete pairs of scissors are similarly decorated (Nos.370 and 371).

1 *Pattern welding.* The four pattern-welded blades are from contexts dated between the late 12th and mid 13th centuries. The pattern was achieved by twisting rods of iron and the final design was determined by the number of rods used, their shape, the number of times they were twisted and how, and the depth to which the surface was etched (Anstee and Biek 1958). The patterned iron was then welded between either a single bent length or two separate strips of iron, one of which might be steel to form a hard cutting edge. The two simplest examples (Nos.4 and 7) have a single layer of twisted iron running along the centre of the blade. The two other pattern-welded blades (Nos.1 and 17) have more complex designs involving two strips of patterned iron, either welded side by side, or a single length folded back on itself. The method used to make these patterns is not clear from x-radiography alone; to be certain the blades would have to be seen in cross-section. The iron back of No.1 does not appear to form a part of the tang, whereas the short roughly made tang of No.17 includes the continuation of the back, patterned strip and cutting edge.

The blade on an unusual knife from a late 14th-century context has a related type of decoration (No.136). The lower part of the blade seems to have been prepared with a 'sawtooth' upper edge. This zig-zag edge was then welded to another piece of iron, possibly with a different hardness. Another length of iron, perhaps the same as the lower section, forms the back. The central section, attached to the sawtooth edge, has corroded very badly compared to the back and lower area, suggesting that different grades of iron were used. However, to be certain of how this knife was made it would need metallurgical analysis.

2 *Overlaid decoration.* Three knives and two shears from mid to late 13th-century contexts, and one unstratified knife, are decorated with an overlaid decoration (Nos.14, 25, 34, 316, 317 and 284). The technique used is described in some detail by Theophilus in his treatise *De diversis artibus* (1110–1140?). First he describes the construction of a machine for keying iron objects with a cross hatched pattern. Then,

'You should also have very fine silver and gold wires, from which you can shape tiny flowers and circles or anything else you like. Lay these on the iron with fine tweezers in any way you wish, but always alternate gold flowers and silver ones. Strike them gently with a small hammer, so that they stick fast. When the whole surface has been filled up in this way, put the iron on live coals until it begins to turn black and strike it carefully with a medium-sized hammer until, wherever iron appears, the cuts are evened out and so the work looks as if were niello.

If you wish to have letters on knives or other things made of iron, engrave them first with an engraving tool, then from thick silver wire that you have made, shape the letters with fine tweezers, lay them in the grooves and embed them by striking them on top with a hammer. In this way you can also make little flowers and circles in iron [things], inlaying them with copper and brass wire.' (Hawthorne and Smith 1979, 185–186).

The cross-hatched keying and attached wire is clearly visible on one of the shear blades (No.316,

Pl.3a). The surfaces of the knife blades are corroded, but one (No.14) seems to have deep cuts running the length of the groove which may be keying, and on its back there are numerous shallow diagonal cuts. In Theophilus' description above, one of the final stages included erasing all traces of keying but this seems to have been omitted on at least two of these examples.

The wire is noticeable on all these blades, but on one it is particularly clear because it has not been flattened into the keying near the tang (No.14, Pl.3b). The wire was identified as silver on four of the blades (Wilthew 1984a). On the two blades from one pair of shears (No.317) small amounts of gold and mercury were also detected in the wire, suggesting either that it may have been mercury gilded, or that silver that had once been gilded was reused. The wire has a definite gold colour. One blade (No.34) is so corroded that it is neither possible to distinguish the design nor analyse the metal used.

The decoration on the two pairs of shears (Nos.316 and 317) covers almost all of the outside of each blade. The designs on all three shear blades are different, but similar in style to the decoration on the three knives. There are faint traces of decoration along the surviving arms which was probably applied by the same method.

3 Inset stamped discs. Another type of ornamentation occurs on a knife from a late 13th-century context (No.36). The knife has a row of brass discs inset along the blade and on the mark side these are set between two parallel grooves. The discs on both sides of the blade have each been stamped with a letter, apparently reading AMOR VNICIT GOMN? for AMOR VINCIT OMNIA (love conquers all). The only parallel, unfortunately not stratified (No.285), is very different in shape, having a small triangular blade and just three inset discs. These are again individually stamped with a letter on both sides of the blade, but in this instance the inscription is unintelligible, the letters appearing to read AVI IIC.

4 Grooves. Straight grooves running parallel with the back of the blade are found on a number of knives. They vary from wide but shallow grooves, which may themselves have been decorative, to narrow grooves which in at least some examples were filled with a non-ferrous metal inlay. The earliest example is on a knife blade from a mid

13th-century context (No.16). This knife has two wide shallow grooves running parallel to the blade back, one on either side of the blade. Single or double grooves became the most common type of decoration during the 14th century, but unlike No.16 they occur only on one side of the blade. Two pairs of shears (from late 14th-century contexts) have grooves on the outside of their blades (Nos.338 and 340). The grooves are shallow with gently sloping sides and one, No.338, has traces of gilding in the grooves.

When visible on the knives, the grooves are usually cut quite deeply into the blade. The tool used may have been either a tracer, which is hammer-struck and does not remove any metal, or a graver which cuts away the surface metal and therefore must be harder than the metal being cut (Hodges 1964, 78–9). The only groove examined metallurgically was made with a tracer (Appendix 1, No.121).

It is not possible to identify how many of the grooves were originally inlaid with non-ferrous metals. Nine still contain an inlay, of which six are brass, one bronze and two unidentified; eleven did not reveal traces of any inlay when x-radiographed. The grooves with no inlay remaining do not seem to have been keyed, but this need not preclude the original presence of inlay, since the grooves are usually deep and steep-sided, capable of retaining an inlay without further treatment. The only knife on which keying is visible has a shallow wide groove (No.130), but half the inlay is missing.

5 Inlaid motifs. Three blades have an inlaid design. On two a line of crosses runs the length of the blade (Nos.73 and 92), the former also having two groups of Y's forming arrows beside the line of crosses. The third inlaid blade (No.98) has a strip of copper soldered onto the back from which, on one side, hangs a line of tin triangles inlaid into the blade; the design extends about a third of the way along the blade. A fourth blade is possibly inlaid: a number of dense areas on the x-radiograph hint at a possible zig-zag design (No.236). Unfortunately the blade is too corroded for any non-ferrous metal to be traced and too encrusted for analysis.

III Marks

Makers' marks have been recognised on 110 knives and 12 pairs of shears (Figs.6–8). The

a

PLATE 3
Overlaid decoration on knife and shear blades:
(a) Shear blade No. 316 with a detail showing
the cross-hatched keying and the silver
wire in relief.
(b) Unattached silver wire on knife blade No. 14.

b

system of arranging the marks within the present collection is derived from that used in the Wallace Collection *Catalogue of European Arms and Armour* (Mann 1962). The marks are grouped in the following sequence: alphabetical, animate, utensils, moon, stars, heraldic (comprising crosses, crowns, fleur-de-lys, heraldic animals, saltires) miscellaneous and indeterminate shapes. Within each group, the order is by catalogue number. Where two marks are present, such as a fleur-de-lys and letter, each will be found in its separate category, with the accompanying mark in outline. Marks on shear blades are included within Figs. 6–8 but with the catalogue numbers suffixed 'S'; a small arrow indicates the direction of the tip of the blade. Although many of the marks have no particular orientation, alphabetical and heraldic stamps are clearly meant to be seen from one direction. It appears that, whilst the majority of marks were placed so that they could be seen from the holder's viewpoint, a number are to be seen from the tip of the blade, and some from the cutting edge.

It is clear that marks such as those on Figs. 6 to 8 were in widespread use by cutlers and bladesmiths across Europe throughout the medieval and well into the post-medieval period. Since records are sparse for the period under discussion, it is impossible to do more than point to various parallels.

An English sword (Royal Armouries IX 2794) of mid 14th-century date from Bullwharf has an eight-pointed star and a 'P' stamped into the fuller on both sides. Although the star resembles No. 176, the 'P' is of a simple upright form unlike either Nos. 56 or 268. A mark very similar to No. 173 (Fig. 6) but with an inlaid crown is on an early 16th-century knife, one of two found associated with a dagger in Southwark. The device depicted with a star on Nos. 175, 330 (shears) and possibly 343 (shears) may represent a bill-hook. No. 124 may be intended as a paten and chalice, a motif which occurs frequently in continental medieval iconography. No. 344 (shears) is perhaps a dagger. The dagger mark became common for London cutlers from 1606 (Hayward 1957, 5), and was compulsory for cutlers not free of the Cutlers' Company. It was apparently also used by members of the Company, and already in use by 1594. The hammer on Nos. 101, 143 and 147 similarly foreshadows the later hammer mark of the Armourers' Company.

The cross is a very common symbol on blades. One example occurs on a late 14th-century French sword in the Wallace Collection (Mann 1962, No. A460) as a small inlaid copper cross on both sides of the blade, similar to Nos. 120 and 170. Several similar, but post-medieval, examples appear in the catalogue of the Wallace Collection. Fleurs-de-lys appear on sword blades throughout the medieval and post-medieval periods. A half fleur-de-lys on a German or Swiss sword of about 1580 (Mann 1962, No. A482) is described as 'traces of a makers' mark', but it is clear from the range of half fleur-de-lys in the private collection that it was used as a complete mark.

No. 180 (Fig. 8) has a very close parallel in the Wallace Collection. This occurs on the blade of a serving knife with the arms of Nicholas Rolin, chancellor of Burgundy under Philip the Good from 1422 to 1462 (Mann 1962, No. A880).

No. 184 (Fig. 8), although on the broken edge of the blade, may have been nearly symmetrical. If this was so, the mark is paralleled on a European pike-head of 15th-century date in the Tower Armouries (VII 1480), another indication of the widespread use of these marks by both cutlers and bladesmiths.

It is worth noting that the earliest mark in the present collection is a deeply-stamped crescent on a small 13th-century knife (No. 31). The marks become increasingly common on 14th-century knives, and by the end of the century just over a half of the knives recovered are marked, compared with only 17 per cent of the shears.

Modern cutlers term the left side of the knife, when held with the tip pointing away from the holder, the 'mark side' and it is this side which consistently bears the makers' marks on knives in this collection. The mark is usually also close to the back and shoulder, which is both the thickest part of the blade, thus preventing distortion to the blade shape during the stamping, and the area least likely to become covered by dirt. The marks on shears are usually near the junction of the blades and arms. In contrast to the knives, the marks may occur on either side of the blade. In this collection four are stamped into the cutting surface, and five onto the outside. One pair of scissors, No. 371, from a 14th-century context also has a possible mark in which five crescents or rings have been roughly stamped onto the top of one blade, near

158 ▲	157 ▲	162 ▲	271 ▼	115 ▲	49 ▼	86 ▼
120 ▼	122 ▼	138 ▼		163 ▼	164 ◄	165 ▼
			146 ▲			
166 ▼	339 S ▲	56 ▲		268 ▲	130 ▲	161 ▲
168 ▼	156 ▲	335 S ▼	173 ▲			
97 ◄		175 ▼	330 S ▲	343 S ▲	124 ▲	344 S ▼
101 ▲	143 ▲	147 ▲		110 ▲	160 ▲	46 ▼
31 ▼	84 ▼		48 ▼	75 ▲	174 ▲	175 ▼
258 ▼	305 ▼	330 S ▲	331 S ▼	343 S ▲		
51 ▲	104 ▲	164 ►	176 ▲			

6 The makers' marks.

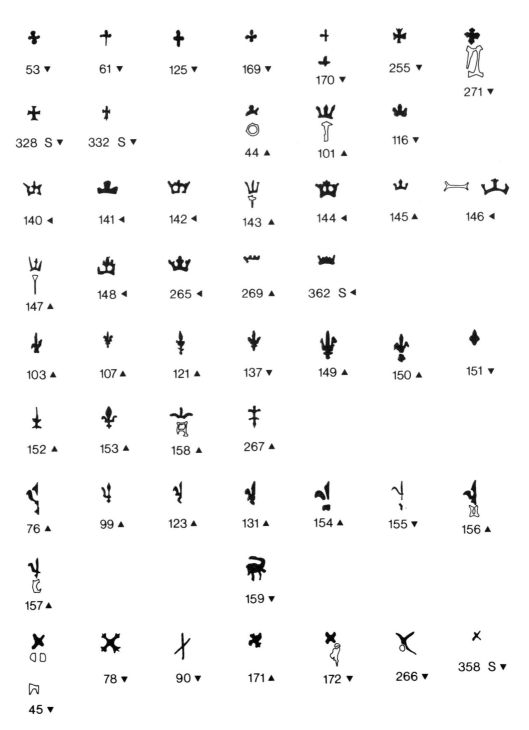

7 The makers' marks.

8 The makers' marks.

the pivot. They are so clumsily executed on what appears to be a quality item, that they may have some other explanation, although their position is similar to that used for makers' marks on knives and shears. Only two out of 119 marks may possibly be from the same punch (Nos. 55 and 72); they are also on similar knives. There is only one maker's mark which seems to have been applied by any other means, a triangle scratched onto a knife blade (No. 129).

An enormous variety of symbols were used as marks. Many were easily identified popular motifs, such as a crown or fleur-de-lys. Few are representational, but the lack of zoomorphic designs is not surprising as they are difficult to depict at such a small scale. There are two in this group, however; one is perhaps a rampant lion with the head section missing (No. 159), and the other resembles a dog (No. 97). Since the dog mark is unusually large and centrally placed on the blade, it may even be a decorative feature. Several marks resemble everyday objects, such as a key (No. 160), a pair of shears (occurring on a knife, No. 46), and a hammer (Nos. 101, 143 and 147). These items may be symbolic of the products of the smith, in the same way that ewers were sometimes shown on the seals of late medieval bell-founders. Another possibility is that they are puns on the makers' names, a popular source of amusement at the time. The small group of letter marks may also be associated with makers' names. The remaining marks comprise a variety of miscellaneous designs, a few of which are purely geometric forms.

There are twenty-one double stamps, of which two are on shears. One component is often either a common symbol such as a crown or 'rosette', or a simple motif, for example a cross or circle. There is only one apparent example of the same stamp being repeated on a single blade (No. 162); this is an elaborate semi-circular mark resembling the letter C.

Almost half of the marks contain a non-ferrous metal inlay (Table 5). Since the inlay was probably hammered cold into the impression, some of the empty marks may have once been inlaid. Although double marked blades usually have the same inlay in both marks, there are two occasions on which different inlays were used (Table 5).

Table 5.   The non-ferrous inlays in the makers' marks.

E–M14th C		L14th C		E15th C	
Tin	2	Tin	13	Tin	2
Tin/Lead	1	Double mark both Tin	4	Double mark both Tin	1
Brass	1	Copper	2	Brass	1
		Brass	11 + 1*		
		Double mark both Brass	1 + 2*		
		Double mark one Brass	2		
		Double mark one Brass one Tin	1		
		Double mark one Copper/Tin one Tin	1		
		Double mark both Gunmetal	1		

  * shears

Table 6.   Materials used for the knife handles.

Material	Date 12th C	E13th C	M–L13th C	E–M14th C	L14th C	E15th C	US	Total
Bone				1	5	2	2	10
Copper					1			1
Brass				1				1
Horn			1		8			9
Horn ?Cattle					2			2
Tin		1						1
Wood – Alder		1			1		1	3
Wood – Beech					1			1
Wood – Birch					1			1
Wood – Box	1		4*	2	14	4	1	26
Wood – Holly					1			1
Wood – Maple				1	7			8
Wood – Oak							1	1
Wood – Pomoideae Fam.		2			1		2	5
Wood – Willow/Poplar							1	1
Wood – Yew			1		1			2
Wood		1	2		4	2	3	12

  * including folding-knife handle

KNIFE HANDLES

Knife handles were made of wood, horn, bone or metal (Table 6). Wood, a cheap, readily available and easily worked material, is by far the most common (71.4 per cent) and most of the species used are both hard and flexible. The only unsuitable wood represented is oak (No.291), which although hard is prone to longitudinal splitting; the unusual shape of this handle suggests that it may have been a replacement. Many of the handles have knots along their length (pers. comm. J Watson), but it is now impossible to determine whether this wood was chosen deliberately for the elaborate grain pattern, or because it was too inferior for any other use. The most common wood is box, which has a subtle grain pattern and is generally pale in colour. It seems to be the wood called 'Digeon' (or 'Dudgeon') by the medieval cutlers (Gerards Herbal 1597, in Murray 1897, 703), and is mentioned in their Ordinances of 1379–80.

> '*Also, in order to avoid deceit of the people . . . be it ordained, that no handles of wood, except digeon, shall be coloured; but let them be sold only according as their right nature demands.*'

(Welch 1916, 261)

This testifies to the practice of dyeing handles, for the prohibition implies that a variety of woods were indeed being coloured.

Having lost some of its handle, one knife (No.281) was reused after breaking by wrapping a strip of textile around the upper section of the blade to form the new handle. Although the fibres of the textile have been completely replaced by iron corrosion, it has been identified by F Pritchard as a medium weight cloth, slightly open-textured, probably linen or canvas.

Knife handles can be classified according to their method of attachment into whittle- and scale-tang handles. Whittle-tang knives are the most common type used in the early medieval period and there are in fact no scale-tang knives in the collection earlier than the early to mid 14th century. Whittle-tang handles are fixed by pushing the pointed end of the knife tang into the handle. Some late examples have tangs which extend the length of the handle while earlier ones have shorter tangs. On scale-tang knives the handle is attached by rivets through the iron tang. This method of attachment makes it easy for more than one material to be used for the handle, although composite whittle-tang handles are also found. The distinction between the two types may have been acknowledged in the medieval period, for Chaucer mentions a Sheffield 'thwitel' in the Reeves Tale (Skeat 1912, line 3933) and in cases heard before the coroners of London in the 14th-century knives called 'thwitels' are often mentioned as weapons of offence.

Whittle-tang Handles

As Table 7 clearly shows, whittle-tang knives not only form the single type found until the early 14th century, but are also still the most common type found until the early 15th century. The tang is usually centrally placed on the blade, rectangular or square in section, and tapering toward the point. During the 12th and 13th centuries the tangs normally penetrate only a short distance into the handle, except in a rare example where the elements of a multi-piece handle were threaded onto the tang (No.15), which is therefore the same length as the handle. On later whittle-tang knives the tang often extends the whole length of the handle.

Table 7. The number of whittle- and scale-tangs.

Date	Whittle-tang	Scale-tang
L12th C	8 (100%)	
E13th C	13 (100%)	
L13th C	15 (100%)	
E–M14th C	24 (92%)	2 (8%)
L14th C	99 (66%)	51 (33%)
E15th C	8 (33%)	16 (66%)

Most whittle-tang handles are cylindrical with a wide diameter to prevent the handle splitting when the knife is flexed. They are generally very similar in shape throughout the medieval period, but rectangular-sectioned handles occur from the 14th century (No.56). There are thirty-nine whittle-tang handles made from wood, three from bone, and three from horn, for example No.90, Pl.4a.

The holes prepared for the whittle tangs are roughly shaped and may not have been made for each tang individually. The tangs may have been burnt into position or held in place with glue or wedges. The fragments of a small and roughly shaped piece of wood were found by the end of one knife tang (No. 79). A sword-hilt recently recovered from the foreshore of the River Thames had two wedges in place on either side of the tang near the shoulder.

The handles on whittle-tang knives are very seldom decorated and few techniques seem to have been employed to ornament them (Pl. 4a). The earliest, and most elaborate, is from a mid 13th-century context (No. 15). This handle consists of tin plates threaded onto the tang, with a similar copper rectangle as a shoulder plate. The looseness of these plates on the tang suggests that they were probably separated by contrasting organic plates which have since decayed. Such a method enables much narrower and more varied handles to be constructed on whittle tangs. A wooden handle from a late-13th-century context (No. 37), was lathe-turned with a ribbed surface. A small mid 14th-century handle is made from a sheet of brass, engraved with a linear design, wrapped around a wooden core (No. 59). Another more elaborate handle of this type has stamped out quatrefoils, which would have allowed a glimpse through to the underlying material (No. 82). The sides of the metal sheets have been soldered together with a white metal.

Five wooden whittle-tang knife handles have a band of metal around the blade end known as the hilt band (Fig. 2a). Two are made of iron (Nos. 55 and 238), two are tin or tinned iron (Nos. 81 and 288), and one is a copper alloy (No. 299). The only other hilt band is from a mid 13th-century context and is made from bone (No. 29). It is a disc 5mm thick, with keying on the handle side to improve the join between the two elements. This may be part of a multi-part handle similar to No. 15.

Scale-tang Handles

The earliest scale tang in the collection is a handle from a mid 14th-century context (No. 63). The source of this development is not known; possibly it was an indigenous invention but equally it may have come from abroad, perhaps from the Low Countries with the increased influence of Queen Philippa and her court. The rapid increase in popularity of scale-tang knives may be explained by a number of factors, the most important perhaps being the greater possibilities for decoration and the production of more elegant handles.

The top of the scale tang is usually a continuation of the blade back and has either parallel sides or more commonly widens towards the end. A frequent feature on the end of the tang from the late 14th century is a small lug (for example Nos. 116 and 118) to aid the attachment of an end plate. There are four anomalous scale-tang knives amongst the large late 14th-century group which have narrow tangs, with rounded ends and have been hollowed out along one side (Nos. 124–5, 141, 213).

The construction of a scale-tang handle requires many more components than a whittle tang and leads to a greater decorative use of metals. The makers of whittle-tang handles could have worked separately from the cutlers. For example, until recently in Sheffield, cutlers ordered handles in bulk from specialist handle makers. By contrast, scale-tang handles have to be constructed on the knife. Indeed they often conform to the tang shape, and give the smith greater control over the final appearance of the knife.

There are twenty-one scale-tang handles made of wood, six of bone and eight of horn. These figures show the more frequent use of bone and horn compared with whittle-tang handles, from 13 per cent to 40 per cent. Although the scales were usually filed down to fit the tang exactly, there are cruder examples where the scales overlap each side of the tang (for example No. 262).

The rivets that attach the scales are made from a number of metals, the most common being brass (46.8 per cent). They are either in the form of hollow tubes, probably shaped from sheet metal (for example No. 125, Pl. 4b), or more commonly

Table 8. The rivets used to attach the scales to the tang.

Material	E–M14th C	L14th C	E15th C
Brass Rods	1	10	1
Brass tubes	1	6	1
Iron rods		10	3
Gunmetal tubes		1	
Silver tubes		1	
Tinned iron?		1	
Tinned iron rods		1	
Brass rods, gunmetal*		1	
Iron rods, brass*		1	
Brass tubes with heads			2
Tin tubes			1
Copper alloy ?rods with heads			1

* Shoulder plate rivets.

solid rods (for example Nos. 119 and 262). There is no obvious correlation between type or size of knife and type of rivet (Table 8).

The scale-tang handles are decorated with a greater variety of techniques than their contemporary whittle-tang counterparts. Ornamented handles occur on knives of all sizes and there does not appear to be any relationship between highly decorated handles and highly decorated blades. The most common non-ferrous metal used on the handles was brass. The earliest decorated scale-tang handle amongst this assemblage is from a mid 14th-century context (No. 64); four late 14th-century handles are similarly decorated (Nos. 134 (Pl. 4c), 138, 166 and 201). All are made of either bone (3) or horn (2). The design was formed by setting tin pins into the handle, the most elaborate has a floral design surrounding 'AVE MARIE' inscribed on one side and a floral scroll on the reverse (No. 138, Pl. 4e and 5c). The design in this instance has been scratched into the bone surface as a guideline for the holes.

There are seven wooden handles decorated with false brass rivets set between the functional rivets (for example Nos. 125, 126 and 127). The decorative rivets are identical to the functional rivets from the same knife. This decoration was perhaps intended to mislead the buyers into believing that the handle was more firmly rivetted than it actually was. Certainly, without the aid of x-radiography it is impossible to distinguish which rivets are functional (Pls. 5a and 5b). There are three similar short wooden handles from a 15th-century context that are decorated with ornamental rivets clustered around the functional ones (Nos. 259, 260 and 261). They are all probably brass tubes but on two knives (Nos. 259 and 261), the tube ends have been blocked with a non-ferrous metal, possibly tin or a tin/lead alloy.

Two other decorative techniques represented in the late 14th-century group occur on bone handles. One handle has a series of hollows cut out on both sides of the scales (No. 135). The surface of the hollows is roughly finished suggesting that they were originally filled, although no metals were detected by X-Ray Fluorescence (XRF) analysis (pers. comm. P Wilthew). The other handle has a series of diagonal grooves inlaid with tin cut into the handle (No. 137). The two scales stop about 30mm from the shoulder, possibly indicating the former existence of an exceptionally long shoulder plate (Pl. 4d).

Scale-tang handles frequently have non-ferrous sheet metal shoulder plates and end plates embellishing the scale ends (Fig. 2b; Table 9). The end plates sometimes consist of two metals, such as copper alloys of contrasting colour (for example No. 261).

There are nineteen knives with shoulder plates, of which fourteen have been identified, while a dense line on the x-radiographs reveals the solder that once held others in place. They are usually plain and extend across the full blade width (for example Nos. 122 and 267). The shoulder plates appear to have been made in the following manner. The shapes are first cut out roughly, then rivetted and/or soldered between the tang and handle scales, bending the metal to form an L-shape over the scale ends. Finally the plates are trimmed. The solder used is often a white metal. The rivets are usually identical to those attaching the scales, but there are two that differ (Nos. 139 and 140). The unusual shoulder and end plates on one knife are composed of a silver casing over the wooden scale ends with a section cut away to reveal a polished bone inset (No. 136). This knife has a number of other unusual features and may perhaps be foreign in origin.

Table 9. The non-ferrous metals used for making the shoulder plates and end plates.

Late 14th C	Shoulder Plate	End Plate	Early 15th C	Shoulder Plate	End Plate
Brass	6	6			3
Brass with arsenic	1				
Copper	1	1			
Gunmetal				2	
Gunmetal with arsenic	1	1			
Silver	1				
Silver and (Bone)	1	1			
Tin					1

PLATE 4

Five decorated 14th-century handles.

(a) Decorated horn whittle-tang handle No. 90.

(b) Wooden scale-tang handle of No. 125 with decorative rivets.

(c) Bone scale-tang handle No. 134 with incised dots.

(d) Bone scale-tang handle No. 137 inlaid with tin.

(e) Bone scale-tang handle No. 138 decorated with tin pins.

a

b

c

d

e

PLATE 5

X-Radiographs of three handles.

(a) Knife No. 125 from the side, showing the tubular decorative and functional rivets.

(b) Handle of No. 126 showing the decorative and functional rod rivets.

(c) Tin pins decorating No. 138. The makers' mark, inlaid groove along the blade, and corroded shoulder and end plates are also visible.

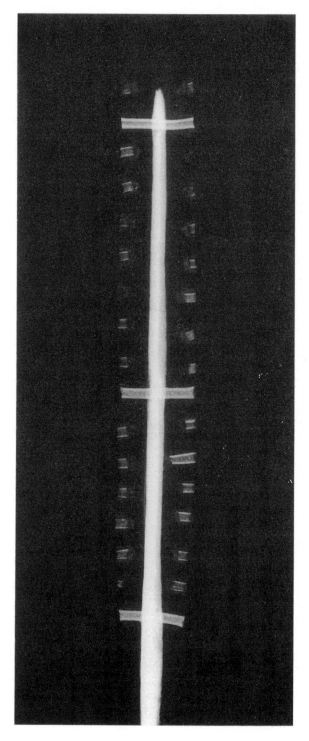

a

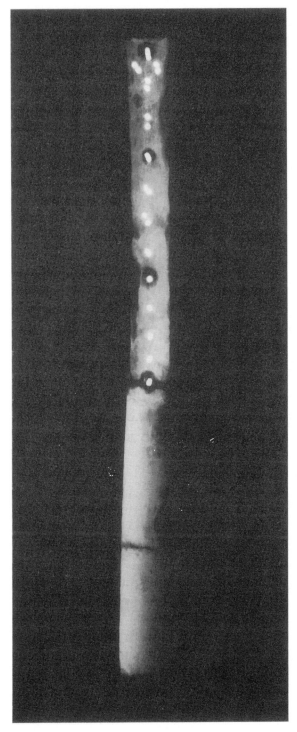

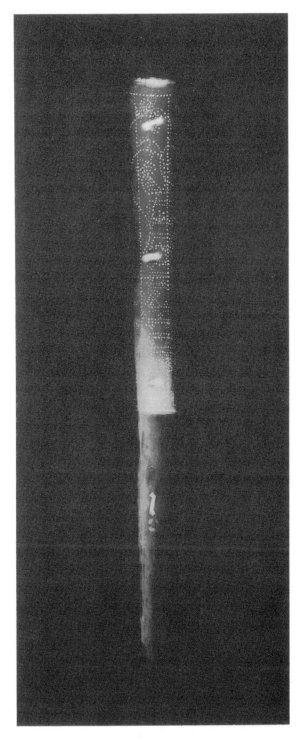

b

c

Although end plates could easily have been attached to whittle-tanged knives, in this collection they are only found with scale tangs. Only seventeen plates are still attached but the former presence of many more is shown by the number of tangs with a lug at the end. The plates were often threaded onto the lug, which was sometimes flattened over the plate to attach it more firmly. Glue or solder, usually a white metal where visible, was also probably necessary. No two plates are the same. They range from plain strips which just cover the end of the tang (for example No. 262) to multi-part plates, usually consisting of a flat sheet covering the handle end and a decorative terminal. The latter is often cone shaped and made from hammered sheet metal (No. 137) or by casting (No. 120).

Documentary Evidence

The crafts involved in the production of knives and scabbards include the Cutlers, Bladesmiths, and Sheathers; the grinders do not seem to have formed any independent association. The most useful source of information appears in the Guild Ordinances or 'rights' which were presented to, and formalised by, the Mayor and Aldermen at the Guildhall. They granted the right to search and assay all work connected with the Guild within the City of London and the suburbs, and were often concerned with particular problems related to the craft.

The History of the Guilds

The Cutlers were perhaps the most powerful, and certainly the best recorded, guild. The earliest reference to them as a group, in an inquisition dated 1285–6, mentions a house of the Cutlers at the east end of Cheapside (Welch 1916, 36). A further reference, in a will of 1311–2, also describes this area as the Cutlery, suggesting that at this date the Cutlers were concentrated there (Welch 1916, 36). The number of members in each guild at any time is not clear from the records, but Girton estimated that in 1442–3 the Cutlers guild probably had about sixty-five members with thirty apprentices and five almsfolk (Girton 1975).

The various crafts related to smithing, including the Bladesmiths, appear to have been represented as a single guild. The earliest definite references to the Bladesmiths implies that they were seeking a separate identity. On the 29 August 1376 six men were sworn into office as 'Masters of the Bladesmythes and Blakesmythes' (Sharpe 1907, 45), but less than two weeks later two different men were sworn in as 'Masters of the Bladsmythes' (Sharpe 1907, 45). Their earliest surviving ordinances were presented in 1408 (Riley 1868, 569–70) and are almost identical to the smiths' ordinances of 1364, only differing in three minor respects.

The Sheathers also appear to have established some degree of organisation by the early 14th century. They presented their first Ordinances in 1327 (Thomas 1926, 39–40).

In 1408, the seemingly ambitious Cutlers presented two petitions at the Guildhall, which appear to have resulted in their domination of the trade. The first was concerned with their relationship with the Sheathers. The petition states that they, as Cutlers, were responsible for the final product, knife and sheath. The problem lay in the fact that they had no control over the quality of the sheaths, even though '. . . as well as the said sheathers, as many others of the said trade of Cutlers applied themselves to making sheaths . . .' (Sharpe 1909, 282–3). The Cutlers were granted the right to search sheaths. The second petition was presented a few weeks later with the Bladesmiths. On the one side, the Cutlers say they will not buy blades with forged marks from non-citizens, and on the other, the Bladesmiths agree not to increase the prices of their blades without first consulting the Cutlers (Riley 1868, 568–9).

Manufacture

In 1408 the Cutlers defined the responsibility of each craft in the manufacturing process. They stated that the '. . . cutlers of the said city (London), were wont to sell knives wholly prepared and decorated, to all buyers whatsoever; but that every knife is prepared separately by three different crafts, *viz*; first, the blade by the smiths called 'Bladesmythes', the handle and the other fitting work by the cutlers, and the sheath by the sheathers; . . .' (Sharpe 1909, 282–3).

The smithing trades were understandably un-popular when practised in the crowded City. In 1394 they were '. . . warned to quit houses, by reason of the great nuisance, noise, and alarm experienced in divers ways by the neigh-bours . . .' (Riley 1868), 537–9). To placate their neighbours they regulated that in future work should only be done between daylight and nine o'clock at night, by modern standards an extreme-ly long workday. The Bladesmiths in their first Ordinances also specified that the points and edges of daggers should be hard throughout, perhaps referring to the necessity of combining iron with a steel edge (p. 8). The grinders responsible for the finishing of the blades seem to have come under the ruling of the Bladesmiths, who accused them of having ruined many blades by their lack of experience and general incompetence. In 1463 the Bladesmiths laid down that the grinders were not to call themselves 'Grinders of Blades' unless they had proved their ability. This also applied to shears, with the exception of Shearmen's shears – 'clothesheris or blades' – presumably because the Shearmen's own guild regulated their grinders. The passage continues '. . . some tyme in stede of gryndyng but whette' (Welch 1916, 335), which perhaps means that instead of properly grinding the blades on a wheel, a whetstone was used to sharpen the finished blades.

The necessity for these rules implies that they were often broken. For example, in 1344 the Cutlers forbade all work at night (Welch 1916, 237–9), but the Sheathers, when they renewed their Ordinances in 1375, rescinded their regula-tion banning night work, giving the reason that the Cutlers always worked then. The reason given for regulations against this work were that the goods produced at night might escape being checked by the Guild, and were likely to be sub-standard. The actual percentage of products checked is not known, but it is unlikely to have been very high.

Makers' Marks

In 1365 Edward III ordered that

'. . . *makers of swords and knives and other arms in the City of London shall put their true marks upon all their work . . . and the work of everyone may be known by his mark.*' (Welch 1916, 248–249).

It was also provided that all work from the suburbs should be marked. All the Smiths' and Bladesmiths' Ordinances include regulations con-cerning marks. There are no references to the marking of blades in any of the Cutlers' Ordinances until their membership included some bladesmiths, suggesting that it was the responsi-bility of the bladesmiths both to mark the blade and protect the quality that it was intended to repre-sent.

The records suggest that the mark belonged to the Master of the workshop, but sheds no light on whether he used one, or a number of marks. When a punch wore out it is also uncertain whether the same motif or another was chosen for the replacement. A respected smith would perhaps have kept to a similar mark as it came to represent quality, as do some modern brand-names, while others may have chosen marks to be associated with (or mistaken for) the good name. There was certainly a problem with the forgery of marks. The continuous counterfeiting of London marks was condemned in the Bladesmiths' Ordinances of 1408 and 1463 (Welch 1916, 285–7, 334–6), and in the 1408 joint Ordinances of the Cutlers and Bladesmiths it was stated that non-citizens fre-quently sold knives and blades marked with marks resembling those of the Bladesmiths free of the City, to cutlers and that many of the knives were faulty (Riley 1868, 568–9).

In 1452 a dispute over a mark was brought before the Court of Aldermen by a widow who had remarried a Skinner. She requested the right to continue using her late husband's mark, a double crescent, which was being used by John Morth. She won her case despite a petition by the Bladesmiths Guild in support of John Morth. There is no information on how John Morth acquired the mark. The owners of marks may have recorded their marks with the Guild, as in the following century. The continued use of a mark, if the motif remained the same, by the same workshop is possible, but it was unlikely to have stayed in the hands of one family for more than one generation, since it was not traditional for a son to follow his father's occupation in the merchant classes (Thrupp 1962, 204–6).

Sale

There are numerous references to the price and value of knives, shears and related objects in wills,

deeds and other records. These vary considerably, and as a result it is impossible to give any
estimates of prices at any specific time. The
Cutlers were only allowed to sell their products in
their house or workshop, but an exception was
allowed in 1379–80, if 'a great lord or respectable
person' requested to see the cutlery for his own
use, then it was permitted to take it to his 'place' or
hostel (Welch 1916, 258–63). The Smiths, and
later the Bladesmiths, were encouraged to sell
from their workshops, but they were also permitted sales on the pavement by St Nicholas Sham-
bles at Gracechurch and near the Tun on Cornhill
(Riley 1868, 360–1, and 568–9). By limiting the
number of places suitable for sales, the guilds
probably hoped to be able to keep a close eye on
the trade, and the standard of the goods sold.
These were the approved locations for sales, but
there is evidence that transactions occurred
elsewhere, street hawking, evening markets, and
hostelries being frequently mentioned.

There are very few references to goods being
imported into, or exported from the City.
Overseas trade in this type of object was almost
non-existent (pers. comm. V Harding), but it is
likely that a lively export trade existed with other
English towns. Goods brought into London for sale
were also supposed to be searched by the relevant
guild. These imports are mentioned as they were
often considered to be sub-standard and were sold
in inns and other unlawful places. Bladesmiths
seem to have been particularly concerned about
non-citizens who sold their wares in the City;
perhaps the continual complaint that they forged
their marks may be one of the reasons for this. In
1463 the Bladesmiths tried to limit these sales to
Leadenhall on market days (Welch 1916, 334–6).
In the same year an act of Edward IV prohibited
the importing of wares 'ready wrought', which
included 'knyves, daggers, wodeknyves, boyt-
kynes, sheres for taillours, cisours, rasours and
shethes'. (Stat. 3 Edw. IV, 4). There are a number
of references which mention exporting goods for
sale outside the City. These are usually concerned
with the fact that the wares should first be
searched, to ensure that the reputation of the
London trades were maintained.

The documentary records serve to remind us
that we can only generalise about these interre-
lated crafts. The cutlery trades produced a wide
range of objects to satisfy the needs of all levels of

society, from the jewelled handles for the nobility
to more simple tools. The craft regulations were
intended to control standards, but the extent to
which they were implemented probably depended
on the mood of the time and the honesty of the
individual workman.

Scabbards

There are 120 scabbards included in this catalogue. The majority were made to carry knives but
a few may have had some other function, eg.
No. 457. All these scabbards were made from
tanned hides. Tanning was a noxious and lengthy
process and often took up to eighteen months to
complete. The preparation of the hides should
include the removal of all the hair, although hair is
clearly visible on some of these scabbards (for
example No. 458). Tanners are mentioned frequently in the documentary records from the late
13th century, but the sources reveal little about
the methods used. The leather was sold in selds (a
kind of covered market) in the City, and it was
from these that the sheathers probably bought
their supplies. The two sides of a piece of leather
are known as the flesh and grain surfaces, the
latter being the outer, hair side. These scabbards
all have the grain on the outside, it being the
tougher and more water resistant surface. To aid
resistance to wear and tear the leather would have
been coated by a currier with grease or oils.

The scabbards were usually made from a single
piece of calf leather, about 2mm thick (Table 10).
This was presumably the approved leather for
scabbards, as in 1350 the Guild of Furbishers (who
refitted armour, weapons and garments) forbade
the use of any other for scabbards (Riley 1868,

Table 10. The type of leather used to make the scabbards.

Period	L12	E13	L13	E14	L14	E15	U/S
Calf	1	14	18	45	11	2	21
Cattle		1			1†		
Sheep/goat				2*			1*
Leather				2	2		1

* Lining or Inner Scabbard
† Calf or cattle

259). Only two outer scabbards were made from other leathers, one from cattle hide (No.383), and the other from sheep or goat skin (No.439). A small group of scabbards recovered in Leicester (Allin 1981, 161–5) were also mainly made from calf leather, but a higher percentage appeared to be sheepskin.

The shape of the knife scabbards reflects their function. They are often asymmetrical, one side being more curved than the other to fit the cutting edge. The upper section which holds the handle is fairly standard in size; only the blade section seems to vary. This pattern is consistent throughout the later 12th to early 15th centuries.

Sixteen of the scabbards are lined, four have an inner scabbard, and two have both (for examples see Fig.9). The earliest examples of both features are from late 13th-century contexts. The leather used for these is often poor quality calf (for example from the stomach area), or sheep/goat which is also a thin leather. With four exceptions the grain surface of the leather usually faces inwards in the linings and additional sheaths. They are often seamed with uneven stitching and occasionally attached to the flesh side of the scabbard with a loose 'whipping stitch'. The linings are all similar in shape to their outer scabbards. The inner sheaths are generally a miniature version of outer scabbards, except one which is made from a flat scrap of leather (No.403). One knife was found inside two decorated scabbards (Nos.397 and 398, Pl.6), the inner scabbard (No.397) was complete except that it lacked suspension slots while the outer was very worn and degraded. Four examples, probably originally non-knife scabbards (Nos.393, 433, 457 and 459), have a lining that projects beyond the top of the scabbard, and may have once had a cap.

When the decoration was completed the leather was moulded into shape, stretching and rounding the upper section to accommodate the handle, and folding in the sides of the blade section to create the seam. One side of the blade section was often made thicker than the other, to take account of the wedge-shaped section of the blade. The moulding was done when the leather was wet and elastic, probably using a wooden last of standard shape and size. The few scabbards that may have been commissioned to fit a specific knife (for example No.391, Pl.8) may have been moulded around the knife itself.

PLATE 6
Knife No.39, within scabbards Nos.397–8.

9 Stylised drawings of some lined scabbards and
   scabbards with additional sheaths.

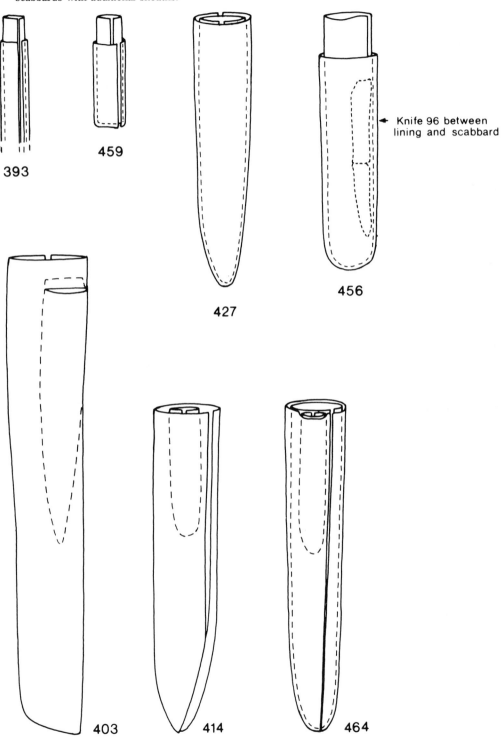

393

459

427

456

← Knife 96 between
   lining and scabbard

403

414

464

PLATE 7
Knife No. 96 with lined scabbard No. 457; a
small damaged section of the scabbard
removed to reveal the knife in position.

The seams were probably stitched while the
scabbard was on the last. They vary in position,
but are commonly down one side of the back. The
thread used was probably flax (pers. comm.
F Pritchard). Single or more commonly double
lengths of thread were used, the latter giving
straighter, stronger and 'tidier' seams (Fig. 10).
The holes for the stitches were frequently prepared with a diamond headed awl and are often at
an angle to the line of stitching to prevent the
leather tearing (Fig. 10). The stitches either go
through the flesh and grain sides to form a ridge of
seam allowance on the outside (for example
No. 462) or on the inside and outside (for example
No. 409), or they go through the edge and grain
side to produce a butt seam (Fig. 10b). The
distance between the stitches varies; they may be
as little as 3–4mm apart on some examples (for
example No. 403), or as much as 10–12mm on
others (for example No. 449); the average is about
5–7mm. Occasionally there are stitch holes in
other areas of the scabbards. The purpose of these
is often not known but some are repairs (for
example the slot on No. 427 has been mended) and
on others it is to reinforce the moulded shape. The
latter occurs frequently on the scabbards with
'wings' or an extension to the side of the handle
section, keeping the wing flat (for example
No. 373).

10 Details of the stitching on the scabbards.

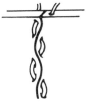

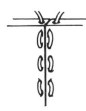

a. Awl holes are often angled

b. Flesh / grain stitch   Edge / grain stitch

c. Double thread   Single thread
   (butt seam)   (butt seam)

PLATE 8
Scabbard No.391: detail showing RICARDIE
and fleur-de-lys stamps, and rouletting.

Several scabbards have been altered, either to give a better fit or for reuse. The most common method employed seems to have been to slit the scabbard at the top, or more rarely at the bottom. At least ten scabbards have been cut in this way. In most cases the cut was deliberately made to allow more room for the knife handle, although occasionally it may have been caused accidentally by the careless withdrawal of a knife. In all but one example, where it is in the centre at the front (No.475), the cut runs down one side from the top to the handle/blade division (for example No.429) or just below (for example No.484). The few scabbards that have been cut along one side at the bottom (for example No.384), may again have been to allow space for a larger knife than the maker originally intended. Another alteration that occurs is the shortening of the scabbards by either cutting off the top (No.455) or the bottom (No.394). The latter is more common, probably because it retained the handle section, which was likely to fit a range of knife sizes (see above). The cuts across the base are usually at right angles to the sides, but one has been curved to give a more normal scabbard shape (No.379). The slits at the bottom have been seamed by a variety of stitches, the most common being a running stitch.

The decoration of medieval scabbards

MARGRETHE de NEERGAARD

Over 100 of the scabbards in this catalogue, which range in date from the mid 12th to the mid 15th centuries, feature some form of decoration on one or both surfaces. As with the knives and shears, the majority of the examples listed were found in 14th-century deposits, making any work on the development of decorative motifs and the combination of methods at times misleading. Perhaps it is also misleading to judge the decoration of the scabbards as it now appears to us, given that some were probably painted, and some even enhanced by gilding (Russell 1939, 133). Some scabbards when found still bore traces of the original paint, eg. Nos. 479 and 487, and examples have also been noted on the Continent (Baart 1977, 96, Fig. 28 No. 3. 7. 1972). Analysis of the pigment on No. 479, showed this to be vermilion. Red and possibly blue colouring were noted on a scabbard from the Austin Friars site at Leicester and were suggested to be either vegetable dye or iron oxide/red earth pigment (Allin 1981, 161). Black dye was also used throughout the medieval period, a combination of tannin and iron oxide. Other colours were achieved with a variety of vegetable dyes; brazil for brown, indigo for blue and pomegranate for yellow (Waterer 1956, 156).

Although there are exceptions, in general the quality of craftsmanship is not the highest, and does not achieve the standards of contemporary leatherwork on the Continent. One should not judge the quality of the decoration on the basis of examples such as No. 484. This crude engraving was probably executed by the owner, and should be regarded as graffiti. With the likely exceptions of No. 425, which couples the arms of England with those of Navarre, and of No. 391, the 'Ricardie' scabbard, the scabbards were probably decorated in accordance with current styles and preferences, but not to the requirements of a particular client. Many designs are stylised to the point of being virtually identical in terms of motifs, form and treatment of surface space (cf Nos. 405–408, 414 and 417).

Decoration seems to have been a concern of the scabbard makers from the earliest times onwards. Indeed, a Neolithic dagger scabbard displays incised linear decoration (Waterer 1956, 150) of the same type which occurs as a space filler on the backs of the later scabbards.

Engraving was the earliest and most common method of decoration during the medieval period. The depth of the engraving varied a great deal according to the pressure exerted, with a greater depth for the main outline and borders, and shallower, lighter lines for detail and background hatching (eg. No. 473). The leather was first dampened for easier working and laid flat. The division of the scabbard into front and back zones, as well as handle and blade sections were first engraved, and then ruled out with a graver. No. 435, with a moulded handle section, was probably engraved first and then moulded; the lines at the base of the section curve slightly over the moulding.

The division of the scabbard into two decorative panels on the front, roughly conforming to the knife handle and the blade seems to have been established by the 10th or 11th century (Russell 1939, 135; cf MacGregor 1982, 143, Fig. 73 No. 681, MacGregor 1978, 55, Fig. 35). The division is sometimes further emphasised by the use of different motifs and even methods of decoration in the two sections (cf Nos. 435, 436 and 437). The back also is often divided to indicate the handle and the blade but the method of decoration remains the same, even if the designs are only linear space fillers. The convention is so strong that it occurs on the above mentioned No. 484.

The relationship between the decorative motifs chosen for these early scabbards and the decorative treatment given to carved stone surfaces (cf Lang 1978, Pl. 1d) is quite startling, and it is possible throughout the Middle Ages to see a relationship between the treatment of motifs featured in sculpture and the selection of particular motifs for scabbard decoration. It is also possible indirectly to trace back a relationship through sculpture to marginal decoration in illuminated manuscripts. Richardson uses motifs in marginal illustrations as a means of dating the Hungate scabbards from York (Richardson 1959, 102, 3), and although comparison with some of the material in the catalogue seems to contradict this dating, (see below) it otherwise confirms the validity of the relationship.

The earliest and most obvious motif is interlace, which was used on scabbards long after its popularity for sculpture had ceased. Indeed, to quote Russell 'the persistence of old styles well into the new styles is characteristic of the minor decorative arts' (Russell 1939, 135). One side note to offer is that whereas the decorative effectiveness of interlace could be appreciated whatever the angle of suspension and could therefore be displayed to advantage horizontally (cf the Middleton cross), from the 12th century onwards there was an increased emphasis on the verticality of the decoration, most effectively displayed if the scabbard was worn suspended vertically from the belt. The decoration on most scabbards remains consistently frontal throughout the medieval period, and the two factors, angle of suspension and arrangement of decoration, may be related. There is also the fact that, except on the short wide handle sections on rondel dagger scabbards such as No. 488, both handle and blade sections were longer than they were wide, and thus well suited to vertical decoration.

None of the catalogued examples display panels of interlace of the intricacy shown on Anglo-Scandinavian examples from London (Waddington 1927, 526 and Pl. LXV) and elsewhere in the country (MacGregor 1978, Fig. 35). Modified interlace survives into the mid 14th century, eg. No. 410, but rather than interwoven fronds and elongated beasts, here there are looped and knotted rope patterns. No. 469 displays a loose simplified interlace on the front handle section with a design representing two overlapping fibrous strands on the blade section. The blade section of No. 409 has a three-plaited braid with engraved lines to simulate fibres, whilst the handle decoration consists of plaiting resembling a woven tabby with engraved lines and pricked dots to indicate the different fibres or even types of fibres. Pricked decoration was not usual but occasionally occurs to provide a textured background effect which contrasts with the main decoration. The pricked

decoration on the handle section of No. 413 forms a particularly effective background for the loose curling fibre encircling a single straight strand. Nos. 405, 407 and 408 have the same woven effect mentioned above, but the impression of a textile is achieved by lightly engraved parallel lines. No. 464 has this same loose plaiting against a lightly criss-crossed background, and the effect is that of a series of four-petalled flowers.

From the mid 13th century extending into the 14th, many decorated scabbards feature zoomorphic decoration outlined with a blunt tool, occasionally embossed, frequently in combination with a background of single stamped dots. Not only has the front decoration continued to be divided into sections indicating the knife components, but the designs in each panel are often enclosed in entwining circlets of foliage which fill any gaps with three lobed leaves. In some instances, the intertwining tendrils have been simplified into linked ovals or circlets with single oval leaves filling the gaps (cf Richardson 1959, Fig. 29 No. 4), reminiscent of biblical scenes enclosed by linked circular frames in the borders of medieval manuscripts (cf. BL Ms Harl 1527 II f38v). Russell believed that such embossed zoomorphic decoration encircled by plant tendrils derived from the influence of Gothic sculpture (Russell 1939, 137). This is confirmed by examples such as a mid 13th-century window soffit in the north transept of Westminster Abbey, where the heads and torsos of the central figures are enclosed in a circular frame formed by the tendrils of a long vine, with the empty corners filled with trilobate leaves. Although scabbards never display human heads or figures, the overall treatment of space is very similar to Nos. 379 and 380. In most cases, the animals are recognisable as hares, boars, cats, or birds. It has been suggested that these scabbards may have held hunting knives and No. 377, on which a hound pursues a horned goat along the scabbard length, lends support to this theory. Along with engraving and occasional embossing, two less common methods of decoration seem to have been used on some of these scabbards. Small areas of the background were lightly scraped back with a sharp tool, creating a contrasting surface effect, or a hot implement was impressed upon the leather, leaving some areas darker than others (cf Nos. 414 and 419).

The combined zoomorphic/foliate decoration on

one group of 13th-century scabbards is very different, and yet is probably derived from similar sources. All have stamped ring and dot backgrounds. Nos.378 and 475 feature long-bodied crested birds with tail feathers extending into a three-feathered curl similar to the curling plant tendrils that form the central decorative elements of No.383. No.489 has another winged beast set against a background of stamped ring and dot, contorting its awkward contours into the tapering scabbard space. This last example, a similar motif treated differently, because of its highly moulded relief is almost overtly sculptural in overall effect. Similar long-bodied beasts with elongated tails and necks also extend their considerable lengths around the borders of contemporary manuscripts (Such as BL Ms Burney 345 f127) or coil themselves within decorative capitals (BL Royal Ms 12 C XIX f67).

Embossing, creating low relief raised decoration on leather, had its origin in Spain (Waterer 1956, 180), and on scabbards involved the modelling in the round of animals, leaves and flowers. The designs were either worked from the back of the softened leather, or moulded with flat and pointed tools from the front. The thin leather was stretched over a wooden frame, the motifs outlined with blunt tools and the borders graved (Russell 1939, 135). Two of the later scabbards, Nos.418 and 464, have raised decoration supported by the insertion of cubes of leather. The cubes seem to have been pushed into place and held there by pressure. Whereas embossing by the usual method created an even and continuous effect, this method of stuffing the leather is lumpy and uneven, with the cubes seemingly positioned to coincide with heads and bodies. In both instances, the decoration is completed with engraved zoomorphic motifs, executed prior to the insertion of the cubes. It would have been a faster, less expensive and simpler way of approximating embossing, and it is difficult to judge its effectiveness from the scabbards in their present state.

The decoration of the scabbard back was dealt with as a matter of secondary importance and was generally of inferior workmanship to that on the front. The arrangement and composition of the decoration seems to have been dictated to a great extent by the position of the seam, with 40 examples having a centre back seam, 32 a side back seam, 11 a split seam and 17 a side seam. In the case of the most common centre back seam, the decoration had to be composed symmetrically on either side of this central feature, usually involving pairs of opposing horizontal or diagonal engraved lines (cf Nos.387, 437, and 438). A side seam allowed more flexibility in surface treatment with the back decorated as a single panel. Several such scabbards have a number of half quatrefoils or trilobate arches positioned vertically along one or both of the long edges (cf Nos.414 and 417). This decoration is one of the features which led Richardson to assign a 13th-century date to the York example (Richardson 1959, 103 and Fig.29.1), but the examples in the present collection have all been dated to the mid 14th century on the evidence of associated pottery. As with the interlace decoration noted above, the different motifs noted by Richardson probably continued in use on scabbards long after they ceased to be fashionable in other art forms. Richardson links these particular elements to the three-arched frames popular in Romanesque architecture and thence to 13th-century illustrations (Richardson 1959, 103). It seems more likely that their vertical use on scabbards, and the fact that these motifs occur as elements in their own right, not as frames, creates essentially a floral effect, and that the double edge suggests petals. When this same three-lobed element occurs on a mid 14th-century scabbard from Baynard's Castle, as the main blade motif, the floral effect was obtained by short, curving, engraved lines indicating the folds of the petals (No.435).

Possibly it would be more accurate in some instances, rather than to trace particular influences back to other contemporary art forms, to say simply that the same overall principles of artistic approach and attitude applied. All display the same *horror vacui*, less a fear of empty space than the feeling that decoration must be adapted to cover all available visible frontal surfaces. All these media for decoration display a love of symmetry, the adaptation of individual motifs to fit particular and peculiar spaces and the tendency to compartmentalise space.

Decoration derived from heraldry first occurs in the present collection on a late 13th-century scabbard, No.391, and reaches a peak in the mid 14th century. With the popularity of heraldic motifs comes the fashion of using repeated heraldic stamps to form the decorative background. In some cases, the fine stamping is the only decoration, creating almost a textural effect, and for the first time the interplay of empty and filled space is used for deliberate effect. Both shields and lozenges occur framing individual or combinations of motifs. Only those scabbards with shields representing or imitating coats of arms have been described as heraldic in the catalogue text. This is not strictly accurate. By far the most popular form of decoration in the 13th century was the stamping of individual heraldic elements such as fleur-de-lys (Nos. 392, 395, and 396), or a combination of the most common elements. It would be tempting to see in this an heraldic shorthand indicating specific allegiances, but with few exceptions, the stamps are the most basic of heraldic components; for example, No. 447 has four lions *passant gardant* in rectangular frames on the handle section, with three fleurs-de-lys set end to end in lozenges on the blade. A possible interpretation is that the lion represents the descent of the male line while the fleur-de-lys in the lozenges is the female, but the earliest proven example of the lozenge enclosing a woman's coat of arms is that of Frances Brandon (d. 1559). The use of heraldic elements is more than decoration, reflecting the extent and influence of heraldry as a social phenomenon.

Stamping was actually quite an early method of scabbard decoration, although used primarily and in its most developed form on leather bookbindings. As with engraving, the leather was probably decorated when wet and flat, otherwise the stamping would be uneven, and it would be difficult to leave a complete impression. The field dividers would be ruled on the leather after the placement of the stamps, as is shown by No. 399 (Pl. 12) on which the tip of a stamped quatrefoil in a lozenge has been obscured by a thick engraved line. The stamps used for the scabbards were probably similar to the mid 12th-century bookbinding stamp found at Belvoir Priory (Antiq. J. 1924, 272). This was 20mm square, 4mm thick with a 30mm tang on the back to take a wooden handle. The design was of an animal with bird's feet, against the background of a three-branched tree. Stamps of this size and complexity do not occur on the scabbards until the 13th century, but Hobson notes the use of 12th-century Romanesque stamps on 15th-century leatherwork (Hobson 1929, 5). The range of stamps used on the scabbards is limited (see Fig. 11, Pl. 8–25 and compare with Blomquist 1938, 161, Bild 34), compared with the range and complexity of the stamping to be found on earlier (mid to late 12th-century) leatherwork on the Winchester and Durham bindings. This seems to reflect both the decline in the quality of craftsmanship when this particular aspect of leatherworking ceased to be centred in the monastic workshops, and perhaps the conventional tastes of the market.

Most stamps, for example the fleur-de-lys and single dots, seem to have borne single motifs, impressed repeatedly upon the leather to create an overall surface effect. On some, single circular stamps have been placed to create a central zoomorphic figure. For example, on Nos. 444 and 462, each lion is different, which would not be the case if the lions themselves were stamped. In addition to the single dots, stamps with several dots in a row were used, for example on No. 404, where the stamp had a row of six small circles placed very closely together across the decorative field. Another method of stamping dots on scabbards as background fillers was that of roller-stamping or rouletting, possibly using small wheels with raised dots on the edge which would leave the almost parallel lines of impressed dots seen on scabbards such as Nos. 391 and 392.

According to Russell, the most popular form of leather decoration in the late 14th to 15th centuries was incision, using a sharp tool to cut the leather through approximately half its thickness (Russell 1939, 139), and it is certainly within this period that the few incised examples in the collection should be placed. The depth of the incision coupled with the thickness of the leather made both precision and sharply angled cuts difficult. Nonetheless, combined with painting, as on No. 479, the designs would have been both effective and easily visible. Only two archaeologically-recovered scabbards have incised decoration, with a third coming from the Museum of London collection, of which only No. 450 can be dated to the mid 14th century. In the material discussed here, engraving and stamping remain the dominant methods of decoration amongst the 14th-century finds. The sharpness of the knife coupled with the depth of the incision seem to have made it difficult to achieve the fineness of execution and detail seen elsewhere, especially when it came to fine incisions, small motifs and curves.

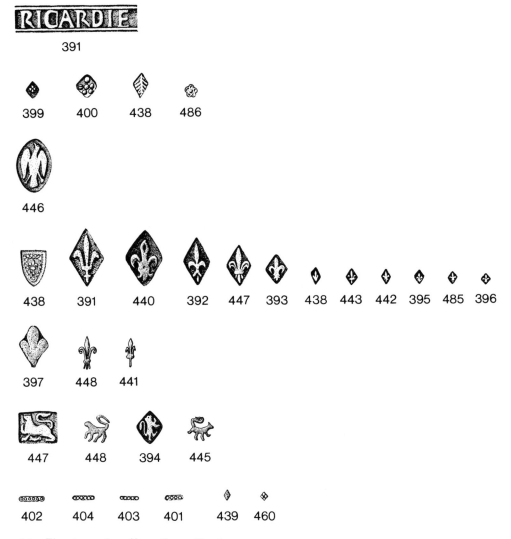

11 The stamped motifs on the scabbards.

No. 479, probably late 14th century, bears this out with its deeply cut lines and the awkwardness that is particularly evident in the curved lines on the back. A later incised scabbard, not from London (Northampton Museum of Leathercraft Acc. No. 487.56), has deep incisions limited to long, slow curves and straight lines, with more intricate and delicate lines more lightly and finely incised.

Chaucer's description of Sir Topas in *The Canterbury Tales* includes the observation that 'his jambeaux were of quirboilly' (Skeat 1912, line

2065). *Cuir boilli* was a method whereby the leather was soaked in oil or wax to increase the suppleness of the materials and thus increase the ease with which it could be worked. On drying, the object became very hard indeed. None of the scabbards in the catalogue seem to have been treated in this fashion; its use would seem to have been restricted to highly modelled scabbards to aid in holding the shape of the decoration, or, in the instance of multi-compartmented scabbards, simply in holding the overall shape.

A note on the heraldic decoration of the scabbards

TONY WILMOTT

The question of how far it is possible to identify heraldry on medieval objects is a difficult one, particularly in the absence of either inscriptions or colour. This is largely due to the number of possible identifications, in different tinctures, which could be applied to any basic linear design. The question of whether the decoration is meant to be representative or merely an imitation of current fashion also affects any attempt at identification. The only permissible comparative material for medieval heraldry is contemporary (Wilmott, forthcoming). Any later source may include material added to the medieval corpus at a later date. Unfortunately contemporary medieval heraldic sources do not embrace the complete corpus of medieval heraldry, so there will always remain a number of arms which are unidentifiable. Despite these problems, it is sometimes the case that the decorative devices or combination of devices is distinctive enough for an identification to be suggested, or a number of potential identifications from which unlikely candidates can be eliminated on the basis of the object's find spot, date or other criteria.

In a previous note (Wilmott 1981), the frequency in scabbard decoration, distribution and identification of the arms *a fess between two chevrons* (Fig. 12 No. 20) was examined. In the present catalogue, these occur singly on three scabbards and in combination with other arms on a further four (Fig. 13). After studying alternative identifications, it was established that those who held these arms were mostly connected with the Fitzwalter family, who bore *or, a fess between two chevrons gules*. The Fitzwalters held the lordship of Baynard's Castle from 1111 until 1275 (Kingsford 1916, 60), and claimed the title of hereditary standard bearer to the City of London militia from the twelfth century until 1437 (Brooke 1975, 215). If painted in their correct colours, it seems unlikely that the arms would be mistaken for those of

anyone other than the Fitzwalters. The possibility that the scabbards should be seen as items of livery equipment was suggested (Wilmott 1981, 138). A further scabbard with this motif has been excavated in Norway (Bryggen Museum Acc No. 1537; pers. comm. G Bolstad), and since the arms, A *fess between two chevrons* does not seem to occur in Norwegian medieval heraldry, this seems to confirm the theory that many scabbards found in Norway parallel English examples and were probably imports (Russell 1939, 137; Herteig 1951, 184).

The arms shown on the scabbards are shown in Figs. 12 and 13, and are described below in the form of an ordinary, a conventional means of listing arms in alphabetical order of charges, eg. Bar, Beast etc.

The Ordinary

The first group of arms are shown conventionally on shields.

1 Barry of seven
2 Three Leopards
3 A bend
4 A bend compony between two cotises
5 A bend compony between two cotises, (or ? a bend paly between two cotises)
6 A bend cotised wavy(?)
7 Two bends, a bordure
8 Three bends
9 Chequy
10 Chequy, a bordure
11 Chequy, a chief

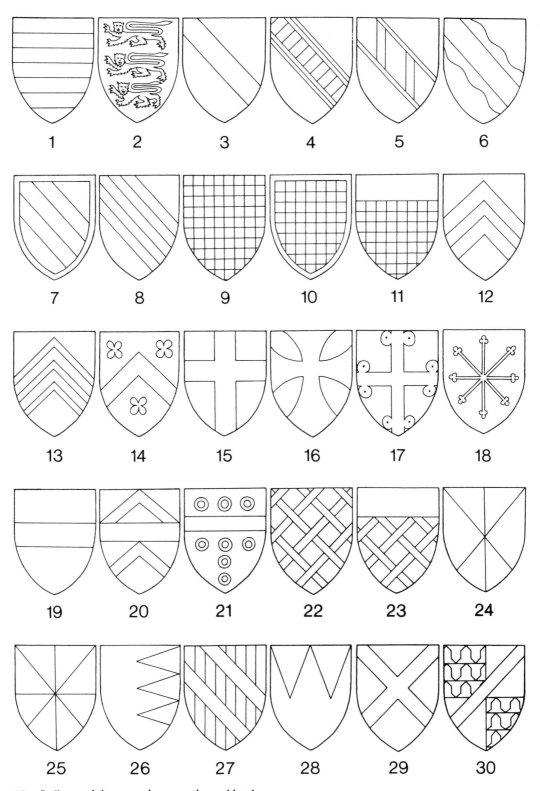

12 Ordinary of the arms shown on the scabbards.

12 Two chevrons

13 Three chevrons

14 A chevron between three quatrefoils

15 A cross

16 A cross patee throughout

17 ?A cross botonny

18 An escarbuncle

19 A fess

20 A fess between two chevrons

21 A fess between eight annulets, three and five (?)

22 Fretty

23 Fretty, a chief

24 Gyronny of six

25 Gyronny of eight

26 Per pale indented

27 Paly, two bends

28 Two piles

29 A saltire

30 Quarterly, one and four vair, a bend sinister

31 Quarterly, a bend

32 Quarterly, a bend within a bordure

33 Quarterly, two and three a fess, overall a bend, a bordure

Further heraldic designs occurring on lozenges.

34 A castle triple towered

35 A cross voided pommetty

36 A fleur-de-lys

37 A fleur-de-lys dimidiating a castle triple towered

38 A mascle fleury (or pommetty)

A Semee de lys dimidiating semee of castles triple towered; arms probably represented by Ordinary No. 37

B A cross voided pommetty; arms probably represented by Ordinary No. 35

Discussion

There are several factors to be taken into account when considering these devices. Firstly, while in some instances there may be some significance in the combination of devices on a scabbard, for the most part the likelihood is that there is not. The repetition on several scabbards of complex arms of the sort which might not readily leap to the mind of a leatherworker decorating his wares may be an indication that such a significance should be sought. Scabbards with arms unique to themselves, especially when only single shields, should be especially instructive, and there may be some significance in the object's provenance.

Identifications have been attempted using medieval heraldic sources, chiefly the rolls of arms. These are listed in brackets after each identification using the alphabetical codes laid down in the *Catalogue of English Medieval Rolls of Arms* (C.E.M.R.A., Wagner 1950). Given the dates assigned to the scabbards, rolls of arms from the earliest, *c.*1244, to *c.*1350 have been consulted.

The fleur-de-lys and the castle seldom occur separately, and are most frequently found in their dimidiated form as ordinary No. 37. This leads to the suggestion that the charges are not arbitrary, but are intended to be meaningful in combination. It is probable that, as they occur in lozenges, they are not arms in themselves but derived from and alluding to arms. The dimidiation of the two charges, and their association in any other way appear in medieval heraldry only as the arms of Alphonse, Count of Poitou, whose arms were *azure, semee-de-lys or, dimidiating gules, semee of castles tripled-towered or* (C; FW, Fig. 13 A). Alphonse was the sixth son of Louis VIII of France and Blanche of Castile, and died in 1271 without heirs (Humphery-Smith 1973, 57). Engraved castles dimidiated with fleurs-de-lys occur on four examples, of which one, No. 488, also carries the design ordinary No. 35. The arms shown in Fig. 13 B are a possible interpretation of this device which is presented on a lozenge. The arms *gules, A cross voided pommettee argent* (C; FW; MP) are those of Count Raymond VII of Toulouse who died in 1279 leaving his daughter Jeanne as his heir (Pinches and Wood 1971, 86). Jeanne was married to Alphonse of Poitou (Powicke 1962, 100–102), and

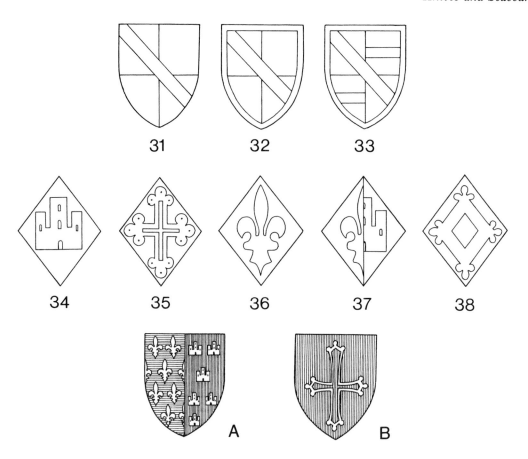

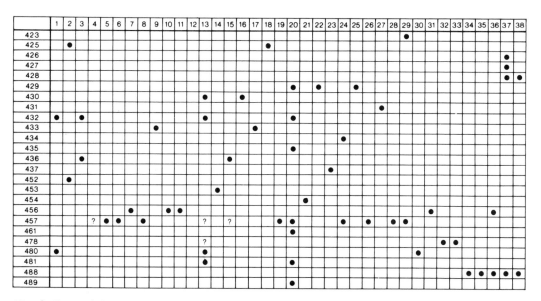

	1	2	3	4	5	6	7	8	9	10	11	12	13	14	15	16	17	18	19	20	21	22	23	24	25	26	27	28	29	30	31	32	33	34	35	36	37	38
423																													•									
425		•																•																				
426																																					•	
427																																					•	
428																																					•	•
429																				•		•			•													
430													•		•																							
431																															•							
432	•		•										•							•																		
433									•								•																					
434																								•														
435																				•																		
436			•											•																								
437																							•															
452		•																																				
453													•																									
454																				•																		
456							•			•	•																		•					•				
457				?	•	•		•					?		?				•	•			•		•	•	•											
461																				•																		
478													?																				•	•				
480	•												•																	•								
481													•							•																		
488																																		•	•	•	•	•
489																				•																		

13   Ordinary of the arms shown on the scabbards,
and concordance with catalogue numbers.

the heraldry on these scabbards may therefore reflect this marriage and the union of Toulouse and Poitou under Alphonse.

The only other Continental arms identifiable on the scabbards are those shown on catalogue Nos. 425 and 456. On No. 425, the familiar arms of England, *gules, three leopards or* (Ordinary No. 2, found in many rolls of arms) are combined with the equally distinctive Ordinary No. 18, the arms of the Kingdom of Navarre. The early arms of Navarre were *gules, an escarbuncle or* (MP; C). In the 14th century, an *orle* of chains was added. It is uncertain at what precise date these became a regular feature of the arms, although they do appear on arms on a mid-13th century sword-belt (Collin 1955, 10). Other continental arms appear on another scabbard from the Custom House site, catalogue No. 456, where the arms of the Duke of Burgundy (*bendy or and azure, a bordure gules*; MP; B; C; FW etc) seem to be represented (Ordinary No. 7).

The question arises as to why scabbards showing Continental arms should occur in London. Clearly, the function of the City as a port would be one explanation, but the arms of Navarre do occur in association with those of England. During the 14th century, the royal houses of England and Navarre were closely connected (Powicke 1962, 268), perhaps the closest relationship being the proposed betrothal in 1273 between the heir of Edward I, his son Henry who died young, and Jeanne, the daughter of Henry of Navarre (ibid. 238). It is probable that the scabbard reflects such a connection.

Only one scabbard features a single shield with the design on the shield sufficiently individual to represent authentic arms. Catalogue No. 437 displays the arms *fretty, a chief* (Ordinary No. 23). In the rolls, the simple *fretty* coat occurs for over 20 families, and it is therefore impossible to suggest any identification. With the addition of a *chief* however, two possibilities emerge as likely candidates. The Yorkshire family of Fitzhugh is represented in the rolls by one Henry (B, E, M. N, PO, P) who flourished 1300–1356 (Ktds. Edw. I, II, 40). He bore *azure, fretty and a chief or*. Two members of the St. Leger family of Kent, Sussex and Surrey (Kts. Edw. I, IV, 232) used the arms *azure fretty argent*, Ralph with the *chief or* and William with the *chief gules* (FW). It is not possible to say which of these families the arms on the

scabbard are meant to represent, although proximity to London might suggest the St. Legers. The next design to be considered also has possible Yorkshire connections.

Catalogue No. 480 shows one shield which is especially significant, featuring the fur *vair*. The implication of this is important, as to all intents this indicates the colour which should be applied to part of the arms, in turn suggesting that a specific coat is intended. The accuracy is marred by the fact that the arms have been engraved in mirror image, as shown (Fig. 13 No. 30). It is likely, then, that these are the arms of the Constable family of Flamborough during the early 14th century and subsequently. The arms appear in the 14th century for William and John Constable in many rolls (L, M, PO, WNR, Q, LM, AS), and are blazoned *quarterly, 1 and 4 gules, 2 and 3 vair, overall a bend or*. These arms are combined on the scabbard with the arms *three chevrons* and *barry of seven* (Ordinary Nos. 13 and 1). Each of these arms is recorded for in excess of ten families, rendering identification and the significance of the arms in combination impossible to recover. These two shields also occur with the arms of the Fitzwalters on No. 432.

One scabbard, catalogue No. 457, features a very distinctive shield, ordinary Nos. 4(?) and 5, *a bend compony between two cotises*. This does not appear in any of the contemporary late 13th–early 14th century rolls, but in later sources, in particular in the heraldic decoration of the later 14th century in the cloisters of Canterbury Cathedral, the arms appear only for the Hertfordshire family of Leventhorp (Griffin 1915, 507). This family bore *argent, a bend compony gules and azure between two cotises azure*. The same arms appear elsewhere on two scabbards in the Museum of London (A3664 and MIV 69 4634), not included in the present collection.

The remaining arms are too general in their designs and have too many possible attributions for an identification to be attempted. This does not necessarily mean that they were all purely decorative. On the contrary, the use of a few arms distinctive enough to identify suggests that many more were meant to be recognized. It should be remembered that at this early stage in the development of heraldry, arms comprised just such simple devices as are shown on these scabbards.

Roll of Arms Consulted

AS Ashmolean Roll *c.*1334 (Heraldry Soc. of Scotland 1983)

B Glover's Roll *c.*1255 (Stanford-London 1967)

C Walford's Roll *c.*1275 (Stanford-London 1967)

E St. George's Roll *c.*1285 (Heraldry Soc. of Scotland 1983)

FW FitzWilliam Roll *c.*1270–80 (Humphery-Smith 1973)

L First Dunstable Roll *c.*1308 (Heraldry Soc. of Scotland 1983)

LM Lord Marshall's Roll *c.*1310 (Heraldry Soc. of Scotland 1983)

M Nativity Roll *c.*1300 (Brault 1973)

MP Matthew Paris Shields *c.*1255 (Tremlett 1967)

N Parliamentary Roll *c.*1312 (Heraldry Soc. of Scotland 1983)

P Grimaldi's Roll *c.*1350 (Grimaldi 1835)

PO Powell's Roll *c.*1350 (Greenstreet 1889, 1890)

Q Collins' Roll *c.*1295 (Heraldry Soc. of Scotland 1983)

The use of knives, shears, scissors and scabbards

MARGRETHE de NEERGAARD

Most of the artefacts in this catalogue were probably the possessions of the common man. They were implements carried about the person for use as and when the need occurred. Only towards the end of our period can any specialisation be seen with the development of the table knife.

Knives are far and away the most common type, 308 in all, reflecting their importance and the wide variety of potential uses. Knives need flexible blades and a sharp cutting edge but the size of the blade and the shape, especially that of the cutting edge and tip, determine their precise function. The range in the complete knife lengths, handle, tang and blade, is from 92mm to 236mm, with the blades alone varying from 42mm to 198mm. Handle length and the material used may also have affected usage; longer handles allowing more pressure to be exerted, the blade used horizontally or slightly angled, and the shortest handles held almost vertically and using only the tip. Those measured ranged from 54mm to 134mm, with 19 of the 42 between 86 and 98mm. Wood was the most common material used for handles, being both flexible and strong if the right wood was chosen. The tendency of wood to swell and split when wet was recognized and combatted by the use of hilt bands.

It would have been difficult to exert much pressure on knives with very slender blades, such as No. 131, making these, as well as the small decorated blades such as No. 14 and No. 25, more suitable for delicate work. A long thin blade would be likely to snap if subjected to much pressure. Most, however, would be suited for preparing food and eating at table. The presence of a whittle- or a scale-tang handle does not necessarily imply a difference in function between the two, although the supplanting of the whittle-tang knives by those with scale tangs from the 14th century onwards (see Table 6) coincides with the increasing specialisation of knives and the emergence of the

'table knife' as an entity distinct from the multi-purpose knife.

The longer, broad-bladed, parallel-sided knives, such as No. 72, and those with blades which widen from the shoulder, Nos. 1, 54, 55, and 73, could have been used at the table for the carving and presentation of meat, 'carving knives', or as trencher knives. Knives of this shape occur in small numbers in all periods. The large wide blade of No. 76 with its thick section, 6mm, may also have been a carving knife of some kind. Knives with squared single or double notched blades feature in manuscripts from the 12th century onwards specifically for eating fish at table (Fig. 14) and these may represent the earliest specialised table knives. No identical knives survive from London, although the wide swelling blades of Nos. 112 and 113 have been suggested as fish knives and are similar to the present-day form.

The increased number of longer, more elegant blades in the 14th century, coupled with extensively decorated scale-tang knife handles, may be another reflection of the emergence of the table knife. Carrying knives around in scabbards seems to have been much less common during this period and the display factor involved in laying decorated knives upon a table should be considered. Certainly the forms of No. 136, both handle and blade, as

14 Notched 'fish knives'. There are no known archaeological examples. 12th century, from Gregory's Moralia, Paris, Bibl Nat Ms Latin 15675 f8v.

well as the handles of Nos. 134, 135, 137 and 138 are very close to the table knives of the 16th and 17th centuries (cf. Hayward 1957, P1.1) and indeed are largely retained by the table knives of the present day. A knife manufactured specifically for use in cutting cooked foods would not have needed a very high quality cutting edge. For example, knives made from piled wrought iron would have possessed a soft edge (Fig. 5 No. 7). Table knives, subject to less rough use than a general purpose knife, may not have needed particularly hard cutting edges. Other knives are easier to identify as carving knives and cleavers. The breadth of No. 111 is paralleled by surviving carving knives and in manuscript illustrations (Fig. 15). No. 70 displays the characteristics of a solid, utilitarian cleaver, such as is shown in the scenes of food-preparation in the Luttrell Psalter.

15 Cook wielding large-bladed cleaver. Note the rivetted handle. 14th century, from BL Add Ms 42130 f207b.

It has not been the intention to include tools in this catalogue. However, with many knives and knife-tools, the dividing line is not distinct. Specialist knives were used in various crafts, notably wood- and leather-working. Specialisation was a gradual process, and, as with cloth shears (see below), multi-purpose knives may have been used prior to the development of a particular implement.

Knives used in leather-working remained largely unchanged from the 11th to the 19th century (Waterer 1956, 154). Some are unmistakable in shape and purpose, for example a currier's knife has an edge set at right angles to the blade; others, like the butt knives and the straight and curved-edged knives, were and are virtually indistinguishable from the multi-purpose knives. Straight flat knives were used for flat cutting such as trimming leather from the flesh side of the skin. Currier's knives required such sharp and delicate edges that they needed sharpening every few minutes. Indeed, the extreme thinness of knife No. 35, 1mm as opposed to the average 2–3mm, and its long parallel-sided blade has led Dr Ian Goodall to suggest that it was used in some aspect of the leather-working process (pers comm). The types of knives used varied according to the branch of the craft concerned. Harness-makers and glovers had to work with very thick leather, the glovers used deer-skin, requiring more effort to trim off the inner layers of skin. This necessity is reflected in the relatively wide thick blade of No. 304, a 15th century glovers knife.

It would be tempting to identify No. 102 as some sort of tool, with its width of 13mm, a thickness of 6mm, and a very long tang, although the ridges along the blade back appear to be decorative. Both the shape and proportions of this knife are unique in the present collection. No. 306, which has an uncomfortably short handle and a short triangular blade may also have been a tool, perhaps used by carpenters for marking measurements.

Indications of wear and sharpening have been noted in the text where they have been definitely identified, but analysis of sharpening and wear patterns has not been done. A knife with a soft cutting edge would be more likely to display a pronounced shape due to a combination of wear and repeated sharpening (for example, No. 16). Many of the blades seem to have been discarded due to breakage, which has occurred most fre-

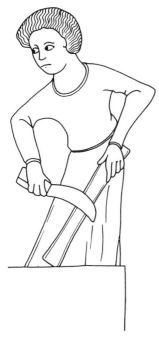

quently at mid-blade in all groups. After repeated use, all knives would have required sharpening to a new edge, and this would have been achieved using a hone-stone, in London usually of Norwegian Ragstone, a light grey schist (Figs. 16 and 17; also Bodl. Ms. 264 f.113b), sometimes worn suspended from the belt. The amount of sharpening required depended on the use, the care of the blade and the method of constructing the edge (see above; Manufacture). One 16th-century complaint claimed that 'if one pours on steel with a ladle, another comes and wipes it off with a feather' (quoted in Tylecote 1981, 48) implying that some knives required sharpening after only a little use.

Being both common and much-used utensils, knives were often carried about the person suspended from the belt in leather scabbards, or tucked in the top of hose, as mentioned by Chaucer in *The Reeve's Tale* (Skeat 1912, line 3933). It is probable that both men and women carried knives with them, although there are no illustrations showing women wearing scabbards. A passage in *The Knight of La Tour Landry*, describing young girls cleaning muddy skirts and hose with their knives, implies that they were carrying the knives

16 Knife being sharpened on whetstone. 14th century, from BL Add Ms 42130 f107b.

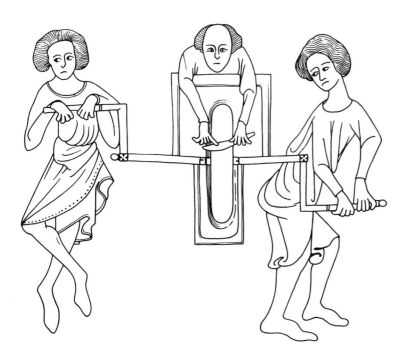

17 Two men turning a grindstone whilst a third sharpens his knife. 14th century from BL Add Ms 42130 f78b.

18 Scabbard tucked diagonally behind belt. There is no indication of a suspension loop. 14th century, from BL Add Ms 42130 f198.

19 The figure on the right seems to be wearing a knife without a scabbard, simply thrust through his purse. BL Ms Burnley 257 f13v.

with them but does not specify where or how (Rawlings 1902, 87). Chaucer's Friar kept knives tucked in his tippet as a treat for young girls (Skeat 1912, line 233).

Scabbards, or sheaths of leather, were used from prehistorical times onwards to protect knives, daggers and swords whilst being transported. A Neolithic scabbard found near Hamburg was similar in shape to those found in the present catalogue: it had a sheepskin lining, was seamed up the centre back, and had simple incised lines as decoration. A long thong wound around the outside was probably used to suspend it from a belt (Waterer 1956, 150; 156, Fig. 119).

The method of wearing the scabbard seems to have depended upon a combination of style and personal preference. The crude, almost haphazard insertion of slots for suspension, coupled with the fact that the thongs passed across and were not integrated into the decoration suggest that the slots were cut after purchase by the owner. Thus the scabbards could be tucked behind the belt (Fig. 18) or through a purse (Fig. 19), suspended horizontally (as shown on the Middleton cross and Fig. 20), vertically (Fig. 21) or diagonally using a leather thong or a metal ring. Of the 61 scabbards on which an indication of the method of suspension survives, only two, Nos. 393 and 456, may have hung from rings. The rest were used with thongs although they only survive on Nos. 425 and 483. In both cases, leather strips are threaded continuously around the open upper edge, laced through a single thickness of leather. The thong is knotted at one corner and then knotted again, making a loop over the belt.

Examination of the positioning of the extant slots suggests that the majority (on 44 scabbards) were cut so that the sheath hung vertically; 11

20 Scabbard tied horizontally at waist with suspension holes in the widened handle flap. The tip of the knife blade protrudes from the scabbard. 13th century, from *Roman de Toute Chevalerie*, Paris, Bibl Nat Fr 23464.

21 Scabbard suspended vertically from thong looped over the belt. 14th century, from BL Add Ms 42130 f170.

hung diagonally, and seven were suspended horizontally. Vertical suspension was the most common method in all periods and it should be noted that Fig. 21 shows only one of a number of ways of doing this (for comparison, see the Devonshire Hunting Tapestries; Falconry). The leather slots were often found to be torn, possibly the reason for their disposal, although several had been reused by the cutting of new slots (for example, No. 483) while others have had the suspension slots completely cut off.

With the contrivance of an additional inner scabbard (cf. Nos. 417, 418 and 428), it was possible to carry more than one knife. A single addition was most common but multiple scabbards such as No. 491 and the four-compartment dagger sheath in Northampton (Northampton Museum Acc No. 497.56) are known, though relatively rare. Two knives could be carried in a single scabbard by

slipping the second knife between the outer scabbard and the lining, as was done with No. 457. For hunting, a set of knives would be required to complete the kill correctly, and it would be necessary to carry several knives together. A 13th-century scabbard from King's Lynn tentatively identified as the scabbard of a hunting knife is an almost exact parallel for No. 438 in the present collection (Clarke & Carter 1977, 365–6, Fig. 169 No. 89).

Before the 14th century, only the host or favoured guests would expect to find a knife set before them at meal times. Others had to provide their own or share. Feasting scenes in manuscripts show an average of two knives per seven diners, with one knife centrally placed by the hand of the most important guest. Sharing a knife was considered an act of some significance, a mark of confidence or trust (Henisch 1976, 178).

The etiquette of knife usage at table was carefully set down in a series of treatises on courtesy and carving. It was up to the owner to keep his knife sharp and clean. *Stans Puer ad Mensam*, one of several 15th-century courtesy books for the young, states that one should

> *Bringe no foule knyfe unto ye table*
> (Furnivall 1868, 590).

The *Boke of Curtasye* stipulates that

> (Do not) *foule ye borde clothe with yi knyfe*
> (Furnivall 1868, 180).

The *Romaunt of the Rose* contains a slightly derisive reference to '*he . . . that likketh his knyf. . .*' (Skeat 1912, line 6502). The rusty blade carried by the Reeve in the prologue to *The Canterbury Tales* (Skeat 1912, line 620) indicates that standards were not always maintained, and Dr Wilthew has suggested that the contrast between tin inlay in cutlers marks and the iron of the blades would not be so great if the blades had been kept polished. It would seem that a casual wipe across a piece of cloth or clothing sufficed as knife cleaning for many.

Other actions not to be committed at the dinner table with knives included paring fingernails, picking teeth, and transferring chunks of meat from the trencher to the mouth which, in the days before forks came into common use, ought to be done with the fingers. Conversely, the knife should be used when lifting salt from the salt dish to the trencher. When cutting portions of food into mouth-sized pieces, the *Boke of Nurture* states that one should

> *Hold alwey thy knyfe sure*
> *by self not too tene*
> *and passe not ij fyngurs and a thombe*
> *on thy knyfe so kene;*
> *in mydde wey of thyne hande set*
> *the ende of ye haft Sure.*
> (Furnivall 1868, 21).

However, it must be stated that 'knife etiquette' was not rigorously followed by all, and *The Babees Book* warns the budding page-boy or servitor.

> *Kutte nouhte youre mete eke as were Felde men*
> *That to theyre mete haue suche an appetyte*
> *That they ne reke in what wyse where ne when*
> *Nor how ungoodly they on theyre mete twyte.*
> (Furnivall 1868, 256).

Knives are shown in the greatest number and variety in manuscript illustrations of feast scenes (Figs. 22 and 23). Carvers and Panters, guardians of the lord's bread, prepare to perform the functions allotted to them by the dictates of custom and ceremony with the specified knives. Elaborate instructions were available on the carving and presentation of each and every type of fish, fowl and meat. While some knives were inlaid with names and blessings (No. 36 carries the blundered inscription '*Amor Vincit Omnia*'; the handle of No. 138 has the words '*Ave Maria*') some serving knives were inscribed with the graces to be said before and after a meat course. In one case, the Latin prayers are accompanied by the music for the first tenor (Victoria and Albert Museum M310.1903). The Panter had no fewer than four particular knives: the chaffer, for large loaves; the parer; the trencher knife for smoothing edges; and the mensal knife, reserved for removing the select upper crust for its presentation to the lord (Figs. 24 and 25). The knives shown in manuscripts often bear little resemblance to what has survived from archaeological excavations and in museum collections (Ward-Perkins 1939, 51). Often the artistic emphasis given to a particular action means that a knife is shown much larger than it actually would have been. Knives are depicted being used to gut fish (Fig. 26); to sever purse strings (Fig. 27); to sharpen writing quills (Fig. 28); to cut notches in a tally-stick (Fig. 29), as well as to cut and carve food during the course of a meal. Fine-bladed knives or fleams were used by the medical profession for blood-letting (Fig. 30) and circumcision. Performers used them for juggling and they seem to feature as part of some games or competitions.

Figure 31 shows a shaving scene with the beard held in one hand by the barber and the razor wielded with the other. Razors and shears seem to have been interchangeable for the task of beard cutting and hair trimming as, for example

> *My berd, myn heer that hongeth long adoun*
> *That never yet ne felte offensioun*
> *Of rasour nor of shere. . .*
> (*The Knight's Tale*, Skeat 1912, line 2415ff.)

In *The House of Fame*, Chaucer writes that

> *And mo berdes in two houres*
> *Withoute rasour or sisoures*
> *Y-maad. . .*
> (Skeat 1912, line 689ff)

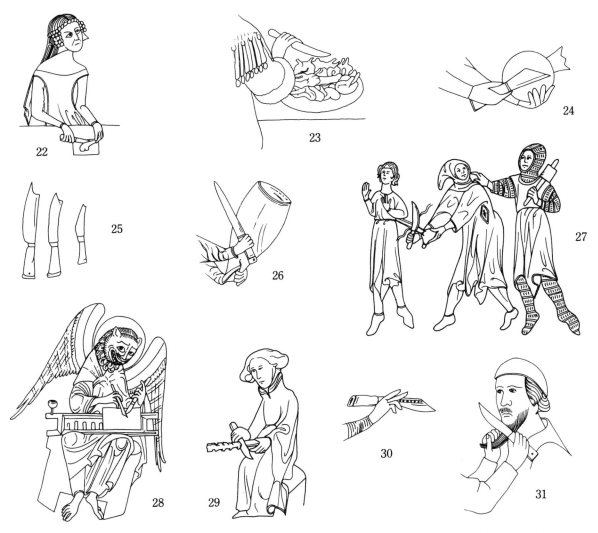

22 Lady Luttrell using a small knife to cut a chicken leg. 14th century, from BL Add Ms 42130 f208.

23 The Carver, waiting to serve Jean, Duc de Berry, holds a carving knife with a straight back and curving blade. Early 15th century, French, from *The Très Riches Heures* of Jean, Duc de Berry (January).

24 Panter slicing bread. Dated *c.*1250, Pierpont Morgan Ms Facs.

25 The three knives of the Panter – chaffer, parer and trencher knives. 15th century. Oxford Bodl Lib Ms Douce 374 f17.

26 Gutting fish with a long triangular-bladed knife. The handle has a rivetted end cap and a shoulder plate. From BL Add Ms 39943 f28v.

27 A cut-purse caught in the act. From BL Add Ms 49622 f153.

28 St Mark sharpening a writing quill using a short 'pen knife'. The tip of the blade is inserted in the end of the quill to split it. 12th century, Hereford Cathedral Ms 0.1.VIII.

29 Cutting notches in a tally stick. 14th century, from Bodl Lib Ms Bodl 264 f244r.

30 Surgical knife. Note angled back and decoration. Early 13th century. Trinity College, Cambridge Ms 0.1.20.

31 Man having beard trimmed with a large knife. The size and shape of the blade make it likely that this shows a knife not a razor. From BL Ms Nero Eii f67.

Shears first appear in the Iron Age *c*.1000 BC when two knives joined by a central spring could be made in iron. The blades could be worked together in a single-handed simultaneous cutting action, leaving the second hand free to hold or steady the item being cut. The use of shears made it possible to obtain an entire fleece of wool, instead of the tufts of wool obtained by combing. It is unlikely that shears began to be used for cutting cloth until the end of the Roman period when cloth began to be woven in lengths (Granger-Taylor 1982, 22). Shears with a wide plain handle and an angled upper blade were found in a sealed Middle Iron Age deposit in Fifield Bavant (Devizes Museum DM1750), and a large pair of Late Iron Age shears survives from Hertford Heath (Hussen 1983, 17, 33, Fig.15). Hussen remarks on the frequent discovery of shears during this period in association with razors and scissors, which has led to their identification as toilet implements suited for hair-cutting. The practices of combing sheep and weaving cloth to shape possibly account for their absence from all but the later Iron Age sites.

The 57 shears in the catalogue range in date from the mid 12th to the mid 15th centuries and in overall length from 74mm to *c.* 318mm. The form remains remarkably consistent throughout, as it has from the earliest examples onwards. The earliest medieval shears consist simply of two wide blades, the upper blade straight or sloping, blades tapering to the tip and a plain handle. The bow holds the tension; all are oval or circular and average *c.* $\frac{1}{3}$ of the total arm length. Shears dated to the 14th century have rectangular-section handles, with central ridges, possibly decorative, possibly as a means of strengthening the loop. Proportionately longer handles than blades meant that greater leverage could be achieved and more pressure exerted. A wide span across the diameter of the handle bow would mean that a very strong cutting action could be attained. It is easier to achieve a continuous cutting action with the combination of a long handle and long blades, whilst accurate and continuous cutting required long and relatively slender blades. Small shears can only be held in the palm of the hand, and closed with the combined action of the finger and thumb. This makes continuous cutting difficult if not impossible, but means that they are suitable for a single exact cut, such as cutting thread. Only fullers' shears seem to have had a shape peculiar to

their function and size is therefore the main criterion when determining use. Most of the shears would have been suitable for domestic uses, such as thread-trimming and hair-cutting, whilst those with the longest blades could have been used for cloth-cutting and sheep-shearing. The shears used to penetrate a sheep's fleece required long slender pointed blades with an overall length of between twelve and eighteen inches (Carus-Wilson 1957, 107). When the wool had been shorn and washed, small shears and forceps were used to remove small particles of dirt and soil (Patterson 1956, 193).

Within the cloth industry, it is necessary to differentiate between cloth shears and fullers' shears, although originally cloth shears were used in the fulling process. Like sheep shears, cloth shears were quite large, with broad pointed blades that helped to ensure a straight cut. Goodall cites a pair of shears from Seacourt, Oxon (overall length *c.* 248mm, blade width *c.* 20mm) as being an appropriate size for cloth-cutting or some aspects of tailoring (Goodall 1981, 54). In the present collection, only Nos. 314, 365 and 368 are of sufficient length to warrant such an hypothesis. The handle and blades of No.314, for example, are virtually the same length (112mm as opposed to 114mm), the long handle making the blades easy to grip when guiding them evenly through the substance being cut.

It is more likely, however, that sheep and cloth shears were of a comparable size to No.368, which combines all the features necessary for either of these two tasks. The shears are both long and broad, with wide tapering blades (*c.*164mm long; 28mm wide), and a handle slightly longer than the blades. The handle loop is also very broad, 58mm in diameter. The length of the handles would allow a good grip to be maintained, whilst the wide diameter span of the handle bow would require considerable pressure to close the blades in a strong cutting action.

Fullers' shears were used in the cloth finishing process to crop the fibre ends raised by the teazels, and give an even soft surface to the fabric. The craftsmen who performed this task were specifically known as shearers, and the tools of their trade were both expensive and valued possessions (see Carus-Wilson 1957, 107 ff). Fullers' shears had long wide blades with a straight upper edge at right angles to the squared tip of the blade. The shears were laid flat upon the cloth with the shearer's left hand inserted through the stirrup grip on the lower blade, allowing the blades to be opened and closed with the same hand.

As with the knives, and with possibly less evidence to go by, most of the shears in the present collection cannot be attributed definitely to a particular purpose. The largest number of those with complete measurable lengths (20 out of 28) fall between 85 and 144mm in length, with 15 of those included being of 14th-century date. Handles were marginally longer than blades until the beginning of the 14th century when this trend was reversed and 80% of the measurable shears had longer blades. No.313 has handles one and half times the blade length, increasing the grip possible on this medium-sized pair of shears (overall length; 138mm).

The smaller shears are very consistent in form. All are late 14th to early 15th century in date, with a single recess, curved upper blades and tapering or angled blade tips. The consistency in form leads to the suggestion that these may represent the development of needlepoint or sewing shears, predecessors of the elaborate needlepoint scissors of the 16th and 17th centuries. Nos. 316 and 317 both have slender blades inlaid with silver, and of a delicacy and elaboration well suited to these tasks.

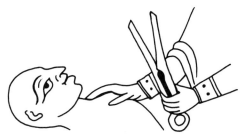

33 Shaving the head with shears prior to surgery. Early to mid 12th century. Durham Dean and Chapter Library, Ms Hunter 100.

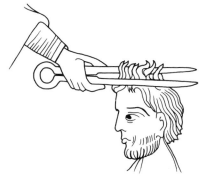

34 Scene of tonsure using shears. The shears have long, slender, tapering blades without a recess. From BL Ms Harl Roll Y 6 Roundel 3.

32 Sheep-shearing using shears. Early 15th century, from *The Très Riches Heures* of Jean, Duc de Berry (July).

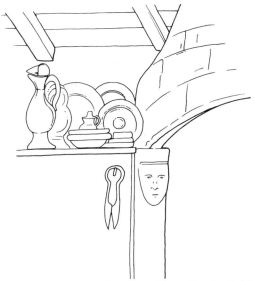

35 Detail of domestic scene with small pair of plain shears hanging by fireplace. *c.*1440, from *The Hours of Catherine of Cleves*, Pierpont Morgan Lib M917 p.151.

Whatever purpose the various shears served, it would seem that they were discarded less because of wear to the blades than because the repeated opening and closing of the blades weakened the bow or spring, and resulted in a central break. Of the 57 shears, 22 are complete, 23 are broken exactly in half and the rest broken in other places.

Shears could be sharpened by holding the blades apart, stroking the edge from blade top, or pivot in the case of scissors, to tip with a whetstone, taking care to keep the original angle of the cutting edge. The grinding of shears was both expensive and difficult, and by the 13th century, had become a specialised profession, for example, William the Schergrinder is mentioned in documents from Lincoln (Carus-Wilson 1957, 107).

The three scissors in the catalogue are probably of late 13th or 14th-century date, the period when they generally came into more common use. As already mentioned, scissor blades must be made to curve or twist inwards from pivot to point so that the blades only touch at the cutting point where pressure is concentrated. Flat blades would be forced apart by the material being cut. On a closed pair of scissors, only the tips touch. The earliest pair of the three, No. 369, has a small notch below the rivet which later became a standard feature, serving as a 'stop' to prevent the blades from completely crossing over each other, rendering them useless. In fact, this is what has happened with the other two examples. Without the 'stop', the only thing preventing the overlap of the blades was the collision of the two handle loops. All three pairs are for use by right-handed persons, as the blades open counter-clockwise.

In the present day, scissors are used more commonly than shears, but, although they were introduced into Europe around the 6th or 7th century, the exact opposite seems to have been true before the 14th century. Medieval sources differentiate between sheep shears, tailors' shears, barbers' shears and fullers' shears but without specifying what the exact differences were. Manuscripts most frequently show shears in scenes of sheep-shearing and hair-cutting (Figs. 32, 33 and 34) including tonsure. In one illustration, a woman sits quietly by the hearth with a small pair of simple unornamented shears hanging from the fireplace (Fig. 35). As with the knives, the shears and scissors are sometimes shown with what seem to be completely unrealistic proportions.

36   Sheep-shearing using scissors. From BL Add Ms 20787 f106v.

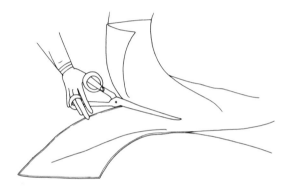

37   Cloth cutting using large scissors. From BL Add Ms 48978 f43.

As shown by the passages from Chaucer cited above, there do not seem to have been definite rules about which implements were used. The preference for shears seems to reflect an element of conservatism, as well as the ready availability of shears and the comparative ease with which they could be manufactured. Scissors occasionally feature in scenes of sheep-shearing (Fig. 36). The finger loops on the handle made scissors easier to use with one hand, and long slender blades eased cutting in a straight line. This may have meant that, while shears were used for domestic purposes, scissors were preferred by tradesmen, such as hatters, glovers, tailors (Fig. 37) and barbers, whose livelihood depended on more precise cutting.

The range of activities, shapes, sizes and quality revealed by this catalogue is great, yet, with few exceptions, most of the knives and shears in the illustrations and in the collections would be suitable for any number of the functions listed above. It is only possible to make vague assumptions about the use to which an object was put and about the status of the owner from the quality of workmanship and the degree of decoration. The small proportion of both knives and shears with inlaid decoration, even in the larger groups, carries with it the implication that these were probably relatively rare and expensive items, more suitable for display or delicate tasks than for day to day use.

For the scabbards, it is the quality of decorative craftsmanship, coupled with the choice of motifs which have implications for their use and/or the status of their owner. Scabbards do not seem a particularly good vehicle for the display of livery, given their small area, the crudity of much of the work, and the fact that they would have been largely obscured by the wearer's garments. Sword scabbards were a different matter, as may be seen on brasses of the period, but the quality of medieval knife scabbards and the likely status of their owners make such a use improbable.

The fact that only three scabbards were found with knives should be pointed out, since it seems likely that knives were purchased and discarded quite separately from the scabbards. A scabbard could be cut back and restitched for reuse with a smaller knife, even if the end was cut through or the suspension loops broken. A knife which had lost its cutting edge or broken in mid-blade could only be discarded and replaced. The position of cut marks within several scabbards indicates that the sizes of the knives and scabbards were not always carefully matched. It must also be noted that although the number of knives recovered from late 14th-century deposits is high, the number of scabbards is not, and indeed declines sharply during this period. This seems to tie in with the development of the table, which brought about a decrease in the number of people carrying knives about with them.

The ubiquity of the knives, shears and scabbards on archaeological sites in the city of London and elsewhere in the country and in Europe is a further final reflection of their importance in medieval life. They were much-used, easily available items, readily discarded and replaced.

38 Stall selling knives and scabbards. It is difficult to tell if the knives slotted through the shelf are in their scabbards. From BL Ms Egerton 1894 f17.

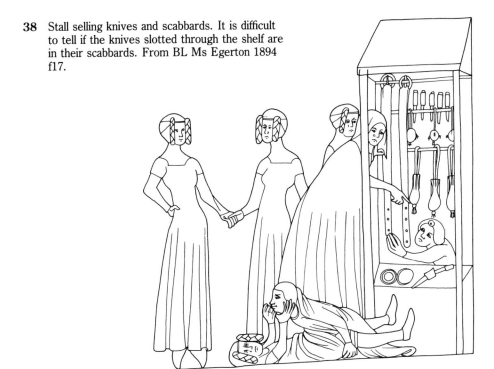

Metallographic examination of medieval knives and shears

PAUL WILTHEW

Ancient Monuments Laboratory, London

A considerable amount of information about the materials and methods of production used by blacksmiths in the past can be obtained from the metallographic examination of the objects they manufactured. Of particular interest are those objects such as tools and blades whose performance could have been improved significantly by the use of an appropriate combination of materials and production techniques.

The effectiveness of a blade is affected by a range of factors, including how sharp an edge can be achieved, how well that edge is retained and how resistant the blade is to breaking. Although the relative importance of these factors depends on the intended use of the blade, particularly if that use is highly specialised, in general a good blade would have to take a sharp edge, retain it reasonably well and not break too easily. This combination of properties was achieved by making the main part of the knife from wrought iron and the cutting edge from steel. Wrought iron is softer than steel, but it is also more ductile, which reduces the risk of breakage, and had the advantage of lower cost (Tylecote 1976). A hard heat-treated steel cutting edge was necessary because wrought iron cannot be sharpened to form a lasting good edge.

Several studies (McDonnell forthcoming; Modin and Pleiner 1978; Tylecote 1976; Tylecote and Black 1980) have shown that a wide range of methods were used by blacksmiths to produce knives and shears during the Anglo-Saxon, Viking and Early Medieval periods, and the resulting objects were of widely varying quality. There is not, however, a great deal of published material for the later medieval period and it was therefore decided to examine a selection of knives and

shears from the present collection. The aim was generally to determine the materials and techniques used in their manufacture and in particular the methods used to achieve steel cutting edges, if present, and the heat treatments applied to the steel. The quality of the blades was also assessed.

Because of the limited time available, only a small number of objects could be examined. Since the methods used require destructive sampling but only analyses of well-preserved metal can produce the required results a choice had to be made between preserving artefacts for display and future study and obtaining a sample. The objects were chosen from amongst those which appeared to retain a reasonable amount of uncorroded metal, particularly along the cutting edge, on the basis of visual examination and inspection of x-radiographs taken by the Conservation Department of the Museum of London. Within this group the sampled objects cover the chronological range of the collection, both knife and shears, and visible variations in manufacturing technique, such as whittle- and scale-tangs.

Sections were cut from the objects and were prepared and examined. Microhardness tests were carried out but chemical analyses were not. The main results and conclusions are summarised immediately below, followed by details of the methods used and the full results for each object:

(1) A wide range of manufacturing methods were used to produce both the knives and the shears. Some were apparently forged entirely from wrought iron but the majority had steel cutting edges. The steel cutting edges were applied in a variety of ways (illustrated schematically in Fig. 5) including scarf or butt welding a

steel edge to a wrought iron back, welding an outer layer of steel round the cutting edge, wrapping wrought iron round a steel core and welding together a series of strips of various composition. A possible example of carburisation of a shear blade was also observed.

(2) In most cases the steel had been heat treated effectively to achieve a hard, quenched and tempered structure.

(3) The quality of many of the blades was very good, but a few were decidedly inferior.

(4) The welds were generally of good quality and some of the weld lines were marked by a white line. This may have been due to segregation of elements such as arsenic (Tylecote 1976; Modin and Pleiner 1978) but microprobe analysis would be required to confirm this.

(5) The high hardness of some of the wrought iron suggested that high phosphorus iron was used in some objects.

(6) In view of the range of techniques used to produce the knives and shears examined, it would be necessary to examine a much larger number of objects from this period to obtain a comprehensive picture of the methods of blacksmiths during the high medieval period.

Method of Examination

Five pairs of shears and ten knives were examined. Sections through the objects were obtained, mounted in polyester resin and polished to a 1 micron diamond finish. All etching was carried out in 2 per cent nital (nitric acid in methanol) or 5 per cent nital. Hardness tests were done using a Vicker's pyramid microhardness tester with a 500g load and the results are given in Tables 11–25. The position at which sections were taken from each object are shown in Figs. 39a–53a. Except where stated below, vertical sections from blade back to cutting edge perpendicular to the plane of the blade were examined and the main features are shown diagramatically in Figs. 39b–53b. The main features are shown diagrammatically using the following conventions:

B: Bainite
F: Ferrite
P: Pearlite
TM: Tempered Martensite
W: Weld.

Knife blade no. 2 (Table 11)

Table 11. Microhardness test results for No.2.

Area	Structure	mHV500
Core	Tempered martensite	423
Centre layer	Bainite + ferrite	330
Back	Piled, Ferrite & ferrite + pearlite	170

Metallography Two sections were examined (Fig. 39a). The blade consisted of a tempered martensite core with a bainite layer around it. The back was formed from two ferrite and ferrite + pearlite sheets of wrought iron welded to either

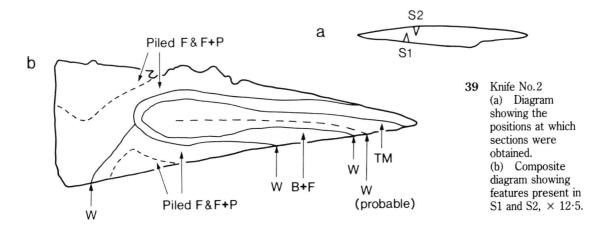

39 Knife No. 2
(a) Diagram showing the positions at which sections were obtained.
(b) Composite diagram showing features present in S1 and S2, × 12·5.

side of the core. Three weld lines were present; between the tempered martensite and the bainite, between the bainite and the wrought iron and separating the two wrought iron pieces. Examination of the core in the unetched state suggested, from the slag distribution, that the tempered martensite region had been folded over, although there was no clear weld line along the centre of this region. It is possible that the bainite layer, which also contained significant amounts of ferrite, was originally of relatively low carbon content and that much of the carbon present diffused in from the high carbon core.

Construction and Quality   The blade was formed from four strips of iron. A high carbon and a low carbon steel were welded together and folded once, with the high carbon steel on the inside. The back was formed by welding a strip of wrought iron to each side of the blade and welding them together at the blade back. In the section examined the cutting edge is formed from the softer bainite layer rather than the harder tempered martensite which would have given a better cutting edge. This was probably not intentional, in other parts of the blade, the cutting edge may have been tempered martensite. The blade would have been of quite good quality.

Knife blade no. 12 (Table 12)

Table 12.   **Microhardness test results for No.12.**

Area	Structure	mHV500
Cutting edge	Tempered martensite	525
Back	Ferrite	119

Metallography   This blade consisted of a tempered martensite cutting edge welded to a ferrite wrought iron back, (Fig.40b). Some diffusion of carbon into the wrought iron had occurred.

Construction and Quality   The blade was made by scarf welding a steel cutting edge to a wrought iron back. The steel was then quenched and tempered to give a hard tempered martensite structure. The blade had been held at high temperature for some time after welding as carbon diffusion across the weld had occurred. The cutting edge would have been resistant to wear and deformation and retained an edge well. The knife was of excellent quality.

Knife blade no. 16 (Table 13)

Table 13.   **Microhardness test results for No.16.**

Area	Structure	mHV500
Cutting edge	Ferrite	161
Back	Ferrite	150
Near tang	Ferrite	145
Near tang	Ferrite + pearlite	175

Metallography   Three sections from this knife were examined (Fig.41a). One horizontal section was taken from the curved part of the blade near the tang (Fig.41b, S3) and two from nearer the tip of the blade (Fig.41c, S1 and S2). The vertical sections showed it to be essentially ferrite, although a ferrite + pearlite area was present in S3.

Construction and Quality   The blade was forged from a single piece of wrought iron. Due to the homogeneous nature of the blade it was not possible to decide for certain if the curved part of the blade had been formed deliberately, or if it was the result of wear and resharpening. The softness of the blade suggests that it would have worn rapidly and required regular resharpening to maintain an edge. It seems likely that the curve is the result of wear and resharpening, and was not deliberate. The knife was of very poor quality.

Knife blade no. 26 (Table 14)

Table 14.   **Microhardness test results for No.26.**

Area	Structure	mHV500
Core	Bainite	519
Centre layer	Ferrite + bainite	385
Back	Ferrite + bainite	398

Metallography   Two sections were examined (Fig.42a), and the blade was found to consist of three strips of steel, butt welded together. The cutting edge was bainite, although some decarburisation had occurred around the weld line between this layer and the central strip. The centre layer had suffered considerable decarburisation around both weld lines and had a bainite structure with ferrite grains also present. The back of the blade was also steel, but probably of lower carbon content. This area had also been decarburised adjacent to the weld and had a bainite structure with some ferrite.

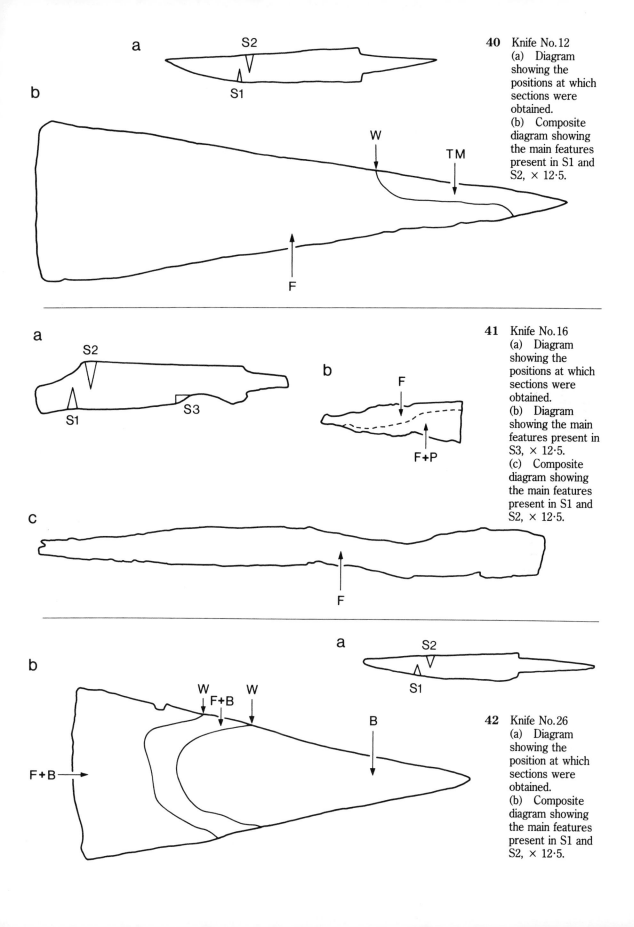

40 Knife No.12
(a) Diagram showing the positions at which sections were obtained.
(b) Composite diagram showing the main features present in S1 and S2, × 12·5.

41 Knife No.16
(a) Diagram showing the positions at which sections were obtained.
(b) Diagram showing the main features present in S3, × 12·5.
(c) Composite diagram showing the main features present in S1 and S2, × 12·5.

42 Knife No.26
(a) Diagram showing the position at which sections were obtained.
(b) Composite diagram showing the main features present in S1 and S2, × 12·5.

Construction and Quality The blade was forged by butt welding three pieces of steel together and was quenched sufficiently rapidly to give a hard bainitic cutting edge. The resulting knife would have been of good quality, but a tempered martensite cutting edge would have had better resistance to fracture.

Knife blade no. 44 (Table 15)

Table 15. Microhardness test results for No.44.

Area	Structure	mHV500
Outer layer 1	Ferrite + pearlite	244
Outer layer 2	Ferrite + pearlite	248
Core	Ferrite	118

Metallography Two sections were examined (Fig.43a). The blade consisted of ferrite + pearlite sides and cutting edge round a ferrite wrought iron core and back. There were white weld lines between the ferrite and the ferrite + pearlite regions. There was also some indication of a weld between the ferrite + pearlite sides at the cutting edge (Fig.43b). All the ferrite + pearlite areas were very fine grained.

Construction and Quality The blade was forged by welding strips of steel onto each side of a wrought iron core. The steel was not cooled rapidly enough from high temperature to prevent the formation of a fairly soft ferrite + pearlite cutting edge. Although the blade could have been of good quality if it had been suitably heat treated, in its actual condition it would not have been a very effective tool. The knife was of poor quality.

Knife blade no. 63 (Table 16)

Table 16. Microhardness test results for No.63.

Area	Structure	mHV500
Cutting edge	Tempered martensite	576
Core	Ferrite + grain boundary cementite	187

Metallography The two sections examined (Fig.44a), were found to consist of a tempered martensite layer wrapped around a wrought iron core. The wrought iron was ferritic, but with some grain boundary cementite. Carbon diffusion into the wrought iron across the weld line had taken place.

Construction and Quality The knife blade was formed by welding a steel layer around a wrought iron core. The steel cutting edge had been quenched and tempered to give a hard (mHV500 = 576) tempered martensite structure. This would have been very resistant to wear and would have retained an edge well. The knife was of excellent quality.

Knife blade no. 84 (Table 17)

Table 17. Microhardness test results for No.84.

Area	Structure	mHV500
Blade	Ferrite	170

Metallography The two sections examined consisted entirely of ferrite containing a high level of phosphorus. There was no evidence that a high carbon cutting edge had ever been present (Fig.45).

Construction and Quality The blade was forged from a single piece of wrought iron. The presence of significant amounts of phosphorus explains the relatively high hardness for wrought iron. The use of a phosphoric iron would have given a better quality blade than low phosphorous wrought iron. The cutting edge was soft (mHV500 = 170) and it would have been a very poor quality knife.

Knife blade no. 121 (Table 18)

Table 18. Microhardness test results for No.121.

Area	Structure	mHV500
Layer 2	Ferrite (fine) + cementite	211
Layer 3	Ferrite (coarse) + cementite	136
Layer 4	Ferrite (fairly fine) + cementite	186
Layer 5	Ferrite (fine) + cementite	197
Layer 6	Ferrite (coarse) + cementite	145

Metallography Two sections were examined (Fig.46a). The blade was forged from a series of strips of wrought iron, all of which had a similar structure. The seven strips visible in the sections examined, consisted of coalesced cementite in ferrite. The welds between the strips were sharply defined and the different wrought iron layers could be distinguished by variations in grain size of the ferrite (Fig.46b).

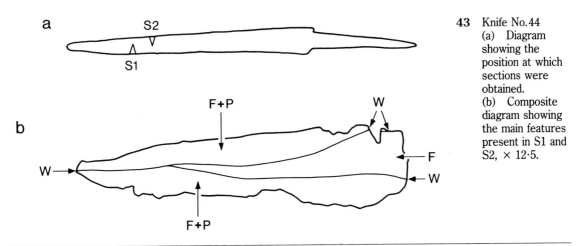

43 Knife No. 44
(a) Diagram showing the position at which sections were obtained.
(b) Composite diagram showing the main features present in S1 and S2, × 12·5.

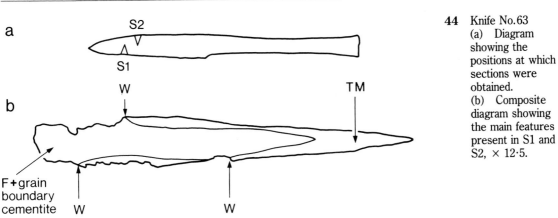

44 Knife No. 63
(a) Diagram showing the positions at which sections were obtained.
(b) Composite diagram showing the main features present in S1 and S2, × 12·5.

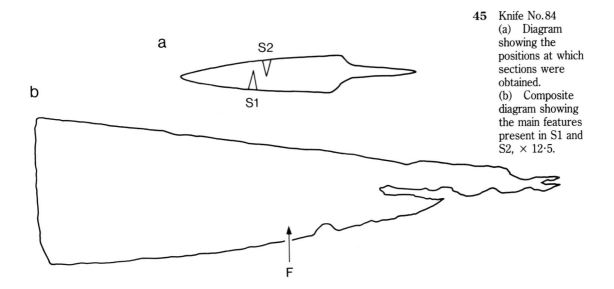

45 Knife No. 84
(a) Diagram showing the positions at which sections were obtained.
(b) Composite diagram showing the main features present in S1 and S2, × 12·5.

Construction and Quality The blade was formed by welding together at least seven strips of wrought iron. The presence of coalesced cementite suggests that the blade was held at moderate temperatures (perhaps about 700 degrees C) for some time, although it is not clear why this was done, if deliberate. All the layers were fairly soft (Table 18), and the blade would have been of very poor quality. The sections cut through a decorative groove in the blade. The metal below the groove was very distorted and there was no evidence that it had been cut during the formation of the groove, which was hammered into the knife and not chiselled out.

Knife blade no. 258 (Table 19)

Table 19. Microhardness test results for No.258.

Area	Structure	mHV500
Area 1	Ferrite	197
Area 2	Ferrite	186
Area 3	Ferrite	179
Area 4 Back	Piled, ferrite & ferrite + pearlite	247
Area 4 Cutting edge	Ferrite + pearlite	231

Metallography The two sections examined showed that the blade was formed from at least three pieces of iron (Fig.47b). The cutting edge and one side of the knife (Fig.47b, area 4) were a single piece of wrought iron with a piled structure including ferrite and ferrite + pearlite areas. This strip was welded to three other pieces of wrought iron (Fig.47b, areas 1–3) which formed the other side of the blade. Areas 1 and 3 were both fine grained ferrite and may have been the same piece of wrought iron which had been split in the particular section examined. Area 2 was a coarser ferrite. There were white weld lines between the areas.

Construction and Quality The blade was formed by welding together three, or more likely, four pieces of wrought iron. No attempt had been made to produce a hardened cutting edge. The cutting edge was a fairly soft ferrite + pearlite structure and would not therefore have retained an edge or been very resistant to wear or deformation. The knife was of poor quality.

Knife blade no. 266 (Table 20)

Table 20. Microhardness test results for No.266.

Area	Structure	mHV500
Layer 1	Tempered martensite	442
Layer 2	Tempered martensite	459
Layer 3	Tempered martensite	400
Layer 4	Ferrite + bainite	266
Layer 5	Ferrite + bainite	310
Layer 6	Tempered martensite	440

Metallography The two sections that were examined (Fig.48a) showed that, like No.121, the blade consisted of a series of strips of iron welded together. The outer three layers on one side and the outer layer on the other side were all tempered martensite. The other two layers were ferrite with some bainite. The latter may have been low carbon wrought iron originally and the carbon now present may have diffused in from the high carbon outer layers. The cutting edge of the section examined was formed from the low carbon layers.

Construction and Quality The blade was formed from a series of at least six strips of iron welded together. The outer layers were steel and were quenched and tempered to give a hard tempered martensite structure in each layer. The tempered martensite layers probably originally formed the cutting edge, although it is now formed by the softer central layers. Wear and repeated resharpening could have resulted in the removal of the high carbon edge leaving the softer, less effective edge observed. Assuming that the cutting edge was originally tempered martensite, the knife would have been a good quality tool.

Shear blade no. 364 (Table 21)

Table 21. Microhardness test results for No.364.

Area	Structure	mHV500
Blade 1		
Cutting face	Tempered martensite	464
Back	Ferrite	149
Back	Ferrite + pearlite	180
Back	Piled, Ferrite & ferrite + pearlite	155
Blade 2		
Cutting face	Tempered martensite	431
Back	Ferrite	125
Handle	Ferrite	132

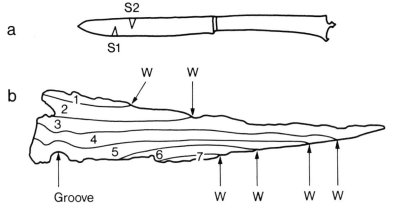

a

b

W   W

1
2
3
4
5   6   7

Groove   W   W   W   W

All the layers were ferrite with cementite, but the ferrite grain
size varied:
    Layers 2,5,7: fine
    Layers 1,4:   fairly fine
    Layers 3,6:   coarse

46 Knife No.121
(a) Diagram showing the positions at which sections were obtained.
(b) Composite diagram showing the main features present in S1 and S2, × 12·5.

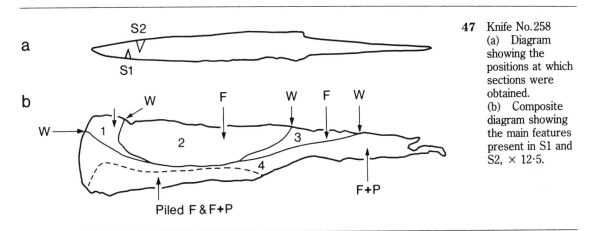

a

b

W   F   W   F   W

W   1
2   3
4

Piled F & F+P

F+P

47 Knife No.258
(a) Diagram showing the positions at which sections were obtained.
(b) Composite diagram showing the main features present in S1 and S2, × 12·5.

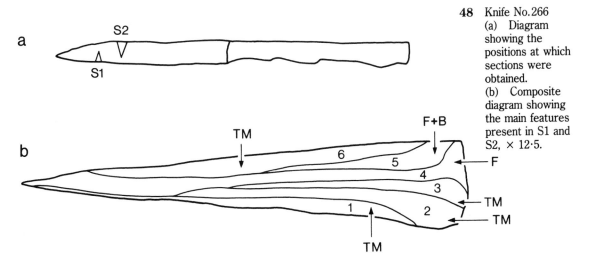

a

b

TM

6
5
4
3
1   2

F+B

F

TM

TM

TM

48 Knife No.266
(a) Diagram showing the positions at which sections were obtained.
(b) Composite diagram showing the main features present in S1 and S2, × 12·5.

a

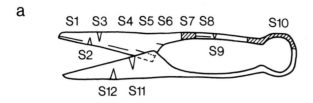

S1 S3 S4 S5 S6 S7 S8   S10

S2   S9

S12 S11

b

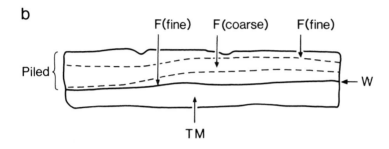

F(fine)   F(coarse)   F(fine)

Piled {

W

TM

49 Shears No.364
(a) Diagram
showing the
positions at which
sections were
obtained.
(b) Diagram
showing the main
features present in
S4, × 12·5.
(c) Composite
diagram showing
the main features
present in S1 and
S2, × 12·5.
(d) Composite
diagram showing
the main features
present in S11 and
S12, × 12·5.

c

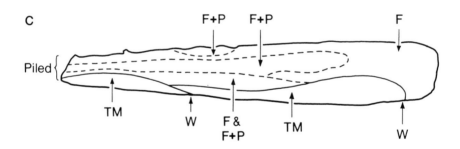

F+P   F+P   F

Piled {

TM   W   F &   TM
                F+P   W

d

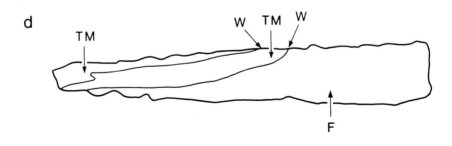

W TM W

TM

F

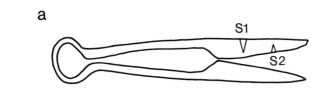

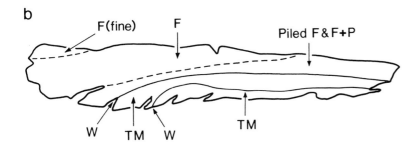

50 Shears No.313
(a) Diagram showing the positions at which sections were obtained.
(b) Composite diagram showing the main features present in S1 and S2, × 12·5.

Metallography A series of twelve sections were examined (Fig.49a), which included vertical (S2 and S3) and horizontal (S1, S4, S5, and S6) sections through one blade and vertical sections (S11 and S12) through the other. The handle was sectioned vertically (S9), horizontally (S8) and in the plane of the object (S7 and S10). The cutting faces of both blades were similar, consisting of two steel strips welded together and welded onto a wrought iron back (Fig.49c). Both layers of each cutting face were tempered martensite and there were white weld lines both between the steel layers and between the wrought iron and steel. It has been suggested that white weld lines are sometimes the result of nickel segregation to the weld, but this could not be investigated in this work. Some carbon diffusion had occurred across the weld from the high carbon steel into the low carbon wrought iron. The back of blade 1 (Fig.49c) consisted of a piled structure with ferrite and ferrite + pearlite regions. There was no evidence for welds between these layers, and the banding was probably due to variations in carbon within one piece of wrought iron, possibly as a result of phosphorus segregation but this has not been confirmed analytically. The back of the second blade had a uniform ferrite structure, as did the handle. The wrought iron back of each blade folded over the steel at the top of the cutting face.

Construction and Quality Both welds were constructed by scarf welding two steel plates to a wrought iron back. The fact that significant carbon diffusion had occurred across the weld into the wrought iron region indicates that the shears were held at a high temperature for a fairly long time after the steel and wrought iron were welded together. The steel cutting faces were quenched and tempered to give a hard tempered martensite structure. This would have been capable of being sharpened and resistant to wear and deformation and would have resulted in a good quality pair of shears. There was no evidence from the sections examined that the backs of the blades and the handle were not all forged from a single piece of wrought iron.

Shear blade no. 313 (Table 22)

Table 22. Microhardness test results for No.313.

Area	Structure	mHV500
Cutting face outer steel layer	Tempered martensite	491
Cutting face inner steel layer	Tempered martensite	395
Back	Ferrite	151
Back	Piled, Ferrite & ferrite + pearlite	242

Metallography Two sections from one blade were examined (Fig.50a). The blade was very similar to those of No.364. It consisted of two layers of steel, both with a tempered martensite structure, welded together and to a wrought iron back with a piled structure including ferrite and ferrite + pearlite regions. Again white weld lines separated the three layers, although carbon diffusion had occurred across the weld into the wrought iron area. As in No.364, the wrought iron back was probably a single piece of iron with an inhomogeneous carbon distribution, possibly due to phosphorus segregation.

Construction and Quality   The shears were made by scarf welding two steel plates to a wrought iron back. The shears had been held at a high temperature for some time after welding as carbon diffusion into the wrought iron had occurred. The steel had been quenched and tempered to give a hard tempered martensite structure which would have been resistant to wear and deformation and would have been capable of being sharpened, resulting in good quality shears.

Shear blade no. 320 (Table 23)

Table 23.   Microhardness test results for No.320.

Area	Structure	mHV500
Blade	Tempered martensite	446
Blade	Ferrite + pearlite	193
Blade	Ferrite	153

Metallography   Two sections from this blade were examined (Fig.51a). The microstructure of the blade was very inhomogeneous and consisted of high carbon regions in ferrite. The carbon concentration at the edge of the high carbon regions decreased gradually on moving towards the ferrite area, but there was no positive evidence of welds. The high carbon regions were tempered martensite but ferrite + pearlite areas were present between the tempered martensite and the ferrite regions.

Construction and Quality   The blade appears to have been forged from a single piece of wrought iron. The inhomogeneous carbon distribution, with the high carbon areas around the edge of the blade, suggests that an attempt was made to carburise the blade. The result was very uneven and resulted in a less efficient cutting tool than a uniformly carburised surface would have pro-

duced. The blade was quenched and tempered to give a hard tempered martensite structure in the high carbon areas, including the cutting edge. The shears were probably quite effective.

Shear blade no. 325 (Table 24)

Table 24.   Microhardness test results for No.325.

Area	Structure	mHV500
Blade	Bainite	716
Blade	Ferrite + pearlite	198

Metallography   The three sections examined (Fig.52a) produced no evidence for welds. The blade was a single piece of steel, but with an inhomogeneous carbon distribution. The cutting edge was ferrite + pearlite, but the proportion of pearlite was lower towards the sides of the blades, although much of this area had been lost due to corrosion. The low carbon areas were probably the result of decarburisation during forging. The back of the blade was bainite and the carbon content appeared to increase towards this area (Fig.52b).

Construction and Quality   The shear blade was forged from a single piece of steel with an inhomogeneous carbon distribution. It had not been quenched rapidly enough from high temperature to suppress the formation of ferrite + pearlite in the lower carbon regions. As a result the cutting edge was fairly soft, although other areas were very hard. The blade had not been tempered. The cutting edge would have blunted and deformed fairly easily and the shears would have been of poor quality.

Shear blade no. 359 (Table 25)

Table 25.   Microhardness test results for No.359.

Area	Structure	mHV500
Cutting face	Tempered martensite	610
Back	Ferrite	148

Metallography   Two sections from one blade were examined (Fig.53a). The blade consisted of a steel cutting edge scarf welded onto a wrought iron back. The steel had a tempered martensite

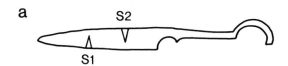

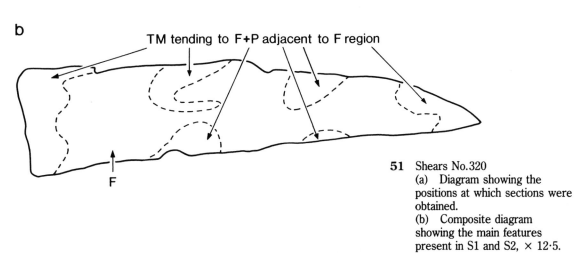

51 Shears No.320
(a) Diagram showing the positions at which sections were obtained.
(b) Composite diagram showing the main features present in S1 and S2, × 12·5.

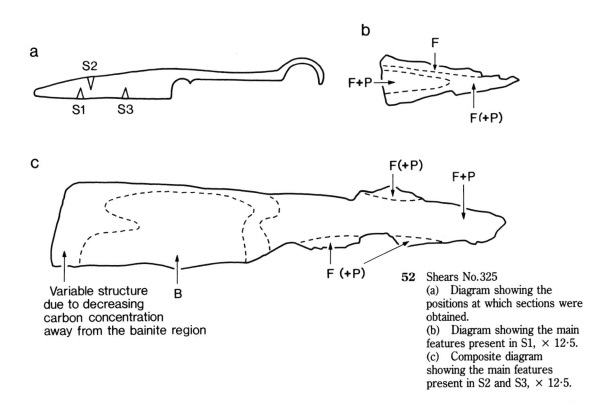

52 Shears No.325
(a) Diagram showing the positions at which sections were obtained.
(b) Diagram showing the main features present in S1, × 12·5.
(c) Composite diagram showing the main features present in S2 and S3, × 12·5.

a

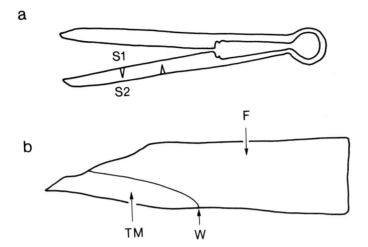

b

53 Shears No.359
(a) Diagram showing the positions at which sections were obtained.
(b) Composite diagram showing the main features present in S1 and S2, × 12·5.

structure and the wrought iron was ferrite, although it showed some indications of cold working. The two regions were separated by a white weld line. Some carbon diffusion had taken place across the weld into the ferrite region.

Construction and Quality The blade was made by scarf welding a steel cutting edge to a wrought iron back. The blade was held at high temperature for some time after welding as carbon diffusion across the weld has occurred. The indications of cold working in the ferrite region may explain its slightly high hardness. The steel had been quenched and tempered to give a very hard tempered martensite structure. This would have resulted in a very wear-resistant edge, capable of being sharpened, and the shears would have been of excellent quality.

Bibliography

ADAMS, A, 1937 *The history of the Worshipful Company of Blacksmiths: from early times until the year 1647*, London

ALLAN, J P, 1984 *Medieval and post-medieval finds from Exeter 1971–1980*, Exeter

ALLIN, C E, 1981 *The medieval leather industry in Leicester*, Leicestershire Mus Archaeol Rep **3**

ANSTEE, J W and BIEK, L, 1961 A study in pattern welding, *Medieval Archaeol*, **5**, 71–93

ANTIQ J, 1924 A note on a bookbinder's stamp found at Belvoir priory, *Antiq J*, **4**, 272

BAART, J et al, 1977 *Opgravingen in Amsterdam*, Amsterdam

BARRON, E J, 1911–13 Notes on the history of the Armourers and Brasiers Company, *Trans London Middlesex Archaeol Soc*, **2**, 300–19

BERESFORD, G, 1975 *The medieval clay-land village; excavations at Goltho and Barton Blount*, Soc Medieval Archaeol Monogr Ser **6**, London

BLOMQUIST, R, 1938 Medeltida Svard, Dolkar och Slidor funna i Lund, *Kulturen*, 134–69

BRAULT, G J, 1973 *Eight thirteenth-century Rolls of Arms*, Pennsylvania

BROOKE, C N L, 1975 *London 800–1216: the shaping of a city*, London

CAM, H (ed), 1968 *Year books of Edward II vol 26 part 2; The Eyre of London 14 Edward II vol 2*, Publ Seldon Soc **86**

CARUS WILSON, E, 1957 The significance of the secular sculpture in the Lance Chapel, Cullompton, *Medieval Archaeol*, **1**, 104–17

CHERRY, J, 1978 Medieval Britain in 1977, *Medieval Archaeol*, **22**, 155–88

CHERRY, J, 1980 Medieval Britain in 1979, *Medieval Archaeol*, **24**, 236–64

CHEW, H M and KELLAWAY, W, 1973 *London assize of nuisance 1301–1431*, London Record Ser **10**, London

CLARKE, H and CARTER, A, 1977 *Excavations in King's Lynn 1963–1970*, Soc Medieval Archaeol Monogr Ser **7**, London

COLLIN, B, 1955 *The riddle of a 13th century sword-belt*, Heraldry Soc Monogr

COSMAN, M P, 1976 *Fabulous Feasts*, London

CUNLIFFE, B, 1977 *Excavations at Portchester Castle. III: Medieval, the Outer Bailey and its defences*, Report of the Research Committee of the Society of Antiquaries of London **XXXIV**, London

DUNNING, G C, 1932 Medieval finds in London, *Antiq J*, **12**, 177–8

FORBES, R J, 1952 *Studies in ancient technology*, Leiden

FURNIVALL, F J, 1868 *Early English meals and manners*, London

GANIARIS, H, KEENE, S, and STARLING, K, 1982 A comparison of some treatments for excavated leather, *The Conservator*, **6**, 12–23

GIRTON, T, 1975 *The mark of the sword: a narrative history of the Cutlers Company 1189–1975*, London

GOODALL, I H, 1981 The medieval blacksmith and his products, in *Medieval Industry* (ed D W Crossley), CBA Res Rep **20**, 51–62

GRANGER-TAYLOR, H, 1982 Weaving cloth to shape in the Ancient World, *Textile History*, **13 (1)**, 3–25

GREENSTREET, J, 1889 Powell's Roll of Arms, *Jewitt's Reliquary*, **3**, 145–52 and 231–40

GREENSTREET, J, 1890 Powell's Roll of Arms, *Jewitt's Reliquary*, **4**, 93–7

GRIFFIN, R, 1915 Heraldry in the Cloisters of the Cathedral Church of Christ at Canterbury, *Archaeologia*, **66**, 447–568

GRIMALDI, S, 1835 Grimaldi's Roll of Arms, *Collectanea Topographica et Genealogica*, **2**

HARBEN, H A, 1918 *A dictionary of London*, London

HAWTHORNE, J G and Smith C S, (trans), 1979 *Theophilus: On divers arts*, New York

HAYTON, D, 1956 *The Worshipful Company of Cutlers of London*, London

HAYWARD, J F, 1957 *English cutlery*, London

HENSICH, B A, 1976 *Fast and feast*, Pennsylvania

HERALDRY SOC. SCOTLAND *English medieval Rolls of Arms*, series of transcripts produced by the Heraldry Soc Scotland

HERTEIG, A E, 1959 The excavation of Bryggen, the old Hanseatic wharf in Bergen, *Medieval Archaeol*, **3**, 184

HILL, C, MILLETT, M, and BLAGG, T, 1980 *The Roman riverside wall and monumental arch in London*, London Middlesex Soc Special Pap **3**

HIMSWORTH, J B, 1953 *The story of cutlery*, London

HOBSON, G D, 1929 *English binding before 1500*, London

HODGES, H, 1964 *Artifacts*, London

HUMPHERY-SMITH, C R, 1973 *Anglo Norman Armory*, Canterbury

HUSSEN, C M A Late La Tène Burial at Hertford Heath, Hertfordshire; 1983

KINGSFORD, C L, 1916   *Historical notes on mediaeval London houses*, London Topogr Rec **10**

LAMBERT, J J, 1933   *Records of the Skinners of London; Edward I to James I*, London

LANG, J T, 1978   Anglo-Scandinavian Sculpture in Yorkshire, in *Viking Age York and the North* (ed R A Hall), London, London, 11–20

LEATHERSELLERS' COMPANY, 1982   *The mistery or art of the Leathersellers of the City of London*, London

MACGREGOR, A, 1978   Industry and commerce in Anglo-Scandinavian York, in *Viking Age York and the North* (ed R A Hall), London, London, 34–57

MACGREGOR, A, 1982   *Anglo-Scandinavian finds from Lloyd's Bank, Pavement, and other sites*, The Archaeology of York: The Small finds **17/3**, London

MANN, SIR JAMES, 1962   *Wallace Collection Catalogue: European Arms and Armour II: Arms*, London

MARYON, H, 1971   *Metalwork and enamelling*, New York

MCDONNELL, J G, forthcoming   in *Iron Artifacts and Ironworking from Coppergate*, The Archaeology of York, London

MILNE, G and MILNE C, 1978   Excavations on the Thames waterfront at Trig Lane, London, 1974–6, *Medieval Archaeol*, **22**, 98

MILNE, G and MILNE, C, 1982   *Medieval waterfront development at Trig Lane London*, London Middlesex Archaeol Soc Special Pap **5**

MODIN, S and PLEINER, R, 1978   The Metallographic Examination of Locks, Keys and Tools, in *Excavations at Helgo V:1, Workshop II*, Stockholm

MOOR, C, 1929–32   *Knights of Edward I vols 1–5*, Publ Harleian Soc **80–84**

MORGAN, R and SCHOFIELD, J A, 1978   Tree rings and the archaeology of the Thames waterfront in the City of London, in *Dendrochronology in Europe* (ed J Fletcher), Oxford, Oxford, 223–38

MORONEY, M J, 1980   *Facts from Figures*, London

MURRAY, J A H (ed), 1897   *A new English dictionary on historical principles*, Oxford

NOBLE, T C, 1889   *A brief history of the Worshipful Company of Ironmongers*, London

PATTERSON, R, 1956   Spinning and weaving, in *A history of technology 2* (ed C Singer, E J Holmyard, A R Hall and T I Williams), Oxford, 191–220

WARD PERKINS, J B, 1940   *Medieval catalogue*, London Museum Catalogue **7**, London

PINCHES, R H and WOOD, A, 1971   *A European Armorial*, London

PLATT, C and COLEMAN-SMITH, R, 1975   *Excavations in Medieval Southampton 1953–1969. 2: The finds*, Leicester

POWICKE, M, 1962   *The Thirteenth Century*, Oxford

PRIESTLEY, H, 1972   *Heraldic Sculpture Illustrated by the Work of James Woodward*, Ipswich

PRITCHARD, F A, forthcoming   Small finds in *Aspects of Saxon and Norman London*, **1**: *Finds and Environmental Evidence* (ed A Vince)

RICHARDSON, K M, 1959   Excavations in Hungate, York, *Archaeol J*, **116**, 51–114

RAWLINGS, G B (ed), 1902   *The Knight of La Tour Landry trans. William Caxton*, London

RILEY, H T (ed), 1868   *Memorials of London and London life*, London

RUSSELL, J, 1939   English medieval leatherwork, *Archaeol J*, **96**, 132–41

SALAMAN, R A, 1975   *A dictionary of tools used in woodworking and allied trades c 1700–1970*, London

SALZMAN, L F, 1923   *English industries of the Middle Ages*, Oxford

SCHOFIELD, J A, 1975   Seal House, *Current Archaeol*, **49**, 53–7

SHARPE, R R (ed), 1899   *Calendar of letter books of the City of London: Letter Book A. c. AD 1275–98*, London

SHARPE, R R (ed), 1900   *Calendar of letter books of the City of London: Letter Book B. AD 1275–1312*, London

SHARPE, R R (ed), 1901   *Calendar of letter books of the City of London: Letter Book C. AD 1291–1309*, London

SHARPE, R R (ed), 1902   *Calendar of letter books of the City of London: Letter Book D. AD 1309–1314*, London

SHARPE, R R (ed), 1903   *Calendar of letter books of the City of London: Letter Book E. AD 1314–1337*, London

SHARPE, R R (ed), 1904   *Calendar of letter books of the City of London: Letter Book F. AD 1337–1352*, London

SHARPE, R R (ed), 1905   *Calendar of letter books of the City of London: Letter Book G. AD 1352–1374*, London

SHARPE, R R (ed), 1907   *Calendar of letter books of the City of London: Letter Book H. AD 1375–99*, London

SHARPE, R R (ed), 1909   *Calendar of letter books of the City of London: Letter Book I. AD 1400–22*, London

SKEAT, W W (ed), 1912   *The complete works of Geoffrey Chaucer.*, London

STANFORD LONDON, H, 1967   Glover's Roll and Walford's Roll, in *Rolls of Arms Henry III: Aspilogia*, **2**, (ed T D Tremlett and H Stanford London), 87–204

STARLING, K, 1984   *The freeze drying of leather pre treated with glycerol*, preprint of the 7th Triennial Meeting of the International Council of Museums Committee for Conservation Copenhagen **2**

TATE, J, 1984   *Examination and analysis using x-rays*, Scottish Soc Conservation and Restoration **3**

TATTON BROWN, T, 1974   Excavations at the Custom House, *Trans London Middlesex Archaeol Soc*, **25**, 117–219

TATTON BROWN, T, 1975   Excavations at the Custom House Site, City of London 1973 – part 2, *Trans London Middlesex Archaeol Soc*, **26**, 103–70

THOMAS, A H (ed), 1924   *Calendar of early Mayors Court Rolls, AD 1298–1307*, Cambridge

THOMAS, A H (ed), 1926   *Calendar of Plea and Memoranda Rolls, AD 1323–64*, Cambridge

THOMAS, A H (ed), 1929   *Calendar of Plea and Memoranda Rolls, AD 1364–81*, Cambridge

THOMAS, A H (ed), 1932   *Calendar of select Pleas and Memoranda of the City of London, AD 1381–1412*, Cambridge

THOMAS, A H (ed), 1943   *Calendar of Plea and Memoranda Rolls, AD 1413–37*, Cambridge

THOMAS, A H (ed), 1954   *Calendar of Plea and Memoranda Rolls, AD 1437–57*, Cambridge

THOMAS, A H (ed), 1961   *Calendar of Plea and Memoranda Rolls, AD 1458–82*, Cambridge

THOMPSON, M W, 1967   *Novgorod the Great*, London

THOMSON, R, 1981   Leather manufacture in the post-medieval period with special reference to Northamptonshire, *Post-Medieval Archaeol*, **15**, 161–75

THRUPP, S L, 1962   *The merchant class of medieval London*, Michigan

TITE, M S, 1972   *Methods of physical examination in archaeology*, London

TREMLETT, T D, 1967   The Matthew Paris Shields, in *Rolls of Arms Henry III: Aspilogia*, **2**, (ed T D Tremlett and H Stanford London), 1–86

TYLECOTE, R F, 1962   *Metallurgy in archaeology*, London

TYLECOTE, R F, 1976   *A History of Metallurgy*, London

TYLECOTE, R F, 1981   The medieval smith and his methods, in *Medieval Industry* (ed D W Crossley), CBA Res Rep **20**, 42–50

TYLECOTE, R F and BLACK, J W B, 1980   *The effect of Hydrogen reduction on the properties of Ferrous Materials*, Studies in Conservation **25.2**

VEALE, E M, 1969   Craftsmen and the economy of London in the fourteenth century, in *Studies in London History* (ed A E J Hollaender and W Kellaway), London, London, 133–51

VINCE, A G, 1985   The Saxon and Medieval Pottery of London: A Review, *Medieval Archaeol*, **29**, 25–93

WADDINGTON, Q, 1927   Viking Sheath of Leather, *Antiq J*, **7**, 526 and Pl. opposite

WAGNER, A R, 1950   *A catalogue of English medieval Rolls of Arms: Aspilogia* **1**

WATERER, J W, 1946   *Leather in life, art and industry*, London

WATERER, J W, 1956   Leather, in *A history of technology* (ed C Singer, E J Holmyard, A R Hall, and T I Williams) **2**, Oxford, 147–86

WATERER, J W, 1968   *Leather craftsmanship*, London

WATSON, J,   *Identification of knife handles from various Department of Urban Archaeology sites*, Ancient Monuments Lab Rep 4570

WEBSTER, L E and CHERRY, J, 1973   Medieval Britain in 1972, *Medieval Archaeol*, **17**, 162–3

WELCH, C, 1916   *History of the Cutlers Company of London. Vol I*, London

WILLIAMS, F, 1977   *Excavations at Pleshey Castle*, Oxford

WILLIAMS, J H, 1979   *Saint Peter's Street, Northampton excavations 1973–6*, Northampton

WILMOTT, T, 1981   The arms of Fitzwalter on leather scabbards from London, *Trans London Middlesex Archaeol Soc*, **32**, 132–9

WILMOTT, T, forthcoming   The heraldic tiles, in A G Vince and T Wilmott, A lost tile pavement at Tewkesbury Abbey and an early 14th century tile factory, *Trans Bristol Gloucester Archaeol Soc*

WILTHEW, P, 1984a   *Analysis of inlays and fittings on medieval iron knives and shears from the Museum of London*, Ancient Monuments Lab Rep 4311 and 4468

WILTHEW, P, 1984b   *Metallographic examination of medieval knives and shears from the Museum of London*, Ancient Monuments Lab Rep 4538

YOUNGS, S M and CLARK, J, 1982   Medieval Britain in 1981, *Medieval Archaeol*, **26**, 192–3

YOUNGS, S M, CLARK, J, and Barry, T B, 1983   Medieval Britain in 1982, *Medieval Archaeol*, **27**, 191–5

The Catalogue

The numbers allocated to the objects run continuously through the catalogue: 1 to 308 are knives, 309 and 310 folding knives, 311 to 368 shears, 369 to 371 scissors, and 372 to 491 scabbards. Within each of these series, those objects from dated contexts have been divided into six chronological groups. The dividing dates were chosen to minimise the number of objects that overlapped two periods, but when this was unavoidable the object has been assigned to the later of the two. In all cases the date assigned to each object is the date of deposition, not manufacture. Although any chronological divisions are artificial, they do aid the recognition of chronological trends. The number of objects in each group varies considerably. Over half the knives and shears come from late 14th-century deposits, whereas the majority of the scabbards are of early to mid 14th-century date. Inevitably, it is only when the groups are large that less common forms and techniques are likely to be represented.

Within each period the knives and shears are ordered by similarity, particularly of form and size; the whittle tangs precede the scale tangs. The scabbards are grouped within period by similarity of decoration. The catalogue lists all stratified knives and scabbards from the sites concerned, but only a representative selection was chosen to be illustrated; these are described first within each period. All the folding knives, scissors and scabbards are illustrated. Makers marks, including those on unillustrated knives or shears, are included on Figs. 6–8.

Throughout the catalogue, the descriptive details of each object are preceded by the museum accession codes. This code consists of three elements: the DUA site code, the context number (in square brackets) and the object's individual registration number on the site (in angled brackets). All three elements are needed to uniquely identify any artefact from the DUA collections. Some objects from the Museum of London reserve collections have been included to clarify points mentioned in the text; their accession numbers are preceded by the initials MOL.

The complete measurement is given only when the whole object survives and all elements are present. A length is given when the complete length survives or in rare instances where so little is missing that an estimated length has been considered possible. The width and thickness are maximum measurements and similarly only given when the object is in sufficiently good condition for them to be accurate.

KNIVES (Fig. 2)

The basic elements of any medieval knife are the *blade*, the *tang* and the *handle*. The junction of blade and tang is termed the *shoulder*; its shape varies as does the position of the tang on the blade. All the knives have iron blades and tangs. The blade consists of a single sharpened cutting edge, a back and a tip. Amongst the considerable variations in blade shapes, the two most obvious are those with *angled backs* (eg. No. 5), and those with *stepped backs* (eg No. 124). The handle can be attached to the tang in two ways determined by the form of the tang. *Whittle-tang* knives have a tapered tang which is inserted into or through the handle. *Scale-tang* knives have wider and flatter tangs onto which the plates comprising the handle are attached with metal rivets. These scales are often bracketed by decorative metal elements, *shoulder plates* and *end caps*.

Late 12th-century knives Nos. 1–10

The knives in this small group vary in size and shape. The three blades with angled backs reflect the end of the 'Saxon' tradition, in which this was a common feature. Pattern welding is the sole type of blade decoration and this similarly represents the continuation of earlier decorative techniques.

1. (SH74 [536] ⟨224⟩)
Blade, length 139mm, width 23mm, thickness 1.5mm; decorated with pattern welding. Whittle tang, length 52mm, central on blade, straight shoulder, tapering.

2. (SWA81 [2266] ⟨2248⟩)
Blade, length 64mm, width 12mm, thickness 4mm, triangular. Whittle tang, in line with back of blade.

3. (SH74 [578] ⟨688⟩)
Blade, length 70mm, width 19mm, thickness 4mm, edge and back curve to meet. Whittle tang, length 43mm, central on blade, sloping shoulder, parallel sided. May have been sharpened.

4. (BIG82 [4584] ⟨2899⟩)
Blade; decorated with pattern welding, stepped back.

5. (BIG82 [4584] ⟨3091⟩)
Blade, length 120mm, width 18mm, thickness 4mm, angled back. Whittle tang, length 49mm, set just below back, sloping shoulder, tapering.

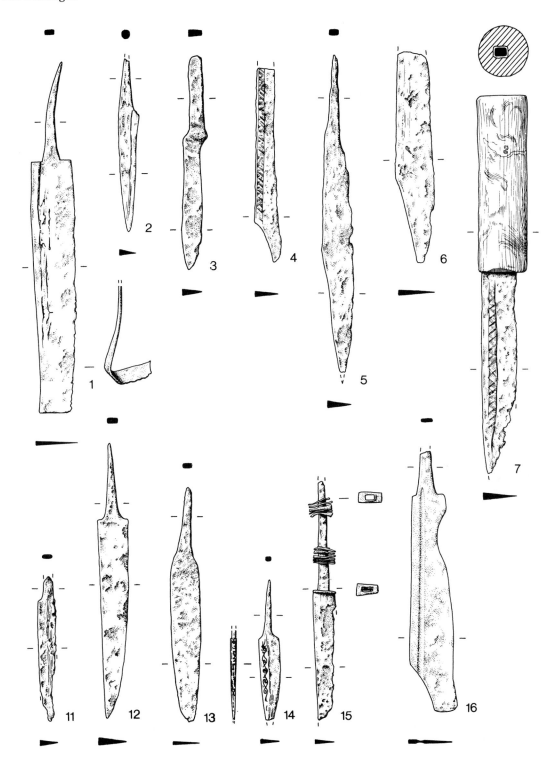

54 Knives, Nos. 1–7 (Late 12th century), Nos. 11–16 (early to mid 13th century). Scale 1:2.

6. (SWA81 [2183] ⟨1532⟩)
   Blade, width 17mm, thickness 3mm, angled back.

7. (SWA81 [2266] ⟨2256⟩)
   Blade, width 19mm, thickness 5mm; decorated with
   pattern welding, edge curves to back. Whittle tang,
   length 38mm, central on blade, straight shoulder,
   tapering. Wooden handle (box), length 92mm, cylindrical.

8. (SWA81 [2187] ⟨1535⟩)   *Not illustrated*
   Blade, width 17mm, thickness 3mm, almost parallel
   sided. Whittle tang, length 55mm, central on blade,
   sloping shoulder, tapering.

9. (SWA81 [2257] ⟨2472⟩)   *Not illustrated*
   Blade, length 67mm, width 19mm, thickness 4mm,
   triangular. Whittle tang, central on blade, sloping
   shoulder. Corroded.

10. (SWA81 [2277] 3517⟩)   *Not illustrated*
    Blade, width 16mm, thickness 2mm, parallel sided?
    Whittle tang, length 41mm, central on blade, sloping
    shoulder, tapering. Very corroded.

Early to mid 13th-century knives Nos.11–24

These knives also vary in shape, but all the large
blades have an indentation on the cutting edge near
the handle. Three techniques of blade decoration are
represented: pattern welding, overlaid wire and
grooves. There is also an elaborate handle (No.15),
constructed by threading a series of elements onto the
tang.

11. (SWA81 [2140] ⟨3098⟩)
    Blade, thickness 3mm, triangular. Whittle tang, central
    on blade, sloping shoulder. Possible weld lines visible
    on the x-radiograph.

12. (SWA81 [2139] ⟨1879⟩)
    Blade, length 105mm, width 17mm, thickness 4mm,
    edge curves to back. Whittle tang, length 39mm,
    central on blade, straight shoulder, tapering.

13. (SH74 [484] ⟨222⟩)
    Blade, length 80mm, width 16mm, thickness 3mm,
    edge and back curve to meet. Whittle tang, length
    47mm, central on blade, sloping shoulder.

14. (BIG82 [2913] ⟨2398⟩)
    Blade, length 50mm, width 17mm, thickness 4mm;
    decorated with applied silver wire in shallow grooves
    and on back, triangular. Whittle tang, length 28mm,
    set just below back, sloping shoulder, tapering. Plate
    3b.

15. (SWA81 [2150] ⟨1243⟩)
    Blade, width 12mm, thickness 2mm, parallel sided.
    Whittle tang, central on blade, straight shoulder, para-
    llel sided. Handled composed of tin and ?organic ele-
    ments, threaded onto tang; decorated with rectangular
    tin plates. Shoulder plate (copper alloy); rectangular.

16. (SH74 [386] ⟨149⟩)
    Blade, length 113mm, width 18mm, thickness 2mm;
    decorated with a groove, angled back. Whittle tang,
    central on blade, straight shoulder, tapering. May
    have been sharpened; whole?

17. (SH74 [386] ⟨152⟩)
    Blade, length 136mm, width 24mm, thickness 2mm;
    decorated with pattern welding. Whittle tang, length
    46mm, central on blade, straight shoulder, roughly
    triangular shaped. May have been sharpened; whole?

18. (SH74 [484] ⟨232⟩)
    Blade, width 28mm, thickness 2.5mm. Whittle tang,
    central on blade, straight shoulder, tapering. Wooden
    handle (pomoideae family), length 92mm, roughly
    shaped. May have been sharpened.

19. (SH74 [386] ⟨192⟩)
    Blade, width 26mm, thickness 1mm. Whittle tang,
    length 50mm, central on blade, sloping shoulder,
    tapering. Wooden handle (pomoideae family), length
    112mm, roughly shaped. May have been sharpened;
    corroded.

20. (BIG82 [3135] ⟨2640⟩)   *Not illustrated*
    Blade, width 23mm, thickness 4mm. Whittle tang,
    length 47mm, central on blade, sloping shoulder,
    tapering. May have been sharpened.

21. (BIG82 [3204] ⟨3411⟩)   *Not illustrated*
    Blade, triangular.

22. (SH74 [386] ⟨140⟩)   *Not illustrated*
    Whittle tang. Wooden handle (alder), length 91mm,
    cylindrical.

23. (SH74 [386] ⟨371⟩)   *Not illustrated*
    Blade, fragmentary. ?Knife.

24. (SWA81 [2150] ⟨4683⟩)   *Not illustrated*
    Whittle tang. Wooden handle, cylindrical.

Late 13th-century knives Nos.25–42

The majority of the blades from this period have a
pronounced triangular shape. Two types of blade
decoration occur, including the only dated example
with inset stamped discs (No.36). The earliest
makers' mark, a deeply stamped crescent, also occurs
here (No.31). Amongst the handles is the only turned
wooden handle in this catalogue (No.37).

25. (SWA81 [2062] ⟨2240⟩)
    Blade, length 82mm, width 14mm, thickness 5mm;
    decorated with applied silver wire in shallow grooves
    and on the back; triangular. Whittle tang, length
    45mm, central on blade, straight shoulder, tapering.

26. (SWA81 [2144] ⟨1130⟩)
    Blade, length 86mm, width 14mm, thickness 5mm,
    triangular. Whittle tang, length 42mm, set just below
    back, straight shoulder, tapering and notch near
    shoulder. Corroded.

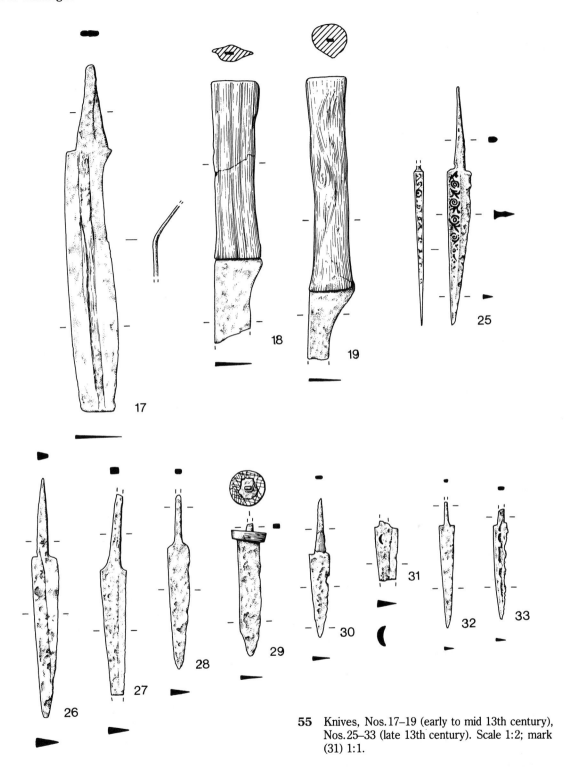

55 Knives, Nos. 17–19 (early to mid 13th century), Nos. 25–33 (late 13th century). Scale 1:2; mark (31) 1:1.

27. (SWA81 [2018] ⟨464⟩)
    Blade width 15mm, thickness 4mm, triangular. Whittle
    tang, central on blade, sloping shoulder, tapering.
    Possible weld lines visible on the x-radiograph. Plate
    1a.

28. (SWA81 [2141] ⟨3399⟩)
    Blade, length 64mm, width 13mm, thickness 3mm,
    triangular. Whittle tang, length 27mm, central on
    blade, sloping shoulder, parallel sided. Corroded.

29. (SWA81 [2051] ⟨676⟩)
    Blade, thickness 3mm, triangular. Whittle tang, central
    on blade, sloping shoulder. Shoulder plate (bone); disc
    5mm thick. Corroded.

30. (SWA81 [2018] ⟨3909⟩)
    Blade, length 48mm, width 10mm, thickness 3mm,
    triangular, back thins near tip. Whittle tang, length
    29mm, central on blade, straight shoulder, tapering.
    Wooden handle.

31. (SWA81 [2039] ⟨2306⟩)
    Blade, width 12.5mm, thickness 4.5mm, marked,
    triangular. Whittle tang, central on blade, straight
    shoulder. Possible weld lines visible on the x-
    radiograph. Plate 1b.

32. (SWA81 [2018] ⟨3890⟩)
    Blade, length 53mm, width 9mm, triangular. Whittle
    tang, central on blade, straight shoulder. Corroded.

33. (SWA81 [2070] ⟨3069⟩)
    Blade, length 51mm, width 9mm, thickness 1.5mm,
    triangular. Whittle tang, central on blade, straight
    shoulder, tapering?

34. (SWA81 [2034] ⟨2309⟩)
    Blade, length 120mm, width 25mm, thickness 2mm;
    decorated with applied wire, widens towards tip, edge
    curves to back. Whittle tang, set just below back,
    sloping shoulder. Corroded.

35. (SWA81 [2018] ⟨460⟩)
    Blade, length 131mm, width 27mm, thickness 2mm,
    widens towards tip. Whittle tang, length 53mm,
    central on blade, sloping shoulder, tapering. Wooden
    handle.

36. (SWA81 [2141] ⟨3274⟩)
    Blade, width 26mm, thickness 4mm; decorated with
    grooves and inset copper/zinc alloy discs stamped
    individually with a letter; widens towards tip. Whittle
    tang, length 42mm, set just below back, straight
    shoulder, tapering. Horn handle.

37. (SWA81 [2051] ⟨1171⟩)
    Blade, width 12mm, thickness 3.5mm, triangular.
    Whittle tang, length 46mm, central on blade, straight
    shoulder, tapering. Wooden handle (box), length
    62mm, cylindrical; decorated with rings turned in the
    wood.

38. (SWA81 [2057] ⟨543⟩)
    Blade, length 126mm, width 25mm, thickness 3mm,
    triangular. Whittle tang, length 64mm, central on
    blade, sloping shoulder, tapering. Wooden handle
    (yew), length 97mm, cylindrical. Possible weld lines
    visible on the x-radiograph; found in scabbard No.391.

39. (SWA81 [2065] ⟨786⟩)
    Blade, width 18mm, thickness 6mm, triangular.
    Whittle tang, length 53mm, central on blade, sloping
    shoulder, tapering. Wooden handle (box), length
    92mm, roughly shaped cylinder. Plate 6.

40. (SWA81 [2018] ⟨2329⟩)   *Not illustrated*
    Blade, triangular?

41. (SWA81 [2030] ⟨3982⟩)   *Not illustrated*
    Blade, triangular. Very corroded.

42. (SWA81 [2137] ⟨3423⟩)   *Not illustrated*
    Blade, triangular.

Early to mid 14th-century knives Nos.43–69

There is a sharp contrast between the earlier knives
and those from this period. The blades are longer and
thinner and are frequently marked. Grooves along one
side only of the blades are the only method by which
they were decorated. Scale tangs first appear in this
group.

43. (TL74 [503] ⟨775⟩)
    Blade, thickness 3.5mm, marked. Whittle tang, central
    on blade, sloping shoulder, tapering. Very corroded.

44. (TL74 [415] ⟨575⟩)
    Blade, width 13mm, thickness 3mm, with double
    mark. Whittle tang, central on blade, straight
    shoulder, tapering. Corroded.

45. (BC72 [261] ⟨3233⟩)
    Blade, length 110mm, width 14mm, thickness 2mm,
    with triple mark, back curves to tip. Whittle tang,
    central on blade, sloping shoulder, tapering. Possible
    weld lines visible on the x-radiograph.

46. (TL74 [415] ⟨347⟩)
    Blade, length 120mm, width 19mm, thickness 2mm,
    marked; decorated with a groove on the blade and
    back, angled back. Whittle tang, length 61mm, set just
    below back, straight shoulder, tapering. Corroded.

47. (BC72 [255] ⟨4752⟩)
    Blade, width 15mm, thickness 5mm; decorated with
    an inlaid groove (copper/zinc alloy) and a groove on
    the back, stepped back. Whittle tang, set just below
    back, sloping shoulder, parallel sided.

48. (TL74 [415] ⟨445⟩)
    Blade, width 16mm, thickness 5mm, with inlaid mark
    (copper/zinc alloy); decorated with a groove. Whittle
    tang, length 45mm, set just below back, sloping
    shoulder, tapering. Corroded.

49. (TL74 [415] ⟨690⟩)
    Blade, width 11mm, thickness 3mm, with inlaid mark
    (tin), triangular. Whittle tang, central on blade,
    straight shoulder, tapering. Corroded.

50. (CUS73 [I 12] ⟨46⟩)
    Blade; fragment with a sloping back.

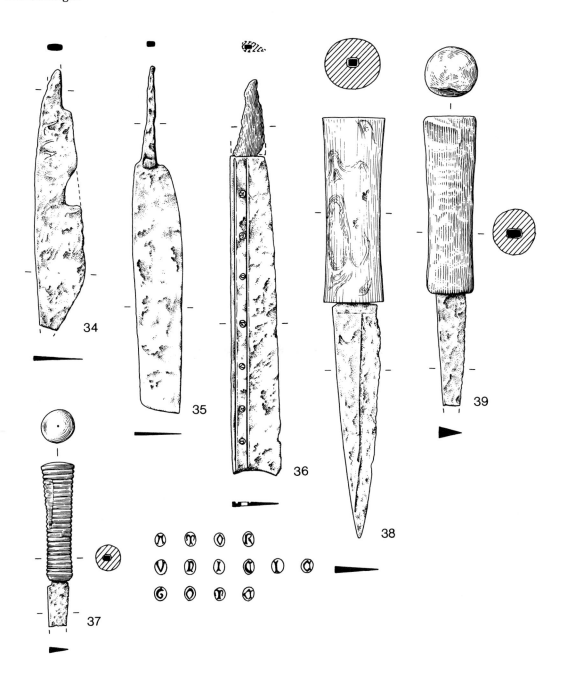

56 Knives, Nos. 34–39 (late 13th century). Scale 1:2; inscription (36) 1:1.

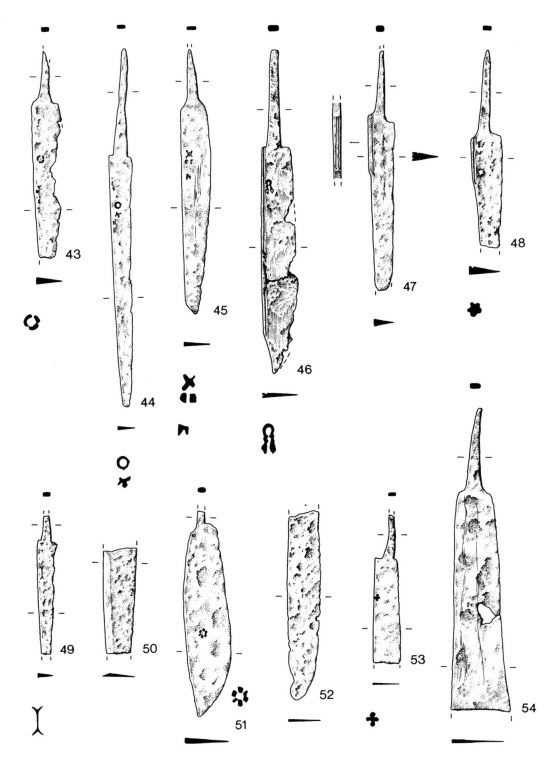

57   Knives, Nos. 43–54 (early to mid 14th century). Scale 1:2; marks 1:1.

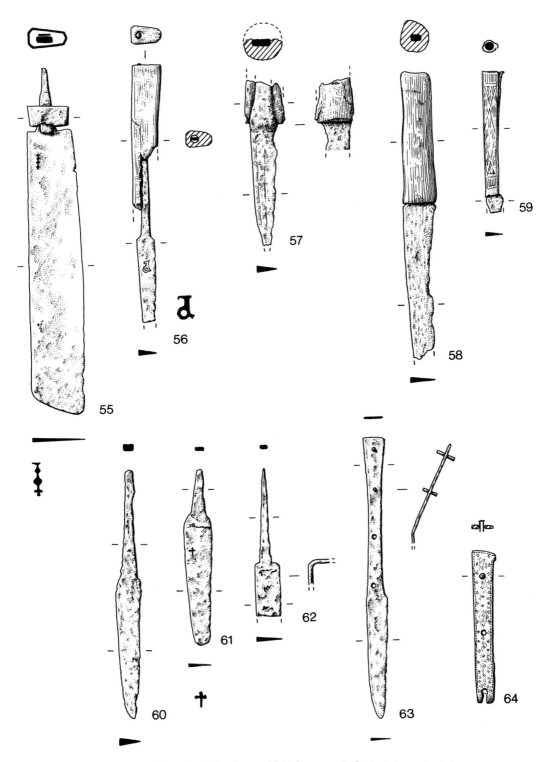

58 Knives, Nos. 55–64 (early to mid 14th century). Scale 1:2; marks 1:1.

51. (BIS82 [494] ⟨165⟩)
Blade, with inlaid mark (tin), edge curves to back.
Whittle tang, set just below back, sloping shoulder.
Corroded; mark in middle of blade.

52. (TL74 [415] ⟨703⟩)
Blade, edge curves to back. Corroded; possible weld
lines visible on the x-radiograph.

53. (BC72 [250] ⟨4624⟩)
Blade, width 12mm, thickness 1.5mm, marked,
widens towards tip. Whittle tang, set below centre of
blade, straight shoulder, tapering.

54. (SWA81 [2042] ⟨4991⟩)
Blade, width 32mm, thickness 2mm, widens towards
tip. Whittle tang, length 45mm, central on blade,
straight shoulder, tapering and twisted. Plate 2b.

55. (CUS73 [III 10] ⟨31⟩)
Blade, length 149mm, width 24mm, thickness 2mm,
marked, widens towards tip. Whittle tang, length
34mm, central on blade, straight shoulder, tapering.
Iron hilt band.

56. (BC72 [255] ⟨3622⟩)
Blade, width 9mm, thickness 2mm, with inlaid mark
(tin/lead alloy). Whittle tang, length 90mm, central on
blade, sloping shoulder, tapering and projects beyond
end of handle. Wooden handle (?box), rectangular with
bevelled edges.

57. (CUS73 [I 12] ⟨63⟩)
Blade, width 18mm, thickness 5mm, triangular.
Whittle tang, central on blade, sloping shoulder.
Wooden handle (?box), cylindrical. Corroded.

58. (CUS73 [IV 48] ⟨1032⟩)
Blade, width 19mm, thickness 3mm. Whittle tang,
length 55mm, central on blade, sloping shoulder,
tapering. Wooden handle (maple), length 69mm,
roughly shaped.

59. (BC72 [250] ⟨4636⟩)
Blade, width 10mm, thickness 1.5mm. Whittle tang.
Copper/zinc alloy and wood handle, length 64mm,
sheet metal tube around a wooden core; with incised
linear decoration.

60. (CUS73 [XV 15] ⟨716⟩)
Blade, length 75mm, width 14mm, thickness 3mm,
triangular. Whittle tang, length 58mm, central on
blade, sloping shoulder, tapering. Corroded.

61. (CUS73 [IV 58] ⟨496⟩)
Blade, width 16mm, thickness 2mm, marked,
triangular. Whittle tang, length 23mm, central on
blade, sloping shoulder, tapering. Corroded.

62. (TL74 [415] ⟨709⟩)
Blade, width 13mm, thickness 2mm, parallel sided.
Whittle tang, length 50mm, set just below back,
straight shoulder, tapering.

63. (CUS73 [VI 26] ⟨509⟩)
Blade, length 65mm, width 11mm, thickness 1.5mm,
back curves to edge. Scale tang, length 83mm, in line
with back of blade, tang handle shape. Handle,
attached with solid rivets (copper/zinc alloy).

64. (BC72 [255] ⟨4751⟩)
Bone handle, length 80mm, flat scale with hooked
end, attached with tubular rivets (copper/zinc alloy);
decorated with copper/zinc alloy pins.

65. (BC72 [250] ⟨4625⟩) *Not illustrated*
Blade, width 13mm, thickness 2mm. Whittle tang,
central on blade, sloping shoulder.

66. (BC72 [250] ⟨4626⟩) *Not illustrated*
Blade, width 12mm, thickness 3mm. Whittle tang,
length 38mm, set below centre of blade, straight
shoulder, tapering. May have been sharpened.

67. (BC72 [261] ⟨3246⟩) *Not illustrated*
Blade, width 13mm, thickness 2mm. Whittle tang,
length 86mm, set just below back, straight shoulder,
tapering. Shoulder plate (bone). End cap (bone oval).

68. (TL74 [414] ⟨823⟩) *Not illustrated*
Blade, width 13mm, thickness 4.5mm, triangular.
Whittle tang, set just below back, straight shoulder,
tapering. Corroded.

69. (TL74 [415] ⟨545⟩) *Not illustrated*
Blade, fragmentary. Corroded.

Late 14th-century knives Nos. 70–252

This is the largest group of knives, and a variety of
forms are represented including several with stepped
backs. Grooves are the most common type of blade
decoration, but there are also some examples with
inlays (Nos 73, 92 and 98). Makers' marks continue to
be common. One third of the knives have scale tangs,
and most of these handles have decorative fittings; the
whittle-tang handles by contrast are usually plain.

70. (BC72 [89] ⟨2512⟩)
Blade, thickness 3mm. Whittle tang, length 112mm,
set just below back, straight shoulder, tapering and
projects beyond end of handle. Wooden handle (box),
length 106mm, rectangular. Possibly a cleaver.

71. (BC72 [150] ⟨4319⟩)
Blade, length 145mm, width 19mm, thickness 3mm,
marked, widens towards tip. Whittle tang, set just
below back, sloping shoulder.

72. (BWB83 [310] ⟨590⟩)
Blade, length 160mm, thickness 3mm, marked.
Whittle tang, set just below back, straight shoulder.
Possibly a cleaver.

73. (BWB83 [359] ⟨404⟩)
Blade; decorated with a line of inlaid 'x's (copper/zinc
alloy), edge curves to back.

74. (SH74 [280] ⟨56⟩)
Blade, length 115mm, edge curves to back. Whittle
tang, set just below back, straight shoulder, tapering.
Wooden handle (holly). Very corroded.

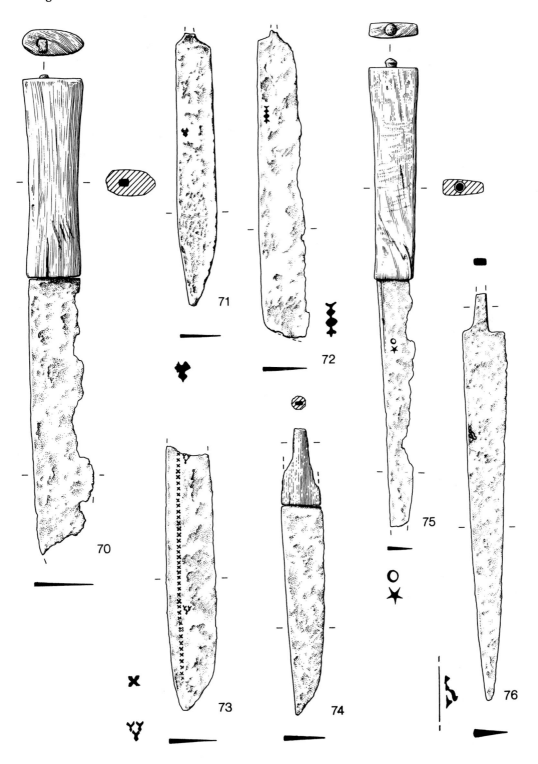

59 Knives, Nos. 70–76 (late 14th century). Scale 1:2; marks and decorative inlay (73) 1:1.

75. (BC72 [119] ⟨2824⟩)
Blade, thickness 4mm, with double mark; decorated with a groove. Whittle tang, length 115mm, set just below back, sloping shoulder, tapering and projects beyond end of handle. Wooden handle (box, length 112mm, rectangular section. End cap (iron), formed from tang end. Corroded.

76. (BC72 [79] ⟨2530⟩)
Blade, length 198mm, width 24mm, thickness 6mm, with inlaid mark (copper/zinc alloy), triangular. Whittle tang, set just below back, sloping shoulder.

77. (BC72 [150] ⟨2985⟩)
Blade, length 96mm, width 19mm, thickness 4mm, triangular. Whittle tang, length 83mm, set just below back, straight shoulder, tapering and projects beyond end of handle. Wooden handle (maple), length 80mm, cylindrical.

78. (BWB83 [332] ⟨309⟩)
Blade, length 89mm, with inlaid mark, back curves to edge. Whittle tang, projects beyond end of handle. Wooden handle (?box), oval section. Corroded; possible weld lines visible on the x-radiograph.

79. (BWB83 [303] ⟨232⟩)
Blade, width 17mm, thickness 5mm, triangular. Whittle tang, set just below back, straight shoulder, tapering and probably projected beyond end of handle. Wooden handle (maple), length 90mm, cylindrical. Corroded; two wedges between the handle and tang end.

80. (BWB83 [256] ⟨105⟩)
Blade, width 21mm, thickness 4mm. Whittle tang, set just below back, straight shoulder, tapering. Wooden handle (alder), cylindrical.

81. (BWB83 [298] ⟨412⟩)
Blade, length 111mm, width 22mm, thickness 3mm, marked, triangular. Whittle tang. Wooden handle (?maple), oval section. Hilt band (tin). Possible weld lines visible on the x-radiograph.

82. (TL74 [2332] ⟨2342⟩)
Copper alloy handle, copper alloy sheet tube; decorated with incised lines and stamped out quatrefoils.

83. (CUS73 [IV 10] ⟨69⟩)
Blade, width 13mm, thickness 4mm, marked, triangular. Whittle tang, set just below back, sloping shoulder, tapering.

84. (BWB83 [369] ⟨760⟩)
Blade, length 89mm, width 18mm, thickness 4mm, marked, triangular. Whittle tang, length 38mm, central on blade, sloping shoulder, tapering.

85. (BWB83 [298] ⟨176⟩)
Blade, length 93mm, width 16mm, thickness 5mm, triangular. Whittle tang, length 49mm, central on blade, sloping shoulder, tapering.

86. (BC72 [150] ⟨4312⟩)
Blade, length 109mm, width 16mm, thickness 2mm, marked; decorated with a groove and notches on the back, stepped back, edge curves to back. Whittle tang, central on blade, sloping shoulder, tapering.

87. (BWB83 [269] ⟨148⟩)
Blade, width 12mm, thickness 2mm, angled back. Whittle tang, length 47mm, central on blade, straight shoulder, tapering and twisted.

88. (TL74 [1998] ⟨2163⟩)
Blade, length 111mm, width 18mm, edge curves to back. Whittle tang, set just below back, straight shoulder, tapering. Corroded.

89. (BWB83 [110] ⟨182⟩)
Blade, width 12mm, thickness 2mm, marked. Whittle tang, length 60mm, set just below back, sloping shoulder, tapering. Corroded.

90. (BC72 [79] ⟨2431⟩)
Blade, width 14mm, thickness 2mm, with inlaid mark (tin). Whittle tang, length 37mm, central on blade, sloping shoulder. Horn handle, length 68mm, cylindrical. Plate 4a.

91. (BWB83 [204] ⟨86⟩)
Blade, length 78mm, width 11mm, thickness 2mm, triangular. Whittle tang, length 31mm, set just below back, sloping shoulder, tapering. Wooden handle (maple), cylindrical.

92. (BWB83 [308] ⟨620⟩)
Blade, width 18mm, thickness 2mm; decorated with a line of inlaid 'x's (copper/zinc alloy). Whittle tang, set just below back, straight shoulder.

93. (BWB83 [292] ⟨189⟩)
Blade, width 14mm, thickness 2mm; notches on the back. Whittle tang, length 39mm, central on blade, sloping shoulder, tapering.

94. (BWB83 [317] ⟨229⟩)
Blade, length 48mm, width 10mm, thickness 3mm, triangular. Whittle tang, length 35mm, set just below back, straight shoulder, tapering. Wooden handle (?box), cylindrical.

95. (BWB83 [2] ⟨31⟩)
Blade, length 45mm, width 8mm, thickness 3mm, triangular. Whittle tang, central on blade, straight shoulder.

96. (DUK77 [501] ⟨131⟩)
Blade, length 42mm, width 11mm, thickness 2mm, back curves to edge. Whittle tang, length 23mm, set just below back, straight shoulder. Wooden handle (pomoideae family), rectangular section. Found in scabbard No.457. Plate 7.

97. (BWB83 [290] ⟨191⟩)
Blade; stamped impression of a dog (?mark), edge and back curves to meet.

98. (BWB83 [318] ⟨565⟩)
Blade, width 17mm, thickness 3mm; decorated with inlaid tin triangles and a copper/zinc alloy strip soldered onto the back. Whittle tang, central on blade, sloping shoulder. Possible weld lines visible on the x-radiograph.

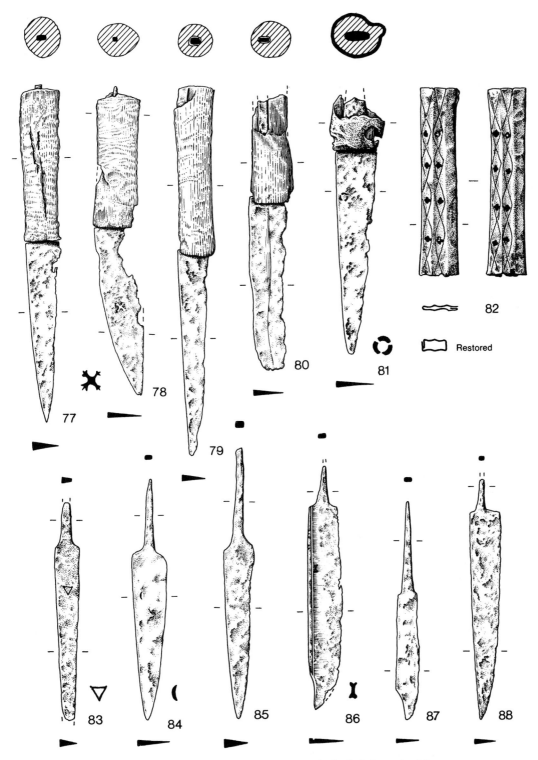

60 Knives, Nos. 77–88 (late 14th century). Scale 1:2; marks 1:1.

Knives and Scabbards

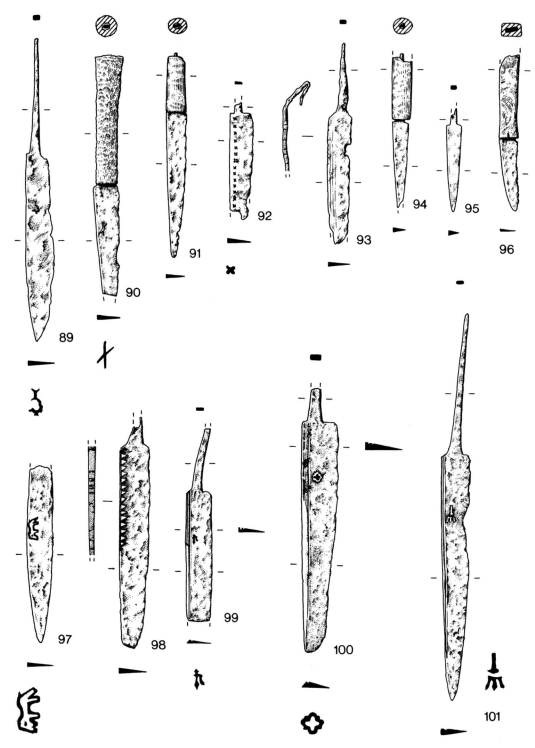

61   Knives, Nos. 89–101 (late 14th century). Scale 1:2; marks, decorative inlay (92) 1:1.

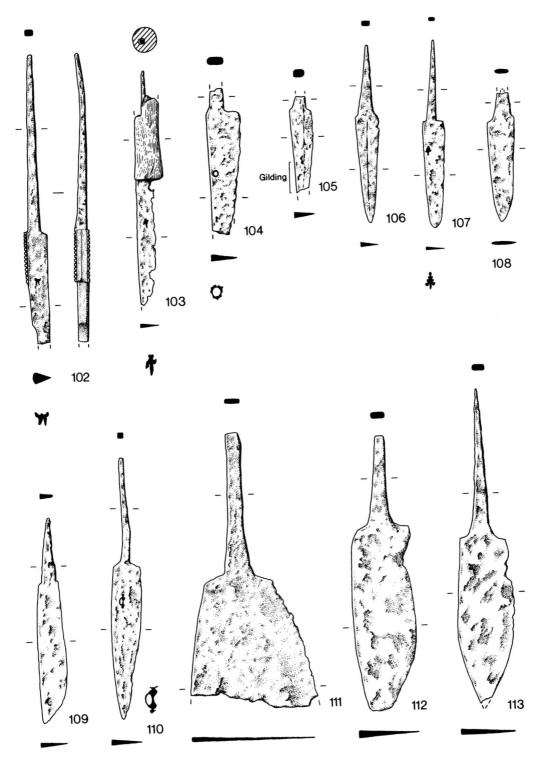

Gilding

62 Knives, Nos. 102–113 (late 14th century). Scale 1:2; marks 1:1.

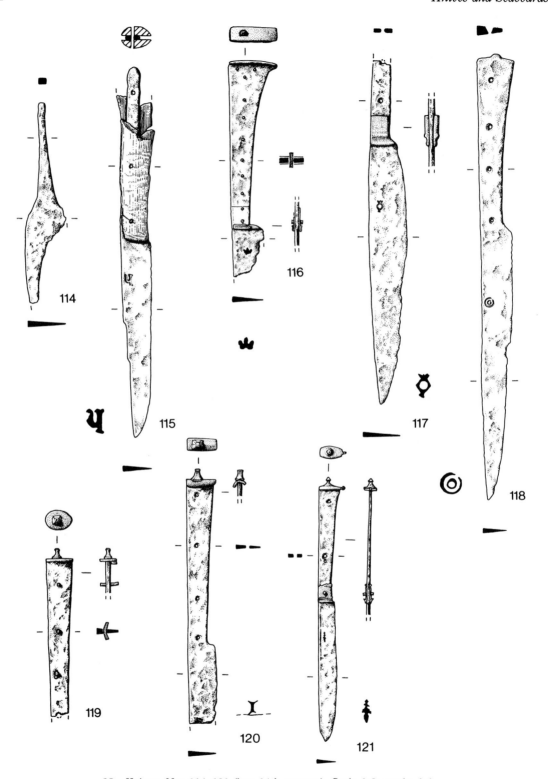

63 Knives, Nos. 114–121 (late 14th century). Scale 1:2; marks 1:1.

99. (BC72 [79] ⟨2430⟩)
Blade, width 14mm, thickness 2mm, marked;
decorated with two inlaid grooves (copper/zinc alloy),
back shaped. Whittle tang, set just below back,
sloping shoulder, tapering.

100. (BC72 [118a] ⟨4260⟩)
Blade, width 20mm, thickness 4mm, with inlaid mark
(copper/zinc alloy); decorated with two grooves.
Whittle tang, set just below back, straight shoulder.

101. (BC72 [150] ⟨4228⟩)
Blade, length 129mm, thickness 3mm; double mark,
one inlaid with copper/zinc alloy, the other with tin;
decorated with an inlaid groove (copper/zinc alloy),
triangular. Whittle tang, length 74mm, set just below
back, sloping shoulder, tapering.

102. (BWB83 [293] ⟨170⟩)
Blade, width 11mm, thickness 7mm, with inlaid mark
(tin); decorated with raised iron ridges on back,
stepped back. Whittle tang, length 94mm, in line with
back of blade, tapering.

103. (BWB83 [307] ⟨230⟩)
Blade, width 14mm, thickness 2mm, marked. Whittle
tang, length 55mm, central on blade, straight
shoulder, tapering. Wooden handle (box), cylindrical.
Corroded.

104. (TL74 [1956] ⟨1611⟩)
Blade, with inlaid mark (tin). Whittle tang, set just
below back, sloping shoulder. Very corroded.

105. (SH74 [58] ⟨79⟩)
Blade, width 11mm, thickness 4mm; decorated with
gilding on the back, triangular. Whittle tang, central on
blade, sloping shoulder.

106. (BWB83 [150 area] ⟨474⟩)
Blade, length 55mm, width 13mm, thickness 3 mm,
triangular. Whittle tang, length 37mm, central on
blade, sloping shoulder, tapering. Possible weld lines
visible on the x-radiograph.

107. (TL74 [1956] ⟨2349⟩)
Blade, length 56mm, width 12mm, thickness 2mm,
marked, triangular. Whittle tang, length 44mm, set
just below back, straight shoulder, tapering.

108. (BWB83 [308] ⟨619⟩)
Blade, length 54mm, width 15mm, thickness 2mm.
Whittle tang, set just below back, sloping shoulder,
tapering.

109. (BWB83 [129] ⟨192⟩)
Blade, length 75mm, width 13mm, thickness 2mm,
edge curves to back. Whittle tang, length 35mm,
central on blade, sloping shoulder, tapering.

110. (TL74 [2659] ⟨2365⟩)
Blade, length 83mm, width 15mm, thickness 3mm,
marked, edge and back curve to meet. Whittle tang,
length 55mm, set just below back, sloping shoulder,
tapering.

111. (BC72 [79] ⟨2420⟩)
Blade, thickness 1.5mm, widens towards tip. Whittle
tang, length 76mm, set just below back, sloping
shoulder, tapering. ?Knife.

112. (BWB83 [275] ⟨470⟩)
Blade, length 98mm, width 30mm, thickness 3mm,
edge and back curve to meet. Whittle tang, length
47mm, central on blade, sloping shoulder, tapering.
Possible fish knife.

113. (BWB83 [299] ⟨498⟩)
Blade, length 93mm, width 25mm, thickness 3mm,
edge and back curve to meet. Whittle tang, length
77mm, central on blade, sloping shoulder, tapering.
Possible fish knife.

114. (BWB83 [282] ⟨771⟩)
Blade, width 21mm, thickness 3mm. Whittle tang,
length 55mm, central on blade, sloping shoulder,
tapering. May have been sharpened.

115. (BC72 [119] ⟨2876⟩)
Blade, length 107mm, width 16mm, thickness 3mm,
marked, double stepped back. Scale tang, length
90mm, in line with back of blade, parallel sided.
Wooden handle (box), expanding to end. Possible weld
lines visible on the x-radiograph.

116. (BWB83 [277] ⟨376⟩)
Blade, width 11mm, thickness 3mm, marked. Scale
tang, length 87mm, in line with back of blade, tang
handle shape, knob on end. Horn handle, attached
with solid rivets (copper/zinc alloy); decorated with
closely spaced copper/zinc alloy rivets. Shoulder plate
(copper/zinc alloy with arsenic). End cap (copper/
zinc/tin alloy with arsenic); rectangular.

117. (BWB83 [207] ⟨114⟩)
Blade, length 138mm, width 15mm, thickness 2.5mm,
marked, widens towards tip. Scale tang, in line with
back of blade, parallel sided. Shoulder plate (copper/
zinc alloy). Rivet holes possibly contain solder.

118. (BC72 [79] ⟨2529⟩)
Blade, length 144mm, width 16mm, thickness 3mm,
marked. Scale tang, length 90mm, in line with back of
blade, tang handle shape, knob on end.

119. (BC72 [79] ⟨2450⟩)
Scale tang, tang handle shape. Handle, attached with
solid rivets (copper/zinc alloy). End cap (copper/zinc
alloy), oval with pointed terminal.

120. (BC72 [150] ⟨4314⟩)
Blade, width 15mm, thickness 2mm, with inlaid mark.
Scale tang, length 87mm, in line with back of blade,
knob on end. End cap (copper/zinc alloy), rectangular
with pointed terminal.

121. (BC72 [83] ⟨2279⟩)
Blade, length 76mm, width 9mm, thickness 2mm,
marked; decorated with inlaid groove. Scale tang,
length 60mm, in line with back of blade, tang handle
shape, knob on end. Handle, attached with solid rivets
(iron). Shoulder plate (copper alloy). End cap (copper
alloy), oval with pointed terminal.

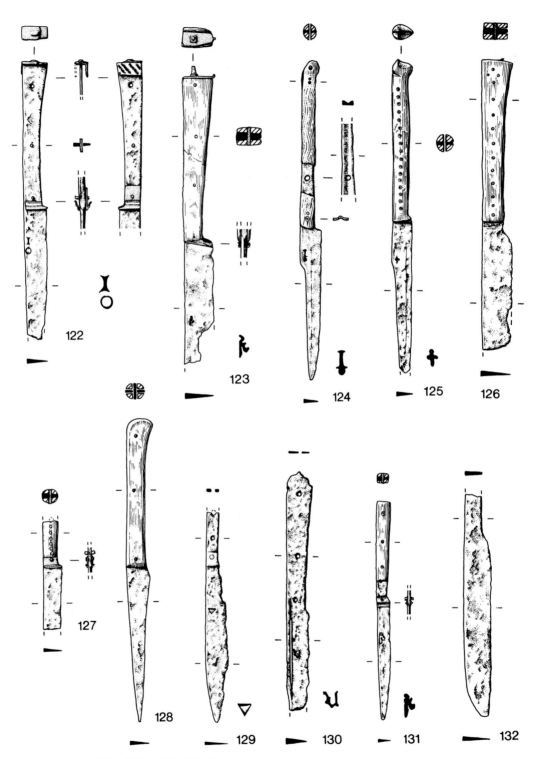

64 Knives, Nos.122–132 (late 14th century). Scale 1:2; marks 1:1.

122. (BWB83 [117] ⟨146⟩)
Blade, width 13mm, thickness 2mm, with double mark inlaid (copper/zinc alloy). Scale tang, length 74mm, in line with back of blade, tang handle shape, knob on end. Handle, attached with solid rivets (copper/zinc alloy). Shoulder plate (copper/zinc alloy). End cap (copper/zinc alloy).

123. (BC72 [79] ⟨2453⟩)
Blade, width 16mm, thickness 3mm, marked. Scale tang, length 89mm, in line with back of blade, tang handle shape. Wooden handle (?maple), length 94mm, attached with ?solid rivets (copper/zinc alloy). Shoulder plate (copper/zinc alloy). End cap (copper/zinc alloy) with pointed terminal.

124. (BC72 [150] ⟨2986⟩)
Blade, length 79mm, width 18mm, thickness 2mm, marked, stepped back. Scale tang, length 84mm, in line with back of blade, hollow. Wooden handle (beech), scale curves down on end, attached with tubular rivets (copper/zinc alloy); decorated with copper/zinc alloy tubes in line with rivets. Possible weld lines visible on the x-radiograph.

125. (BWB83 [117] ⟨1⟩)
Blade, length 90mm, width 10mm, thickness 2.5mm, marked, stepped back. Scale tang, length 70mm, in line with back of blade, hollow. Wooden handle, length 86mm, attached with tubular rivets (copper/zinc alloy); decorated with copper/zinc alloy tubes in line with rivets. Possible weld lines visible on the x-radiograph. Plates 4b, 5a.

126. (BC72 [150] ⟨2990⟩)
Blade, thickness 2mm. Scale tang, length 90mm, in line with back of blade, tang handle shape. Wooden handle (?box), length 88mm, flat scale expanding to end, attached with solid rivets (copper/zinc alloy); decorated with copper/zinc alloy pins in line with rivets. Plate 5b.

127. (BC72 [79] ⟨2528⟩)
Blade, width 14mm, thickness 2mm. Scale tang, in line with back of blade. Horn handle, attached with solid rivets (copper/zinc alloy); decorated with copper/zinc alloy pins in line with rivets. Shoulder plate (copper/zinc alloy).

128. (TL74 [2671] ⟨2201⟩)
Blade, length 80mm, width 12mm, thickness 2.5mm, triangular. Scale tang, length 82mm, in line with back of blade, tang handle shape. Wooden handle (birch), length 82mm, flat scales with bevelled edges, attached with solid rivets (iron). May have been sharpened.

129. (BWB83 [256] ⟨186⟩)
Blade, width 12mm, thickness 2mm, marked, edge and back curves to meet. Scale tang, in line with back of blade. Shoulder plate (very corroded).

130. (BC72 [79] ⟨2433⟩)
Blade, width 12mm, thickness 2mm, marked; decorated with inlaid groove (copper/zinc alloy), notches on the back. Scale tang, length 72mm, tang handle shape, knob on end.

131. (BC72 [150] ⟨4214⟩)
Blade, length 64mm, width 7mm, thickness 1mm, with inlaid mark (tin), triangular. Scale tang, length 52mm, in line with back of blade, tang handle shape. Wooden handle, length 54mm, flat scale expanding to end, attached with tubular rivets (silver). Shoulder plate (silver).

132. (BWB83 [291] ⟨193⟩)
Blade, length 98mm, width 14mm, thickness 2mm, back curves to edge. Scale tang, in line with back of blade.

133. (BWB83 [306] ⟨308⟩)
Scale tang, handle shape. Wooden handle (box), length 101mm, expanding to wedge shape, attached with solid rivets (iron).

134. (BC72 [79] ⟨2439⟩)
Scale tang, handle shape. Bone handle, length 87mm, flat scale expanding to end, attached with solid rivets (iron); decorated with incised dots. Plate 4c.

135. (BWB83 [306] ⟨775⟩)
Blade, thickness 2mm. Scale tang, length 76mm, in line with back of blade, tang handle shape. Bone handle, length 76mm, shaped end, attached with solid rivets (iron); decorated with two rows of circular hollows.

136. (BWB83 [108] ⟨2⟩)
Blade, thickness 4mm; decorated with sawtooth welding. Scale tang, length 95mm, in line with back of blade, tang handle shape. Wooden handle (?maple), length 95mm, expanding to end, attached with solid rivets (tin); decorated with elaborate shoulder plate and end cap. Shoulder plate (silver with a bone inlay). End cap (silver with a bone inlay). Possible weld lines visible on the x-radiograph.

137. (BC72 [79] ⟨2429⟩)
Blade, thickness 2mm, marked. Scale tang, length 98mm, in line with back of blade, tang handle shape, knob on end. Bone handle, length 95mm, expanding to end, attached with solid rivets (iron); decorated with diagonal lines inlaid with tin/mercury. End cap (copper/zinc alloy) sheet metal, two alloys. Large shoulder plate missing. Plate 4d.

138. (SWA81 [2105] ⟨798⟩)
Blade, width 11mm, thickness 2mm, with double mark, one inlaid with a copper/tin alloy, the other tin; decorated with inlaid groove (copper/tin alloy), parallel sided. Scale tang, length 71mm, in line with back of blade, tang handle shape, knob on end. Bone handle, length 71mm, cylindrical, attached with tin rivets; tin pin inscription and floral decoration. Shoulder plate (corroded). End cap (corroded). Plates 4e, 5c.

139. (BC72 [83] ⟨1932⟩)
Blade, width 20mm, thickness 3mm, marked; decorated with two grooves, triangular. Scale tang, length 112mm, in line with back of blade, tang handle shape, knob on end. Wooden handle (?box), length 104mm, attached with solid rivets (copper/zinc alloy). Shoulder plate (copper/zinc/tin alloy with arsenic). End cap (copper/zinc alloy), sheet metal.

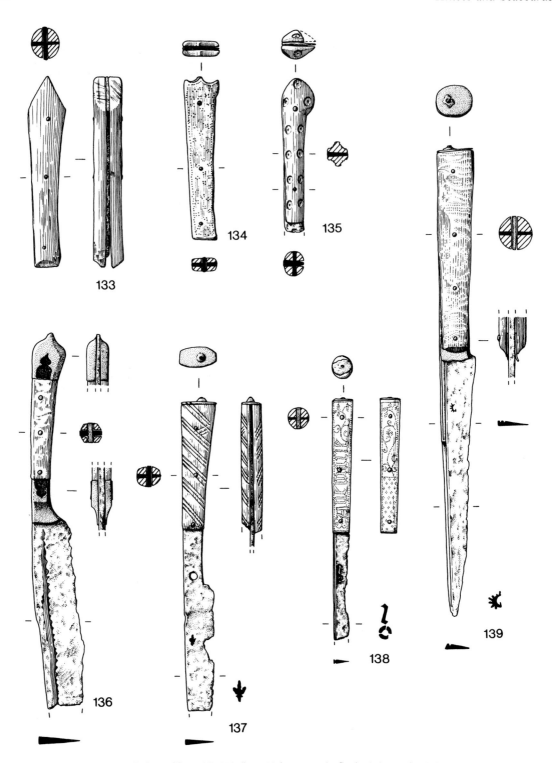

65 Knives, Nos. 133–139 (late 14th century). Scale 1:2; marks 1:1.

140. (BC72 [150] ⟨4324⟩) *Not illustrated*
Blade, length 105mm, thickness 2mm, with inlaid mark (tin). Scale tang, length 84mm, in line with back of blade, tang handle shape. Horn handle, length 84mm, expanding to end, attached with solid rivets (iron and copper/zinc alloy).

141. (BWB83 [379] ⟨540⟩) *Not illustrated*
Blade, thickness 4mm, marked, stepped back. Scale tang, in line with back of blade, parallel sided, hollow. Possible weld lines visible on the x-radiograph.

142. (BC72 [83] ⟨1931⟩) *Not illustrated*
Blade, width 13mm, thickness 2mm, marked. Scale tang, length 67mm, in line with back of blade, tang handle shape. Horn handle, flat scale, attached with solid rivets (copper/zinc alloy). Possible weld lines visible on the x-radiograph.

143. (BC72 [79] ⟨2449⟩) *Not illustrated*
Blade, length 114mm, thickness 3mm, with double mark, triangular. Scale tang, in line with back of blade.

144. (BC72 [79] ⟨2422⟩) *Not illustrated*
Blade, length 128mm, width 13mm, thickness 3mm, with inlaid mark (tin), triangular. Scale tang, in line with back of blade, tang handle shape. Wooden handle (box); decorative pins missing.

145. (BWB83 [310] ⟨564⟩) *Not illustrated*
Blade, width 16mm, thickness 5mm, marked, triangular. Whittle tang, set just below back, sloping shoulder, tapering.

146. (BWB83 [156] ⟨501⟩) *Not illustrated*
Blade, thickness 4mm, double mark (both inlaid with tin), stepped back. Whittle tang, set just below back, sloping shoulder. May have been sharpened.

147. (BC72 [79] ⟨2427⟩) *Not illustrated*
Blade, width 19mm, thickness 6mm, double mark (both inlaid with tin alloy), triangular. Whittle tang, length 65mm, set just below back, sloping shoulder, tapering.

148. (BC72 [150] ⟨4316⟩) *Not illustrated*
Blade, with inlaid mark (copper/zinc alloy), triangular.

149. (TL74 [1956] ⟨1593⟩) *Not illustrated*
Blade, with inlaid mark (tin). Whittle tang, central on blade, straight shoulder. Very corroded.

150. (FLE82 [34] ⟨6⟩) *Not illustrated*
Blade, with inlaid mark. Very corroded.

151. (BWB83 [295] ⟨156⟩) *Not illustrated*
Blade, width 12mm, thickness 4mm, with inlaid mark (copper), triangular. Whittle tang, length 46mm, central on blade, straight shoulder, tapering. Corroded.

152. (BWB83 [269] ⟨455⟩) *Not illustrated*
Blade, width 19mm, thickness 3mm, marked, edge curves to back. Whittle tang, set just below back, sloping shoulder. May have been sharpened; corroded.

153. (BWB83 [301] ⟨781⟩) *Not illustrated*
Blade, length 160mm, width 16mm, thickness 3mm, marked, triangular. ?Whittle tang, set just below back, straight shoulder.

154. (BWB83 [310] ⟨543⟩) *Not illustrated*
Blade, width 11mm, thickness 3mm, marked, stepped back. Scale tang, length 78mm, in line with back of blade, tang handle shape, hollow. Handle, attached with tubular rivets (copper/zinc alloy). Possible weld lines visible on the x-radiograph.

155. (BC72 [79] ⟨2448⟩) *Not illustrated*
Blade, width 13mm, thickness 2mm, with inlaid mark (copper/zinc alloy); decorated with inlaid groove (copper/zinc alloy), triangular. Scale tang, length 69mm, in line with back of blade, tang handle shape, knob on end. Wooden handle (maple), expanding to end, attached with tubular rivets (copper/zinc alloy). Shoulder plate (copper/zinc alloy).

156. (BC72 [79] ⟨2421⟩) *Not illustrated*
Blade, thickness 4mm, double mark (both inlaid with tin alloy). Whittle tang, length 66mm, set just below back, sloping shoulder, tapering.

157. (BC72 [79] ⟨2426⟩) *Not illustrated*
Blade, width 14mm, thickness 2mm, with double mark; decorated with a groove. Scale tang, in line with back of blade.

158. (BWB83 [10] ⟨128⟩) *Not illustrated*
Blade, with double mark.

159. (BC72 [118] ⟨2801⟩) *Not illustrated*
Blade, width 15mm, thickness 2mm, with inlaid mark (copper/zinc alloy), widens towards tip. Whittle tang, length 96mm, set just below back, sloping shoulder, tapering, ?projects beyond end of handle. Unusual shape where edge meets tang.

160. (BWB83 [319] ⟨784⟩) *Not illustrated*
Blade, width 18mm, thickness 2mm, marked; decorated with a groove. Whittle tang, set just below back, straight shoulder. May have been sharpened.

161. (BC72 [79] ⟨2447⟩) *Not illustrated*
Blade, width 10mm, thickness 2mm, with inlaid mark (tin), triangular. Whittle tang, length 36mm, set just below back, straight shoulder, tapering. Wooden handle (box), oval section.

162. (BC72 [119] ⟨3836⟩) *Not illustrated*
Blade, length 124mm, width 15mm, thickness 3mm, double mark (both inlaid with copper/zinc alloy); decorated with a groove, edge curves to back. Whittle tang, set just below back, straight shoulder, tapering.

163. (BC72 [150] ⟨4315⟩) *Not illustrated*
Blade, width 14mm, thickness 4mm, marked, triangular. Whittle tang, length 44mm, set just below back, sloping shoulder, tapering.

164. (BC72 [79] ⟨2488⟩) *Not illustrated*
Blade, thickness 3mm, with double mark. Scale tang, in line with back of blade. Corroded.

165. (BC72 [150] ⟨4313⟩) *Not illustrated*
Blade, width 14mm, thickness 3mm, with inlaid mark (tin), triangular. Whittle tang, length 53mm, central on blade, sloping shoulder, tapering.

166. (BC72 [88] 〈2841〉) *Not illustrated*
Blade, thickness 2mm, with inlaid mark; decorated with inlaid groove. Scale tang, length 72mm, in line with back of blade, tang shaped so that fits scale exactly. Horn handle, attached with solid rivets (iron); decorated with tin pins around the edges with clusters inside.

167. (BC72 [89] 〈2803〉) *Not illustrated*
Blade, length 105mm, width 19mm, thickness 2mm, with inlaid mark (tin), triangular. Whittle tang, set just below back, sloping shoulder.

168. (BWB83 [291] 〈783〉) *Not illustrated*
Blade, length 107mm, width 10mm, thickness 2mm, with inlaid mark (tin), widens towards tip, edge curves to back. Whittle tang, set just below back, sloping shoulder. May have been sharpened.

169. (BWB83 [292] 〈169〉) *Not illustrated*
Blade, width 18mm, thickness 2mm, with inlaid mark (copper/zinc alloy). Scale tang, length 66mm, in line with back of blade, tang handle shape. Bone handle, length 91mm, pointed end, attached with solid rivets (iron).

170. (BWB83 [151] 〈552〉) *Not illustrated*
Blade, width 16mm, double mark (both inlaid with copper/zinc/tin alloy), triangular. Whittle tang, central on blade, sloping shoulder.

171. (BWB83 [293] 〈786〉) *Not illustrated*
Blade, length 117mm, width 13mm, thickness 2mm, with inlaid mark (copper), edge curves to back. Scale tang, in line with back of blade.

172. (BC72 [79] 〈2425〉) *Not illustrated*
Blade, width 17mm, thickness 4mm, with double mark (one inlaid with copper/zinc alloy), angled back. Whittle tang, central on blade, sloping shoulder.

173. (BWB83 [110] 〈464〉) *Not illustrated*
Blade, length 125mm, width 19mm, thickness 5mm, with inlaid mark (copper/zinc alloy), triangular. Whittle tang, central on blade, straight shoulder.

174. (BWB83 [278] 〈126〉) *Not illustrated*
Blade, width 18mm, thickness 3mm, with inlaid mark (copper/zinc alloy), triangular. Whittle tang, set just below back, sloping shoulder, tapering. Corroded.

175. (TL74 [1956] 〈1612〉) *Not illustrated*
Blade, double mark (both inlaid with tin). Very corroded.

176. (BWB83 [204] 〈118〉) *Not illustrated*
Blade, width 13mm, thickness 3mm, marked, widens towards tip. Whittle tang, set just below back, sloping shoulder. Very corroded, possible weld lines visible on the x-radiograph.

177. (BWB83 [157] 〈548〉) *Not illustrated*
Blade, width 16mm, thickness 4mm, with inlaid mark, triangular. Whittle tang, length 62mm, central on blade, straight shoulder, tapering.

178. (BWB83 [162] 〈766〉) *Not illustrated*
Blade, with inlaid mark (copper/zinc alloy), stepped back.

179. (BWB83 [156] 〈478〉) *Not illustrated*
Blade, width 17mm, thickness 4mm, marked. Whittle tang, length 42mm, central on blade, sloping shoulder, tapering. May have been sharpened.

180. (BC72 [79] 〈2428〉) *Not illustrated*
Blade, width 18mm, thickness 2.5mm, with inlaid mark (tin). Whittle tang, set just below back, straight shoulder, tapering.

181. (BC72 [118] 〈3202〉) *Not illustrated*
Blade, marked. Corroded.

182. (BWB83 [274] 〈566〉) *Not illustrated*
Blade, width 20mm, thickness 3mm, with inlaid mark (tin), edge curves to back. Whittle tang, set just below back, sloping shoulder. Corroded.

183. (BWB83 [313] 〈808〉) *Not illustrated*
Blade, thickness 2mm, with inlaid mark (copper/zinc alloy). Whittle tang, length 84mm, set just below back, sloping shoulder, tapering. Very corroded.

184. (BC72 [79] 〈2527〉) *Not illustrated*
Blade, with inlaid mark (copper/zinc alloy).

185. (BWB83 [150 area] 〈472〉) *Not illustrated*
Blade, length 64mm, width 11mm, thickness 3mm, marked, edge and back curve to meet. Whittle tang, length 59mm, central on blade, sloping shoulder, tapering.

186. (BWB83 [278] 〈562〉) *Not illustrated*
Blade, length 120mm, thickness 3mm, marked, triangular. Whittle tang, set just below back, straight shoulder.

187. (BWB83 [156] 〈486〉) *Not illustrated*
Blade, width 16mm, thickness 4mm, marked. Whittle tang, length 68mm, set just below back, straight shoulder, tapering.

188. (BWB83 [157] 〈635〉) *Not illustrated*
Blade, width 17mm, thickness 2mm, marked, widens towards tip. Scale tang, in line with back of blade.

189. (BC72 [79] 〈2111〉) *Not illustrated*
Wooden handle (box), flat scale, attached with tubular rivets (copper/zinc alloy).

190. (BC72 [79] 〈2432〉) *Not illustrated*
Blade, decorated with inlaid groove (copper/zinc alloy), edge curves to back.

191. (BC72 [79] 〈2451〉) *Not illustrated*
Blade, length 113mm, width 21mm, thickness 4mm, edge and back curve to meet. Whittle tang, in line with back of blade.

192. (BC72 [79] 〈2452〉) *Not illustrated*
Blade, thickness 2.5mm. Scale tang, length 74mm, in line with back of blade, tang handle shape. Handle, attached with solid rivets (iron).

193. (BC72 [88] 〈2984〉) *Not illustrated*
Wooden handle (box), length 120mm, attached with tubular rivets (copper/zinc alloy); decorated with copper alloy tubes in line with rivets.

194. (BC72 [88] ⟨4142⟩) *Not illustrated*
Blade, fragmentary.

195. (BC72 [88] ⟨4149⟩) *Not illustrated*
Blade, length 130mm, width 14mm, thickness 2mm; decorated with a groove, back curves to edge. Scale tang, in line with back of blade. Horn handle, attached with solid rivets (copper/zinc alloy).

196. (BC72 [88] ⟨4178⟩) *Not illustrated*
Scale tang. Horn handle (?cattle), attached with solid rivets (copper/zinc alloy).

197. (BC72 [118] ⟨2905⟩) *Not illustrated*
Blade, width 10mm, thickness 2mm. Whittle tang. Wooden handle (yew), length 60mm, oval section.

198. (BC72 [129] ⟨3553⟩) *Not illustrated*
Blade, thickness 2mm, widens towards tip. Scale tang, in line with back of blade, parallel sided.

199. (BC72 [150] ⟨4213⟩) *Not illustrated*
Blade, fragmentary.

200. (BC72 [150] ⟨4218⟩) *Not illustrated*
Scale tang, tang handle shape, knob on end.

201. (BC72 [150] ⟨4274⟩) *Not illustrated*
Blade, thickness 2.5mm. Scale tang, length 85mm, in line with back of blade, tang handle shape, knob on end. Horn handle (?cattle), length 81mm, attached with solid rivets (iron); decorated with pins (?iron), only visible on the x-radiograph. Shoulder plate (copper/zinc alloy). End cap, corroded. Corroded.

202. (BC72 [150] ⟨4291⟩) *Not illustrated*
Blade, width 15mm, thickness 2mm. Scale tang, length 89mm, in line with back of blade, tang handle shape.

203. (BC72 [150] ⟨4311⟩) *Not illustrated*
Blade, width 13mm, thickness 3mm; decorated with a groove, triangular. Whittle tang, set just below back, straight shoulder, tapering.

204. (BC72 [150] ⟨4322⟩) *Not illustrated*
Blade, fragmentary. Whittle tang, central on blade, sloping shoulder. Very corroded.

205. (BWB83 [108] ⟨573⟩) *Not illustrated*
Blade, width 15mm, thickness 2mm.

206. (BWB83 [119] ⟨195⟩) *Not illustrated*
Blade, fragmentary.

207. (BWB83 [131] ⟨459⟩) *Not illustrated*
Blade, fragmentary.

208. (BWB83 [136] ⟨471⟩) *Not illustrated*
Blade, width 13mm, thickness 2mm. Whittle tang, length 49mm, set just below back, straight shoulder. Corroded.

209. (BWB83 [138] ⟨1913⟩) *Not illustrated*
Blade, fragmentary.

210. (BWB83 [150 area] ⟨476⟩) *Not illustrated*
Blade, width 14mm, thickness 3mm; decorated with a groove. Whittle tang, central on blade, sloping shoulder. May have been sharpened.

211. (BWB83 [151] ⟨554⟩) *Not illustrated*
Blade, length 84mm, width 11mm, thickness 2mm, triangular. Whittle tang, set just below back, sloping shoulder.

212. (BWB83 [204] ⟨117⟩) *Not illustrated*
Blade, length 103mm, width 18mm, thickness 5mm, triangular. Whittle tang, length 50mm, set just below back, sloping shoulder, tapering. Possible weld lines visible on the x-radiograph.

213. (BWB83 [256] ⟨115⟩) *Not illustrated*
Blade, width 10mm, thickness 2mm. Scale tang, length 78mm, in line with back of blade, straight shoulder, hollow. Handle, attached with tubular rivets (copper/zinc/tin alloy); decorated with copper/zinc alloy tubes in line with rivets. Very corroded.

214. (BWB83 [257] ⟨779⟩) *Not illustrated*
Blade, width 21mm, thickness 3mm, widens towards tip. Whittle tang, set just below back, sloping shoulder.

215. (BWB83 [257] ⟨780⟩) *Not illustrated*
Blade, thickness 6mm.

216. (BWB83 [265] ⟨110⟩) *Not illustrated*
Blade, length 108mm, width 16mm, thickness 4mm, triangular. Tang, set just below back, straight shoulder. May have been sharpened.

217. (BWB83 [265] ⟨778⟩) *Not illustrated*
Blade, fragmentary. Corroded.

218. (BWB83 [278] ⟨563⟩) *Not illustrated*
Blade, width 14mm, thickness 3mm, parallel sided. Whittle tang, central on blade, sloping shoulder.

219. (BWB83 [279] ⟨124⟩) *Not illustrated*
Blade, length 135mm, width 18mm, thickness 2mm, edge curves to back. Whittle tang, set just below back, sloping shoulder. May have been sharpened.

220. (BWB83 [279] ⟨765⟩) *Not illustrated*
Blade, angled back.

221. (BWB83 [282] ⟨454⟩) *Not illustrated*
Blade, width 20mm, thickness 4mm. Whittle tang, length 58mm, central on blade, straight shoulder, tapering. Corroded.

222. (BWB83 [282] ⟨772⟩) *Not illustrated*
Blade, edge curves to back. Corroded.

223. (BWB83 [289] ⟨469⟩) *Not illustrated*
Blade, thickness 3mm. Whittle tang, length 84mm, central on blade, straight shoulder, tapering. Very corroded.

224. (BWB83 [291 area] ⟨561⟩) *Not illustrated*
Blade, fragmentary.

225. (BWB83 [300] ⟨465⟩) *Not illustrated*
Blade, width 23mm, thickness 5mm, triangular. Whittle tang, length 57mm, central on blade, sloping shoulder, tapering. ?Horn handle.

226. (BWB83 [300] ⟨567⟩) *Not illustrated*
Blade, triangular. Whittle tang, central on blade, sloping shoulder, tapering. Corroded.

227. (BWB83 [301] ⟨782⟩)   *Not illustrated*
Blade, thickness 2mm. Whittle tang, length 40mm, set just below back, straight shoulder, tapering. Corroded.

228. (BWB83 [303] ⟨789⟩)   *Not illustrated*
Blade, fragmentary.

229. (BWB83 [305] ⟨559⟩)   *Not illustrated*
Blade, thickness 3mm, triangular. Whittle tang, length 43mm, central on blade, sloping shoulder, tapering. Corroded.

230. (BWB83 [306] ⟨776⟩)   *Not illustrated*
Blade, angled back.

231. (BWB83 [309] ⟨500⟩)   *Not illustrated*
Blade, thickness 2mm. ?Possible weld lines visible on the x-radiograph.

232. (BWB83 [309] ⟨502⟩)   *Not illustrated*
Blade, thickness 4mm. Whittle tang, central on blade, straight shoulder, tapering. Corroded.

233. (BWB83 [310] ⟨541⟩)   *Not illustrated*
Blade, width 19mm, thickness 4mm. Whittle tang, length 41mm, central on blade, sloping shoulder, tapering. Possible weld lines visible on the x-radiograph; may have been sharpened. Plate 2a.

234. (BWB83 [310] ⟨558⟩)   *Not illustrated*
Blade, length 146mm, width 18mm, thickness 6mm, triangular. Whittle tang, length 46mm, central on blade, sloping shoulder, tapering.

235. (BWB83 [310] ⟨560⟩)   *Not illustrated*
Blade, thickness 3mm. Scale tang, length 85mm, in line with back of blade, tang handle shape, knob on end. Corroded possible weld lines visible on the x-radiograph.

236. (BWB83 [310] ⟨787⟩)   *Not illustrated*
Blade, width 15mm, thickness 2mm; decorated with inlay? widens towards tip. Whittle tang, central on blade, straight shoulder. ?Knife.

237. (BWB83 [313] ⟨788⟩)   *Not illustrated*
Blade, fragmentary.

238. (BWB83 [330] ⟨228⟩)   *Not illustrated*
Blade, fragmentary. Whittle tang, projects beyond end of handle?. Wooden handle (?box), length 80mm, cylindrical. Iron hilt band. Very corroded.

239. (BWB83 [361] ⟨382⟩)   *Not illustrated*
Blade, thickness 2mm. Whittle tang, length 96mm, sloping shoulder, tapering. ?Knife.

240. (BWB83 [367] ⟨769⟩)   *Not illustrated*
Blade, width 14mm, thickness 4mm. Whittle tang, length 28mm, central on blade, straight shoulder, tapering. Wooden handle. Very corroded.

241. (BWB83 [378] ⟨767⟩)   *Not illustrated*
Blade, fragmentary.

242. (BWB83 [378] ⟨770⟩)   *Not illustrated*
Blade, fragmentary.

243. (BWB83 [399] ⟨763⟩)   *Not illustrated*
Blade, thickness 3mm. Whittle tang, set just below back, straight shoulder, tapering. Corroded.

244. (BWB83 [399] ⟨768⟩)   *Not illustrated*
Blade, fragmentary. Whittle tang, set just below back, sloping shoulder, tapering. May have been sharpened. Corroded.

245. (BWB83 [399] ⟨764⟩)   *Not illustrated*
Blade, fragmentary.

246. (OPT81 [51] ⟨115⟩)   *Not illustrated*
Blade, fragmentary. Scale tang. Shoulder plate, corroded. Very corroded.

247. (SWA81 [2102] ⟨2648⟩)   *Not illustrated*
Blade, triangular?

248. (SWA81 [2105] ⟨1115⟩)   *Not illustrated*
Scale tang, tang handle shape. Wooden handle, attached with solid rivets (copper/zinc alloy).

249. (TL74 [683] ⟨909⟩)   *Not illustrated*
Blade, thickness 3.5mm, triangular. Whittle tang, length 33mm, central on blade, straight shoulder, tapering. Corroded.

250. (TL74 [1956] ⟨1597⟩) *Not illustrated*
Blade, edge and back curve to meet. Whittle tang, set just below back, sloping shoulder, tapering. Very corroded.

251. (TL74 [1956] ⟨1615⟩)   *Not illustrated*
Blade, fragmentary. Whittle tang, set just below back, sloping shoulder. Very corroded.

252. (TL74 [1956] ⟨1616⟩)   *Not illustrated*
Blade, parallel sided. Scale tang. Very corroded.

Early to mid 15th-century knives Nos.253–280

None of the knives in this small group have decorated blades. Two thirds of the knives have scale tangs and the extant handles are simpler than in the preceding period with fewer decorative fittings. The only new feature is the shaped ends that are present on two tangs (Nos.267 and 270).

253. (TL74 [306] ⟨254⟩)
Whittle tang, tapering and projects beyond end of handle. Bone handle, length 86mm. ?Knife.

254. (TL74 [306] ⟨906⟩)
Blade, width 15mm, thickness 5.5mm, triangular. Whittle tang, length 34mm, set just below back, sloping shoulder, tapering shoulder, roughly formed. Corroded.

255. (TL74 [306] ⟨255⟩)
Blade, width 18mm, thickness 4mm, marked. Whittle tang, set just below back, straight shoulder, tapering. Corroded.

256. (SWA81 [2097] ⟨754⟩)
Blade, width 19mm, thickness 4mm, parallel sided. Whittle tang, central on blade, sloping shoulder.

257. (SWA81 [2113] ⟨1857⟩)
Blade, width 14mm, thickness 3mm, parallel sided. Whittle tang, length 34mm, central on blade, sloping shoulder, tapering.

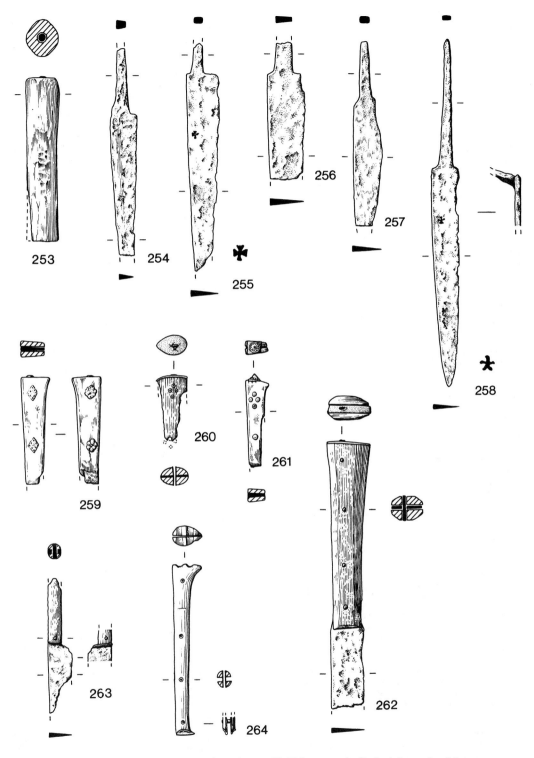

66 Knives, Nos. 253–264 (early to mid 15th century). Scale 1:2; marks 1:1.

258. (TL74 [368] ⟨1229⟩)
Blade, length 117mm, width 15mm, thickness 3.5mm, marked. Whittle tang, length 60mm, central on blade, sloping shoulder, tapering. Possible weld lines visible on the x-radiograph.

259. (SWA81 [2107] ⟨805⟩)
Scale tang, parallel sided, knob on end. Wooden handle (box), attached with ?solid copper alloy rivets with lead/tin heads soldered on; decorated with copper alloy pins in diamond motifs. End cap.

260. (SWA81 [2112] ⟨1168⟩)
Scale tang, tang handle shape, knob on end. Wooden handle (box), attached with tubular rivets (copper/zinc alloy); decorated with copper/zinc alloy tubes in diamond motifs. End cap (copper/zinc alloy) sheet metal.

261. (SWA81 [2112] ⟨892⟩)
Scale tang, parallel sided, knob on end. Wooden handle (box), attached with tubular rivets (copper/zinc alloy); decorated with copper/zinc alloy tubes in diamond motifs. End cap (copper/zinc alloy), sheet metal, two alloys.

262. (SWA81 [2112] ⟨1172⟩)
Blade, width 20mm, thickness 3mm, parallel sided. Scale tang, length 95mm, set just below back, sloping shoulder, parallel sided, knob on end. Wooden handle (box), length 98mm, octagonal section, attached with solid rivets (iron). End cap (copper/zinc alloy) sheet metal. May have been sharpened.

263. (SWA81 [2100] ⟨848⟩)
Blade, width 8mm, thickness 2.5mm. Scale tang, in line with back of blade, parallel sided. Wooden handle, attached with solid rivets (iron). Shoulder plate (tin).

264. (SWA81 [2106] ⟨796⟩)
Scale tang, length 89mm, tang handle shape? Bone handle, length 88mm, hooked, attached with tubular rivets (copper/zinc alloy). Shoulder plate (copper/ zinc/ tin alloy).

265. (TL74 [368] ⟨1111⟩)
Blade, length 170mm, width 23mm, thickness 3mm, with inlaid mark (tin), triangular. Scale tang, length 108mm, in line with back of blade, tang handle shape. Handle, attached with solid rivets (copper/zinc alloy). Corroded.

266. (TL74 [368] ⟨1104⟩)
Blade, length 96mm, width 13mm, thickness 3mm, with inlaid mark (tin), back curves to edge. Scale tang, length 96mm, in line with back of blade, tang handle shape, knob on end. Handle, attached with solid rivets. Shoulder plate, corroded.

267. (TL74 [368] ⟨2735⟩)
Blade, length 116mm, width 13mm, thickness 3mm, marked. Scale tang, length 84mm, in line with back of blade, tang handle shape, decorative end. Handle, attached with solid rivets (iron). Shoulder plate (copper/zinc/tin alloy).

268. (TL74 [368] ⟨1232⟩)
Blade, width 13mm, thickness 3mm, marked. Scale tang, in line with back of blade.

269. (TL74 [368] ⟨2195⟩)
Blade, width 11mm, thickness 2mm, marked. Scale tang, in line with back of blade. Corroded.

270. (TL74 [368] ⟨1098⟩)
Blade, length 176mm, width 13mm, thickness 3mm, with inlaid mark (copper/zinc alloy), triangular. Scale tang, length 106mm, in line with back of blade, tang handle shape, decorative end. Corroded.

271. (BWB83 [111] ⟨572⟩)   *Not illustrated*
Blade, width 13mm, thickness 3mm, double mark (both inlaid with tin), triangular. Whittle tang, length 50mm, set just below back, straight shoulder, tapering.

272. (SWA81 [2082] ⟨967⟩)   *Not illustrated*
Blade, width 9mm, thickness 3mm, parallel sided. Scale tang, in line with back of blade, parallel sided. ?Wooden handle, attached with tubular rivets (tin).

273. (SWA81 [2113] ⟨1855⟩)   *Not illustrated*
Blade, width 11mm, thickness 3mm, parallel sided. Scale tang, in line with back of blade, parallel sided.

274. (SWA81 [2113] ⟨1856⟩)   *Not illustrated*
Blade, width 13mm, thickness 2mm, parallel sided. Scale tang, in line with back of blade.

275. (SWA81 [2113] ⟨1858⟩)   *Not illustrated*
Blade, thickness 2mm, parallel sided. Scale tang, in line with back of blade, parallel sided. Very corroded.

276. (SWA81 [2113] ⟨1859⟩)   *Not illustrated*
Blade, fragmentary.

277. (TL74 [291] ⟨487⟩)   *Not illustrated*
Blade, fragmentary.

278. (TL74 [368] ⟨550⟩)   *Not illustrated*
Blade, width 15mm, thickness 3mm, triangular. Whittle tang, set just below back, sloping shoulder, tapering. Very corroded.

279. (TL74 [416] ⟨819⟩)   *Not illustrated*
Blade; decorated with a groove on x-radiograph? Very corroded.

280. (TL74 [1458] ⟨2769⟩)   *Not illustrated*
Blade, triangular. Corroded.

UNSTRATIFIED KNIVES Nos. 281–308

This selection of unstratified knives is illustrated (Nos. 281–5, 304–8), because they show points of particular interest. The five examples from the Museum's collections include two specialised knife types; a glover's knife (No. 304) and a penknife (No. 305).

281. (BC72 [73] ⟨2050⟩)
Blade, with inlaid mark, triangular. Textile impression on blade.

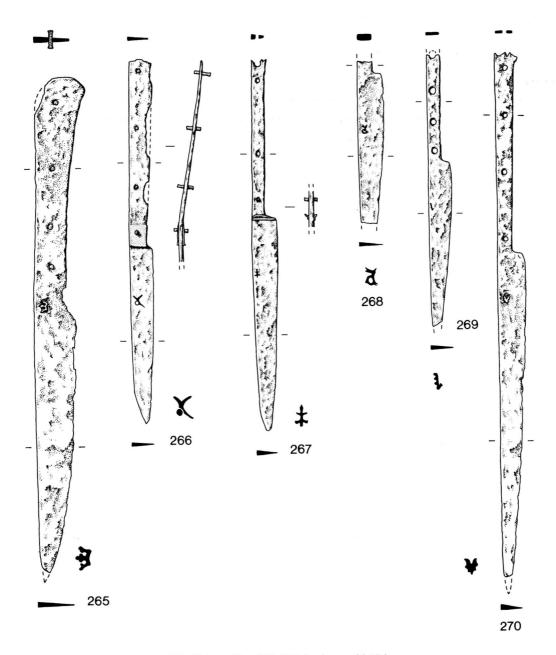

67 Knives, Nos. 265–270 (early to mid 15th century). Scale 1:2; marks 1:1.

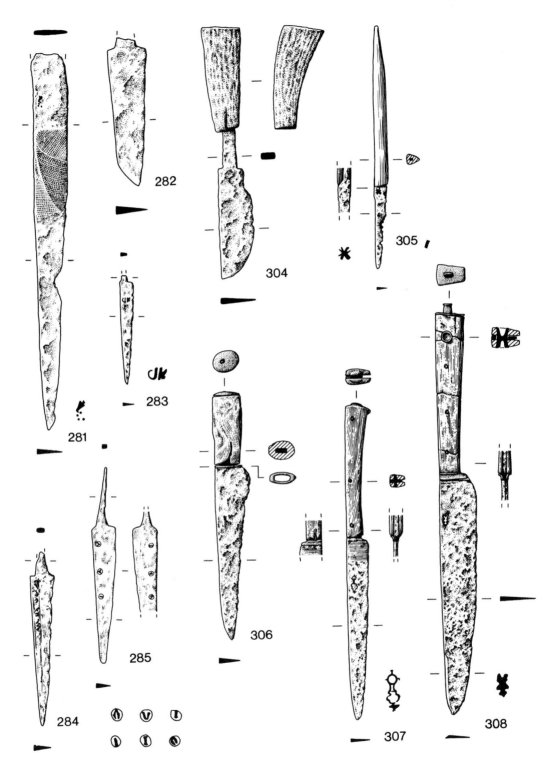

68   Knives, Nos.281–285 (unstratified), Nos.304–308 (Museum of London
Reserve Collection). Scale 1:2; marks and inscription 1:1.

282. (SWA81 [+] ⟨3847⟩)
Blade, length 74mm, width 23mm, thickness 6mm, back curves to edge. Whittle tang, central on blade, straight shoulder.

283. (SWA81 [+] ⟨3951⟩)
Blade, length 55mm, width 8mm, thickness 2mm, with double mark, triangular. Whittle tang, set just below back, straight shoulder.

284. (SWA81 [1189] ⟨654⟩)
Blade, length 90mm; decorated with overlaid wire in shallow grooves and on the back, triangular. Whittle tang, central on blade, straight shoulder. Very corroded.

285. (CUS73 [III 17] ⟨108⟩)
Blade, length 75mm, width 13mm, thickness 3mm; decorated with inset stamped discs (copper/zinc alloy), triangular. Whittle tang, length 32mm, central on blade, straight shoulder, tapering.

286. (BC72 [+] ⟨2825⟩) *Not illustrated*
Blade, thickness 1mm. Whittle tang, set just below back, sloping shoulder, tapering. Wooden handle (pomoideae family).

287. (BIG82 [1823] ⟨2050.9⟩) *Not illustrated*
Blade, triangular. Whittle tang, central on blade, sloping shoulder, tapering. Wooden handle (willow/poplar). May have been sharpened.

288. (BIG82 [2635] ⟨2341⟩) *Not illustrated*
Blade, fragmentary. Whittle tang. Wooden handle (?box), length 101mm, cylindrical with a narrow diameter. Hilt band (tin). Very corroded.

289. (BIG82 [3807] ⟨2910⟩) *Not illustrated*
Blade, fragmentary.

290. (BWB83 [15] ⟨123⟩) *Not illustrated*
Scale tang, parallel sided. Wooden handle, rectangular scale with bevelled edges widens at end, attached with rivets (copper/zinc alloy).

291. (BWB83 [344] ⟨293⟩) *Not illustrated*
Blade, thickness 4mm. Whittle tang, length 65mm, set just below back, sloping shoulder. Wooden handle (oak), length 98mm, cylindrical with a knob on the end, slice removed.

292. (POM79 [194] ⟨522⟩) *Not illustrated*
Blade, length 127mm, back curves to edge. Whittle tang, set just below back, sloping shoulder, tapering. Corroded.

293. (POM79 [656] ⟨400⟩) *Not illustrated*
Blade, fragmentary. Whittle tang, set just below back, sloping shoulder, tapering. Corroded.

294. (POM79 [2048] ⟨437⟩) *Not illustrated*
Blade, fragmentary. Whittle tang, set just below back, sloping shoulder, tapering. ?Wooden handle. Corroded.

295. (POM79 [2327] ⟨403⟩) *Not illustrated*
Blade; decorated with ?pattern welding. Whittle tang, central on blade, sloping shoulder. Very corroded.

296. (SH74 [3] ⟨3⟩) *Not illustrated*
Scale tang, parallel sided. Wooden handle, thin scales, attached with solid rivets (iron); decorated with iron pins. End cap (copper alloy).

297. (SH74 [115] ⟨31⟩) *Not illustrated*
Blade, parallel sided. Scale tang, in line with back of blade, parallel sided. Handle, attached with rivets. Shoulder plate (?copper alloy). Very corroded.

298. (SWA81 [+] ⟨1001⟩) *Not illustrated*
Blade, width 14.5mm, thickness 4mm; decorated with a groove, parallel sided. Whittle tang, central on blade, sloping shoulder, tapering.

299. (SWA81 [+] ⟨2300⟩) *Not illustrated*
Blade, fragmentary. Whittle tang, central on blade, sloping shoulder, parallel sided. Wooden handle (pomoideae family). Hilt band (copper alloy).

300. (SWA81 [+] ⟨2618⟩) *Not illustrated*
Blade, width 18mm, thickness 2mm, parallel sided. Whittle tang, length 40mm, central on blade, sloping shoulder, tapering. Wooden handle (alder).

301. (SWA81 [+] ⟨3198⟩) *Not illustrated*
Whittle tang. Bone handle, length 81mm.

302. (SWA81 [+] ⟨4528⟩) *Not illustrated*
Blade, parallel sided. ?Knife.

303. (TL74 [847] ⟨1090⟩) *Not illustrated*
Whittle tang. Bone handle, length 113mm, roughly shaped grooves cut into sides.

304. (MOL no. 59.94/60)
Blade, length 56mm, width 18mm, thickness 4mm, edge curves to back. Whittle tang, length 74mm, central on blade, straight shoulder. Horn handle, length 53mm, round. 15th-century glover's knife.

305. (MOL no. 9839)
Blade, length 47mm, width 7mm, thickness 1.5mm, marked. Whittle tang, length 23mm, central on blade, sloping shoulder. Bone handle, length 84mm, slender. ? Penknife.

306. (MOL no. 17.026)
Blade, length 91mm, width 20mm, thickness 3mm, back curves to edge. Whittle tang, length 38mm. Wooden handle, length 40mm. Shoulder plate (copper alloy). End cap (copper alloy), oval. Very short handle.

307. (MOL no. 10.894)
Blade, length 96mm, width 12mm, thickness 2mm, marked. Scale tang, length 70mm, in line with back of blade. Wooden handle, length 71mm, hooked, solid iron pins. Shoulder plate (tin).

308. (MOL no. 82.509/2)
Blade, length 128mm, width 20mm, thickness 3mm, with inlaid mark (tin). Scale tang, length 84mm, in line with back of blade, tang handle shape, knob on end. Wooden handle, length 91mm, attached with solid rivets (iron). Shoulder plate (?tin/lead alloy). End cap (tin).

FOLDING KNIVES

The folding knives, Nos. 309–10, are distinguished by the absence of a tang, which may be replaced by a *thumb piece*. There is a hole piercing the *blade* for the *pivot*, which attaches the blade to the *handle*.

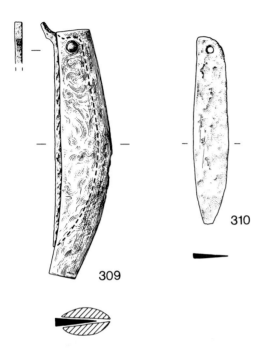

69 Folding knives, Nos. 309 (late 13th century) and 310 (late 14th century). Scale 1:2.

Late 13th century

309. (SWA81 [2018] ⟨414⟩)
Blade, length 112mm, width 14mm, thickness 2mm. Iron thumb piece. Wooden handle (box), length 134mm, single piece of wood, iron pivot. Plate 00.

Late 14th century

310. (BWB83 [285] ⟨145⟩)
Blade, edge and back curve to meet, hole for pivot.

SHEARS (Fig.3)

The basic components of a pair of shears are two *blades* joined by two *arms* to a central sprung *bow*. Both the tip and the top of the blade vary in form. The junction of the blade and handle may have single or multiple semi-circular *recesses*.

Late 12th-century shears No.311

This period is represented by a single complete pair of shears which are a plain shape and lack any recesses.

311. (SWA81 [2266] ⟨1924⟩)
Blade, length 57mm, width 12mm, thickness 2mm, tapering tips. Handle, length 63mm, width 8mm, diameter 20mm, square arm section. Plate 1c.

Early to mid 13th-century shears Nos.312–315

The early to mid 13th-century shears are similar to the 12th-century pair, but three have a recess at the join of the arms and blades. The recess, arms and bow of one pair are decorated (No.314).

312. (SH74 [484] ⟨230⟩)
Blade, length 60mm, width 13mm, thickness 3mm, single recess. Handle, length 83mm, width 7mm, diameter 22mm, round arm section. Tips corroded, slight ridge on interior of bow.

313. (BIG82 [5221] ⟨2811⟩)
Blade, length 58mm, width 10mm, thickness 2mm. Handle, length 81mm, width 4mm, diameter 24mm, round arm section.

314. (SH74 [484] ⟨226⟩)
Blade, length 111mm, width 18mm, thickness 3mm, decorated with small notches on the recess edges; single recess, an angled tip and a tapering tip. Handle, length 114mm, width 11mm, diameter 37mm, round arm section, decorated with diagonal grooves on the arms and notches around the bow.

315. (SWA81 [2270] ⟨2253⟩)
Blade, length 61mm, width 12mm, thickness 2mm, single recess, angled tips. Handle, length 81mm, width 8mm, diameter 24mm, round arm section.

Late 13th-century shears Nos.316–317

The blades are triangular in shape and similar to the knife blades from the same period. Both are elaborately decorated with overlaid silver wire.

316. (SWA81 [2061] ⟨2230⟩)
Blade, length 60mm, width 14mm, thickness 2mm, decorated with overlaid silver wire, angled tip. Handle length 65mm, width 8mm, diameter 22mm, rectangular arm section, decorated with circles inlaid with silver. Plate 3a.

317. (SWA81 [2061] ⟨1953⟩)
Blade, length 52mm, width 10mm, thickness 1mm, decorated with overlaid silver wire, tapering tips. Handle, rectangular arm section. Overlaid silver wire includes traces of copper, mercury and gold.

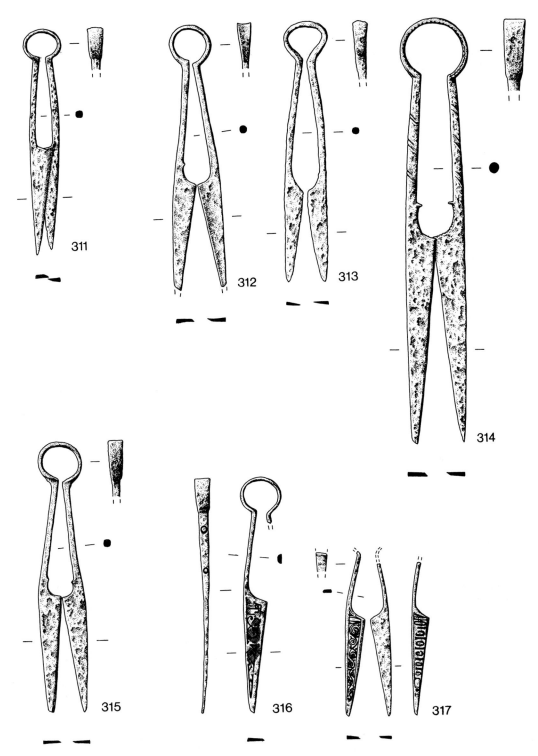

70 Shears, No.311 (12th century), Nos.312–315 (early to mid 13th century) and Nos.316–317 (late 13th century) Scale 1:2.

Early 14th-century shears Nos. 318–323

This group of shears is more varied in both size and shape. All the bows have a central ridge around the outside and one is decorated with notches.

318. (CUS73 [III 10] ⟨29⟩)
Blade, length 50mm, width 12mm, thickness 2mm, single recess, angled tips. Handle, length 35mm, width 6mm, diameter 17mm, semi-circular arm section.

319. (TL74 [415] ⟨721⟩)
Blade, width 15mm, thickness 3mm, single recess. Handle, width 9mm, round arm section, decorated with notches on the back near the recess.

320. (TL74 [415] ⟨625⟩)
Blade, length 66mm, width 12mm, thickness 2mm, single recess, tapering tip. Handle, length 62mm, width 6mm, square arm section.

321. (TL74 [415] ⟨718⟩)
Blade, length 37mm, width 7mm, thickness 1mm, single recess, an angled tip and a tapering tip. Handle, length 41mm, width 4mm, diameter 17mm, square arm section. Possible weld lines visible on x-radiograph.

322. (BC72 [250] ⟨3060⟩) *Not illustrated*
Blade, length 39mm, width 8mm, thickness 2mm, single recess, angled tip. Handle, length 37mm, width 5mm, diameter 16mm, square arm section.

323. (TL 74 [309] ⟨455⟩) *Not illustrated*
Handle, square arm section. Corroded.

Late 14th-century shears Nos.324–357

The blades in this group frequently have slightly curved backs, and some have a makers' mark on one or both blades. Two of the blades are decorated with grooves. A group of three (Nos.334, 336 and 345) are very similar in shape and they all have multiple recesses and decorated arms.

324. (BC72 [79] ⟨2440⟩)
Blade, width 8mm, thickness 2mm, single recess, tapering tips. Handle, length 52mm, width 5mm, diameter 19mm, square arm section.

325. (BC72 [79] ⟨2470⟩)
Blade, length 79mm, width 14mm, thickness 3mm, marked, single recess, tapering tip. Handle, length 78mm, width 10mm, round arm section.

326. (BWB83 [369] ⟨761⟩)
Blade, length 74mm, width 13mm, thickness 3mm, single recess, angled tip. Handle, square arm section.

327. (BWB83 [265] ⟨109⟩)
Blade, length 74mm, width 18mm, thickness 3mm, single recess, angled tip. Handle, length 63mm, width 10mm, round arm section.

328. (BC72 [150] ⟨2861⟩)
Blade, length 58mm, width 12mm, thickness 2mm, marked, single recess, angled tip. Handle, length 66mm, width 9mm, diameter 20mm, round arm section. Possible weld lines visible on x-radiograph.

329. (BWB83 [147] ⟨354⟩)
Blade, length 80mm, single recess, tapering tip. Handle, rectangular arm section.

330. (BWB83 [299] ⟨496⟩)
Blade, length 67mm, width 11mm, thickness 3mm, double mark (both inlaid with copper/zinc alloy) single recess, angled tip. Handle, length 65mm, width 7mm, round arm section. Possible weld lines visible on the x-radiograph.

331. (BWB83 [110] ⟨462⟩)
Blade, length 74mm, width 13mm, thickness 3mm, inlaid mark (copper/zinc alloy), single recess, angled tip. Handle, square arm section.

332. (BC72 [150] ⟨4309⟩)
Blade, length 131mm, width 12mm, thickness 2mm, both blades marked, single recess, angled tip. Handle, length 97mm, width 9mm, diameter 25mm, round arm section, decorated with two square sections mid-way along both arms.

333. (BC72 [83] ⟨2389⟩)
Blade, length 59mm, width 8mm, thickness 2mm, more than two recess, angled tip. Handle, round arm section.

334. (BC72 [55] ⟨1770⟩)
Blade, length 77m, width 8mm, thickness 2mm, more than two recess, angled tips. Handle, length 63mm, width 6mm, diameter 19mm, semi-circular arm section, decorated with raised ridges on arms.

335. (BC72 [79] ⟨2464⟩)
Blade, width 10mm, thickness 2mm, marked, double recess, tapering tip. Handle, width 6mm, round arm section. Possible weld lines visible on the x-radiograph.

336. (BC72 [150] ⟨4221⟩)
Blade, length 88mm, width 9mm, thickness 2mm, more than two recess, angled tip. Handle, width 2mm, square arm section, decorated with raised ridges on arm.

337. (BC72 [83] ⟨2243⟩)
Blade, length 43mm, width 8mm, thickness 2mm, single recess, tapering tips. Handle, length 45mm, width 5mm, diameter 14mm, round arm section. Possible weld lines visible on the x-radiograph.

338. (BWB83 [285] ⟨143⟩)
Blade, length 41mm, width 10mm, thickness 2mm, decorated with grooves on both blades, single recess, angled tips. Handle, length 41mm, diameter 15mm, square arm section. Blades bent apart.

339. (BC72 [88] ⟨4139⟩)
Blade, length 51mm, width 6mm, thickness 2mm, marked, angled tips. Handle, length 37mm, width 5mm, diameter 12mm, round arm section, decorative ridges on bow.

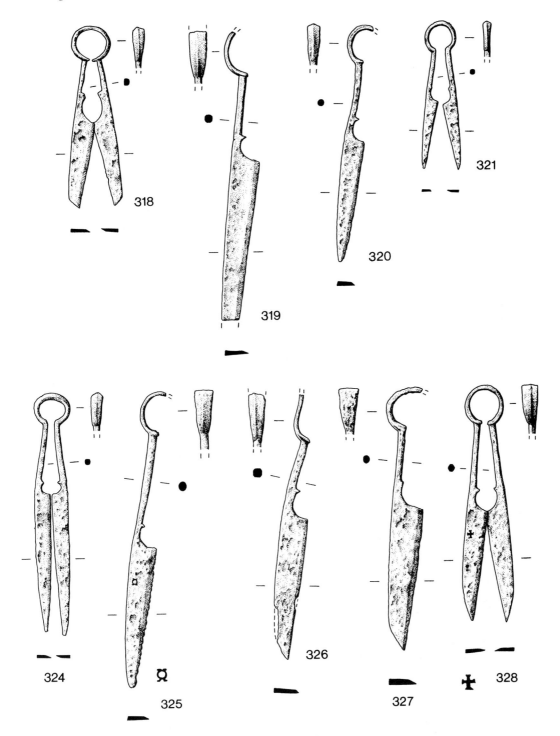

71 Shears, Nos.318–321 (early to mid 14th century), Nos.324–328 (late 14th century). Scale 1:2; marks 1:1.

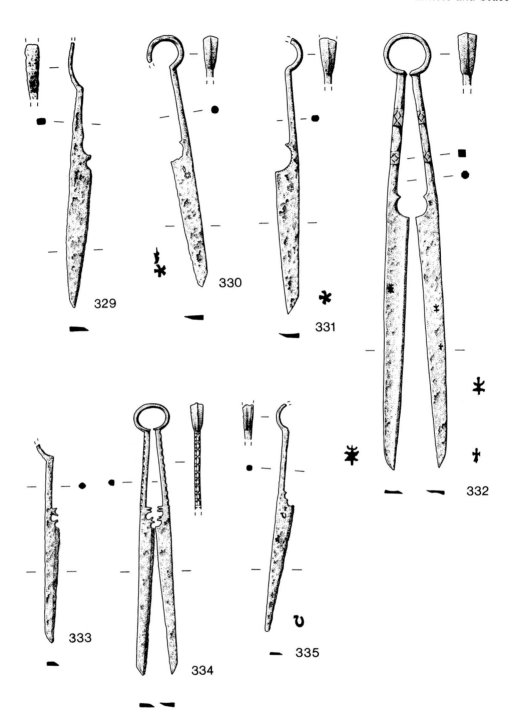

329 330 331 332 333 334 335

72 Shears, Nos. 329–335 (late 14th century). Scale 1:2; marks 1:1.

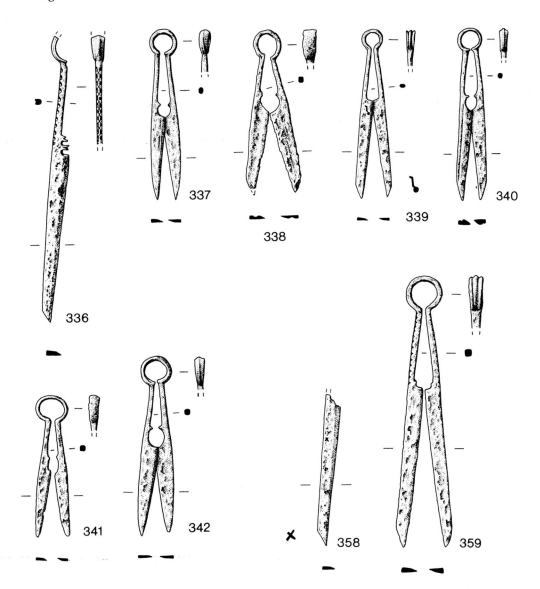

73 Shears. Nos.336–342 (late 14th century), Nos.358–359 (early to mid 15th century). Scale 1:2; marks 1:1.

342. (BWB83 [279] ⟨211⟩)
Blade, length 47mm, width 9mm, thickness 2mm, single recess, tapering tips. Handle, length 46mm, width 4mm, diameter 17mm, square arm section. Possible weld lines visible on the x-radiograph.

343. (BWB83 [285] ⟨556⟩) *Mark illustrated*
Blade, length 58mm, width 11mm, thickness 2mm, double mark (both inlaid with copper/zinc alloy), single recess, angled tip.

340. (BWB83 [279] ⟨125⟩)
Blade, length 48mm, width 8mm, thickness 3mm, decorated with a groove on both blades, single recess, angled tips. Handle, length 42mm, width 5mm, diameter 13mm, round arm section.

341. (BWB83 [257] ⟨120⟩)
Blade, length 35mm, width 7mm, thickness 2mm, tapering tips. Handle, length 39mm, width 5mm, diameter 17mm, square arm section.

344. (BWB83 [298] ⟨807⟩)   *Mark illustrated*
Blade, length 64mm, width 12mm, thickness 2mm, marked, single recess, angled tip. Handle, length 51mm, width 8mm, diameter 13mm, round arm section.

345. (BC72 [79] ⟨2465⟩)   *Not illustrated*
Blade, length 75mm, width 9mm, thickness 2mm, more than two recesses, angled tip. Handle, rectangular arm section, decorated with raised ridges on arm.

346. (BC72 [83] ⟨2919⟩)   *Not illustrated*
Blade, length 52mm, width 10mm, thickness 2mm, single recess, tapering tip.

347. (BWB83 [110] ⟨221⟩)   *Not illustrated*
Blade, length 76mm, width 9mm, thickness 2mm, single recess, tapering tip. Handle, length 59mm, width 6mm, diameter 18mm, round arm section.

348. (BWB83 [147] ⟨351⟩)   *Not illustrated*
Blade, length 53mm, width 10mm, thickness 2mm, single recess, angled tip. Handle, round arm section.

349. (BWB83 [147] ⟨352⟩)   *Not illustrated*
Blade, length 72mm, width 11mm, thickness 2mm, single recess, angled tip. Handle, round arm section.

350. (BWB83 [150] ⟨605⟩)   *Not illustrated*
Blade, length 65mm, width 10mm, thickness 2mm, single recess, angled tip. Handle, round arm section.

351. (BWB83 [157] ⟨609⟩)   *Not illustrated*
Blade, length 67mm, width 10mm, thickness 3mm, single recess, tapering tip. Handle, length 61mm, width 5mm, diameter 21mm, round arm section. Possible weld lines visible on the x-radiograph.

352. (BWB83 [283] ⟨383⟩)   *Not illustrated*
Blade, width 11mm. Handle, round arm section.

353. (BWB83 [308] ⟨613⟩)   *Not illustrated*
Blade, length 52mm, width 10mm, thickness 2mm, single recess, angled tip. Handle, length 50mm, width 6mm, diameter 17mm, round arm section. Possible weld lines visible on the x-radiograph.

354. (BWB83 [314] ⟨604⟩)   *Not illustrated*
Blade, length 61mm, width 11mm, thickness 3mm, single recess, angled tip. Handle, length 56mm, width 5mm, round arm section.

355. (BWB83 [319] ⟨785⟩)   *Not illustrated*
Handle, width 7mm, diameter 19mm, rectangular arm section.

356. (BWB83 [366] ⟨762⟩)   *Not illustrated*
Blade, length 82mm, width 18mm, thickness 3mm, tapering tip. Handle, square arm section.

357. (TL74 [429] ⟨908⟩)   *Not illustrated*
Blade, single recess. Handle, round arm section. Corroded.

Early to mid 15th-century shears Nos.358–361
These generally have both narrower blades and straighter backs than in preceding periods.

358. (TL74 [368] ⟨1105⟩)
Blade, length 75mm, width 8mm, thickness 2mm, marked, angled tip.

359. (TL74 [368] ⟨2668⟩)
Blade, length 86mm, width 8mm, thickness 2mm, single recess, angled tip. Handle, length 58mm, width 7mm, diameter 20mm, square arm section, decorated with small notches on the arms.

360. (TL74 [368] ⟨2196⟩)   *Mark illustrated*
Blade, length 53mm, width 8mm, thickness 1.5mm, marked, angled tip. Handle, rectangular arm section. Corroded.

361. (TL74 [368] ⟨2657⟩)   *Not illustrated*
Blade, single recess. Handle, length 73mm, width 6mm, diameter 21mm, square arm section. Corroded.

UNSTRATIFIED SHEARS Nos.362–8

Four pairs from the Museum's collections are illustrated (Nos.365–8); these include a rare copper alloy pair, originally with iron or steel cutting edges.

362. (TL74 [2806] ⟨2368⟩)   *Mark illustrated*
Blade, length 60mm, width 10mm, thickness 2mm, marked, single recess, angled tip. Handle, length 49mm, width 4mm, round arm section. Bent at both recess and middle of one blade, possible weld lines visible on the x-radiograph.

363. (BC72 [+] ⟨4343⟩)   *Not illustrated*
Blade, length 40mm, width 8mm, thickness 2mm, single recess, angled tip. Handle, length 36mm, width 4mm, diameter 15mm, rectangular arm section. Possible weld lines visible on the x-radiograph.

364. (SWA81 [2096] ⟨2121⟩)   *Not illustrated*
Blade, length 53mm, width 13mm, thickness 1mm, angled tip. Handle, length 77mm, width 8mm, diameter 23mm, rectangular arm section.

365. (MOL no. 8019)
Blade, length 135mm, width 24mm, thickness 3mm, single recess, tapering tip. Handle, length 106mm, width 6mm, diameter 45mm, square arm section.

366. (MOL no. 24615)
Blade, length 53mm, width 9mm, thickness 2mm, single recess, angled tip. Handle, length 30mm, width 3mm, diameter 18mm, square arm section.

367. (MOL no. A 27248)
Blade, length 85mm, thickness 2mm, double recess, angled tip. Handle, length 50mm, width 2mm, diameter 18mm, square arm section. Made from a copper alloy.

368. (MOL no. 15.235)
Blade, length 165mm, width 28mm, thickness 4mm, single recess, angled tip. Handle, length 154mm, width 8mm, diameter 58mm, round arm section. Both blades bent.

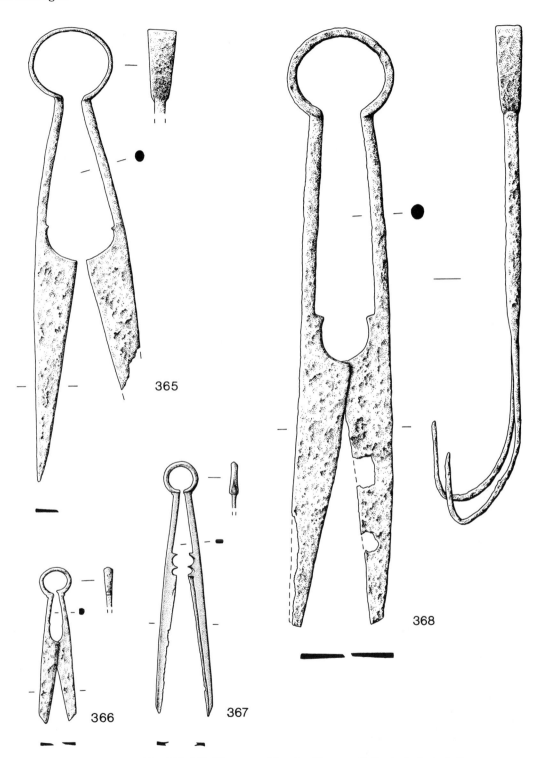

74 Shears, Nos.365–368 (Museum of London Reserve Collection). Scale 1:2.

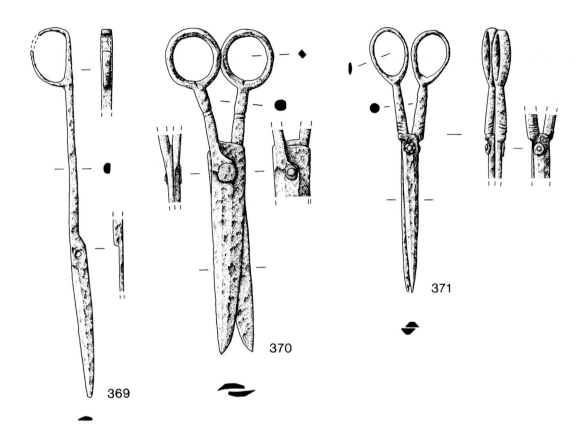

75 Scissors, Nos.369 (late 13th or early 14th century), 370 (late 14th century) and 371 (unstratified). Scale 1:2.

SCISSORS

The scissors, Nos.369–71, consist of a pair of opposed *blades* with *arms*, pivoted together in the centre. At the end of each arm is a *loop* for manipulating the scissors. Above the pivot, at the junction of the blade and arm may be a *stop* to prevent the arms overlapping.

Early to mid 14th century

369. (TL74 [2680] ⟨2369⟩)
Blade, length 83mm, width 8mm, thickness 2mm, tapering tip. Handle, length 108mm, width 5mm, diameter 31mm, rectangular arm section, semi-circular loop.

Late 14th century

370. (BC72 [88] ⟨2274⟩)
Blades, length 111mm, width 20mm, thickness 2mm, angled tips, copper alloy washer on pivot. Handles, length 60mm, width 5mm, diameter 29mm, round arm section, decorated with a single ridge on each arm, circular loop.

Unstratified

371. (BWB83 [1] ⟨1695⟩)
Blades, length 84mm, width 12mm, thickness 5mm, tapering tips, decorated with a floral copper alloy washer on the pivot. Handles, length 60mm, width 6mm, diameter 29mm, round arm sections decorated with incised lines at the base of each arm, oval loop.

SCABBARDS (Figs. 4 and 9)

The scabbards are usually made from a single piece of leather, but occasionally they are *lined* or have small *additional sheaths*. All have *stitched seams*. Most are decorated, the decorative elements occurring both on the front, where they are usually divided into panels corresponding to the division between the knife handle and blade, and on the back, Four decorative techniques have been identified, and these have been further sub-divided into the motifs used. *Slots* were cut into the leather to facilitate suspension from the belt by rings, or a thong.

The measurements given were taken after conservation, but since the degree of shrinkage during conservation will have varied depending on the technique used to dry them, they must be considered approximate in relation to the original size (Starling 1984).

Late 12th-century scabbards No. 372

The sole scabbard from this period is in a form that is associated almost exclusively with plaited decoration, but in this instance this occurs only on the blade section.

372. (SWA81 [2155] ⟨4711⟩)
Calf leather, width 49mm. Flesh/grain and edge/grain stitches. Decorated by engraving.
Design elements:
    Front handle: linear, other motifs.
    Front blade: linear, plaits.
    Back: linear.
Two suspension slots on the front and back. Tip cut off.

Early to mid 13th-century scabbards Nos. 373–386

The greatest variety of scabbard shapes are found in this group. Many also show signs of reuse or have been repaired. Engraving, often with fine portrayals of running animals, was the main technique used, sometimes in association with a single circular stamp.

373. (SH74 [467] ⟨161⟩)
Calf leather, width 59mm. Split seam with edge/grain stitches; stitched repair. Decorated by engraving and stamping.
Design elements:
    Front handle: linear and lattice (engraved), dot (stamped).
    Front blade: linear and lattice (engraved), dot (stamped).
    Back: linear (engraved).
Four suspension slots on the front and back. Deliberate cut, additional stitch holes around the slots.

374. (SH74 [386] ⟨86⟩)
Calf leather, width 58mm. Centre-back seam with edge/grain stitches. Decorated by engraving.
Design elements:
    Front handle: lattice, linear and plaits.
    Front blade: lattice, linear and plaits.
    Back: linear.
Four suspension slots on the front and back, hung diagonally by a thong.

375. (SH74 [386] ⟨88⟩)
Calf leather, length 154mm, width 36mm. Centre-back seam with edge/grain stitches. Decorated by embossing and engraving.
Design elements:
    Front handle: zoomorphic (embossed), linear (engraved).
    Front blade: zoomorphic (embossed), linear (engraved).
    Back: linear (engraved).
Four suspension slots on the back, hung vertically by a thong.

376. (SH74 [467] ⟨163⟩)
Calf leather. Centre-back seam with flesh/grain stitches. Decorated by engraving and stamping.
Design elements:
    Front handle: foliate and linear (engraved), dot (stamped).
    Front blade: linear and zoomorphic (engraved), dot (stamped).
    Back: linear (engraved).

377. (SH74 [386] ⟨90⟩)
Calf leather, length 155mm, width 36mm. Centre-back seam with edge/grain stitches. Decorated by embossing and engraving.
Design elements:
    Front handle: zoomorphic (embossed), linear (engraved).
    Front blade: zoomorphic (embossed), linear (engraved).
    Back: linear (engraved).
Two suspension slots on the back, hung vertically by a thong.

378. (SH74 [394] ⟨139⟩)
Calf leather. Centre-back seam with edge/grain stitches. Decorated by engraving and stamping.
Design elements:
    Front blade: linear and zoomorphic (engraved), dot (stamped).
    Back: linear (engraved).

379. (BIG82 [2545] ⟨2255⟩)
Calf leather, length 236mm, width 43mm. Centre-back seam with flesh/grain and edge/grain stitches. Decorated by embossing and engraving.
Design elements:
    Front handle: zoomorphic (embossed), foliate, zoomorphic and lozenge (engraved).
    Front blade: zoomorphic (embossed), foliate, zoomorphic and lozenge (engraved).
    Back: linear (engraved).
Four suspension slots on the back, hung vertically by a thong. Deliberate cut; reused.

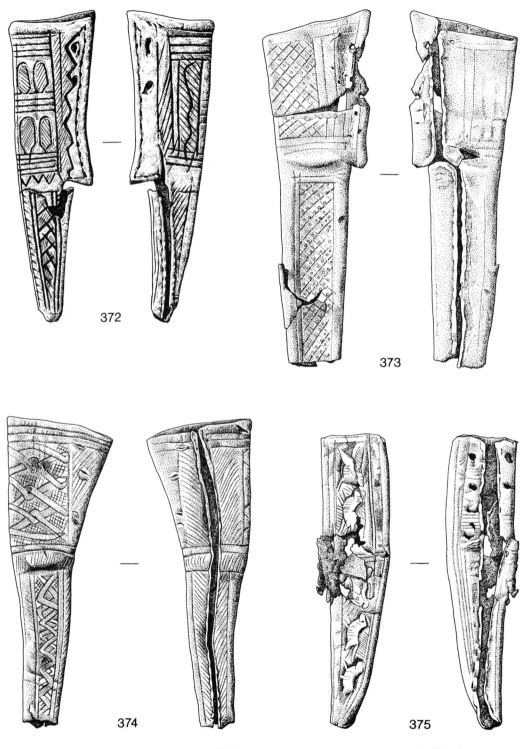

372

373

374   375

76 Scabbards, Nos.372 (12th century) (SM), 373–375 (early to mid 13th century) (JP). Scale 1:2.

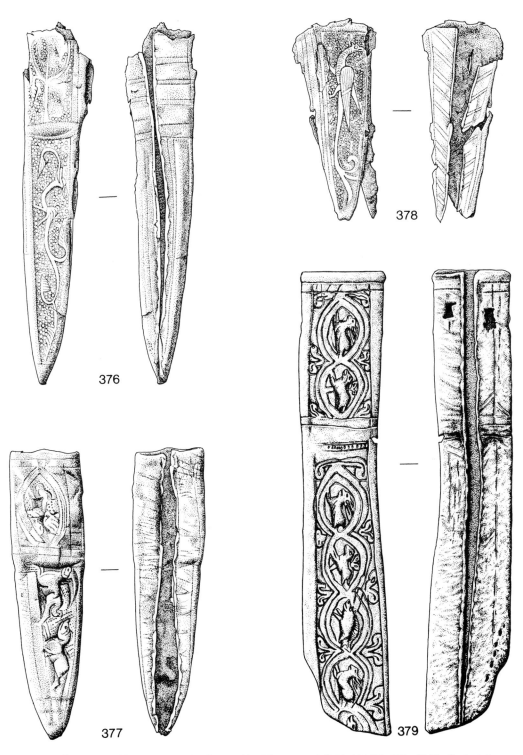

77 Scabbards, Nos.376–379 (early to mid 13th century) (376–378 JP; 379 CLR). Scale 1:2.

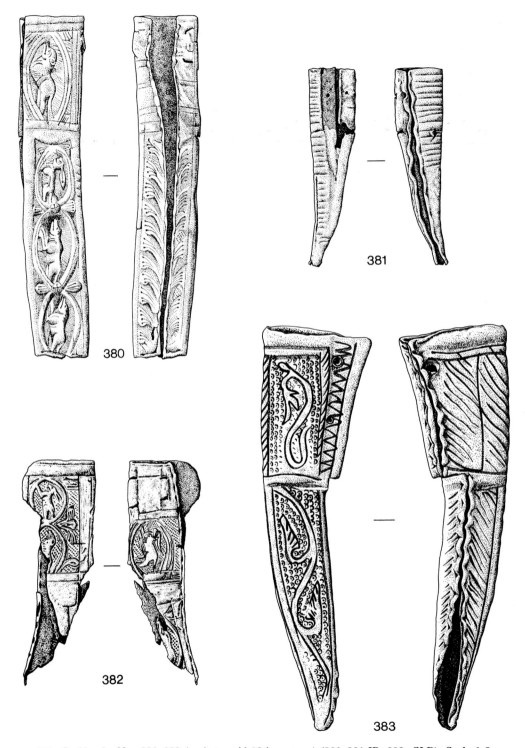

78 Scabbards, Nos. 380–383 (early to mid 13th century) (380–381 JP; 383 CLR). Scale 1:2.

380. (SH74 [386] ⟨108⟩)
    Calf leather, width 30mm. Centre-back seam with
    flesh/grain and edge/grain stitches. Decorated by
    embossing and engraving.
    Design elements:
      Front handle: zoomorphic (embossed), linear
      (engraved).
      Front blade: zoomorphic (embossed), foliate and
      linear (engraved).
      Back: foliate and linear (engraved).
    Five suspension slots on the back, hung vertically by a
    thong. Deliberate cut; reused?

381. (SWA81 [2151] ⟨4799⟩)
    Calf leather, length 104mm, width 24mm. Side of back
    seam with edge/grain stitches. Decorated by
    engraving.
    Design elements:
      Front handle: linear.
      Front blade: linear.
      Back: linear.
    Two suspension slots on the front and back, hung
    vertically by a thong.

382. (LH74 [F 92/93] ⟨2⟩)
    Calf leather. Side seam with edge/grain stitches.
    Decorated by embossing and engraving.
    Design elements:
      Front handle: zoomorphic (embossed), foliate and
      linear (engraved).
      Back: zoomorphic (embossed), foliate and linear
      (engraved).
    Four suspension slots on the back, hung vertically by
    a thong?

383. (BIG82 [5221] ⟨2806⟩)
    Cattle leather, length 204mm, width 55mm. Split seam
    with edge/grain stitches. Decorated by engraving and
    stamping
    Design elements:
      Front handle: foliate and linear (engraved), dot
      (stamped).
      Front blade: foliate (engraved), dot (stamped).
      Back: linear (engraved).
    Two suspension slots on the front and back, hung
    vertically by a thong.

384. (BIG82 [3211] ⟨2426⟩)
    Calf leather, length 210mm, width 44mm. Centre-back
    seam with edge/grain stitches. Decorated by
    engraving and stamping.
    Design elements:
      Front handle: zoomorphic (engraved), dot
      stamped).
      Front blade: foliate (engraved), dot (stamped).
      Back: linear (engraved).
    Two suspension slots on the back, hung horizontally
    by a thong.

385. (BIG82 [4538] ⟨2745⟩)
    Calf leather. Side seam with edge/grain stitches.
    Decorated by engraving.
    Design elements:
      Front handle: foliate and linear (engraved).
      Back: foliate and linear (engraved).

386. (SH74 [484] ⟨248⟩)
    Calf leather, length 114mm, width 18mm. Side of back
    seam with edge/grain stitches. Decorated by
    engraving and stamping.
    Design elements:
      Front handle: linear and zoomorphic (engraved), dot
      (stamped).
      Front blade: linear and zoomorphic (engraved), dot
      (stamped).
      Back: linear (engraved).
    Four suspension slots on the back, hung vertically by
    a thong.

Late 13th-century scabbards Nos. 387–404

The majority of these scabbards have fairly straight
sides and are decorated with stamps, frequently of
heraldically derived motifs. All but five were found at
Swan Lane so that the similarity may be due to a site
bias. Two were found containing knives (Nos. 391 and
397/398), and one was probably not for carrying a
knife (No. 393).

387. (BIG82 [2915] ⟨2363⟩)
    Calf leather, width 56mm. Centre-back seam with
    edge/grain stitches. Decorated by engraving and
    stamping.
    Design elements:
      Front handle: foliate and linear (engraved), dot
      (stamped).
      Front blade: linear and zoomorphic (engraved), dot
      (stamped).
      Back: linear (engraved).
    Six suspension slots on the back, hung by a thong.

388. (TL74 [2417] ⟨1936⟩)
    Calf leather, width 51mm. Edge/grain stitches.
    Decorated by engraving.
    Design elements:
      Front handle: linear and plaits.
      Back: linear and plaits.
    Two suspension slots on the front and back.

389. (TL74 [2467] ⟨2510⟩)
    Calf leather. Edge/grain stitches. Decorated by
    engraving.
    Design elements:
      Front handle: linear.
      Back: linear.
    Four suspension slots on the front and back.
    Deliberate cut.

390. (BIG82 [3136] ⟨2435⟩)
    Calf leather. Centre-back seam with edge/grain
    stitches. Decorated by engraving.
    Design elements:
      Front blade: linear and plaits.
      Back: linear.
    Wooden ?lining; deliberate cut.

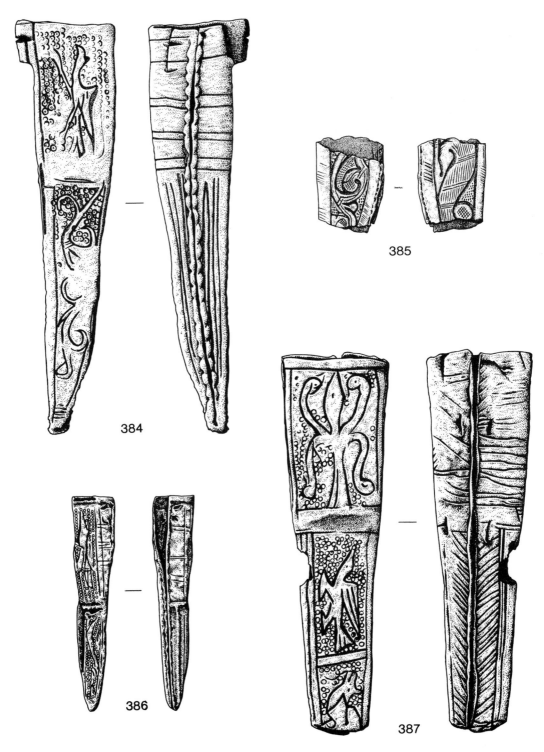

79 Scabbards, Nos.384–386 (early to mid 13th century), 387 (late 13th century) (384, 387 CLR). Scale 1:2.

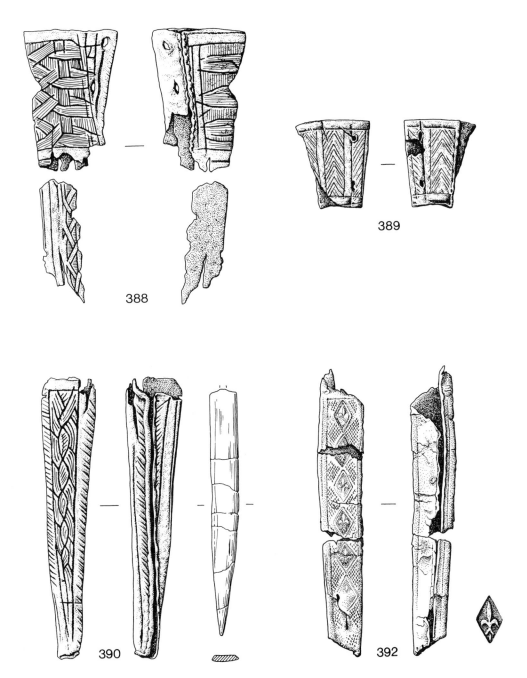

80 Scabbards, Nos.388–390, 392 (late 13th century) (388 SM; 390 CLR; 392 JP). Wooden lining(?) with 390. Scale 1:2; details of stamp 1:1.

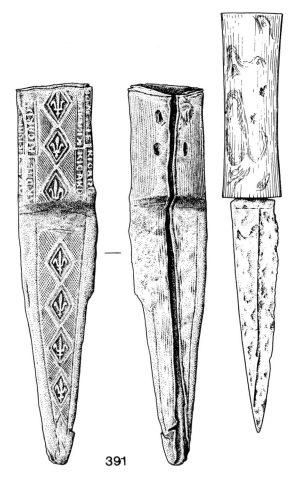

391

RICARDIE

81   Scabbard, No. 391 and knife 38 (late 13th century). Scale 1:2; details of stamps 1:1.

391.   (SWA81 [2057] ⟨543⟩)
Calf leather, length 197mm, width 44mm. Centre-back seam with edge/grain stitches. Decorated by engraving and stamping.
Design elements:
    Front handle: linear and lozenge (engraved, dots, fleur-de-lys and inscription (stamped).

Front blade: linear and lozenge (engraved) dots and fleur-de-lys (stamped).
    Back: linear (engraved).
Four suspension slots on the back, hung diagonally by a thong. Complete knife found in scabbard (No. 38). Inscription reads 'RICARDIE'. See Plate 8 for detail of stamp.

392.   (SWA81 [2061] ⟨4935⟩)
Calf leather. Side of back seam with edge/grain stitches. Decorated by engraving and stamping.
Design elements:
    Front blade: linear and lozenge (engraved), fleur-de-lys and dots stamped).
    Back: linear (engraved).

393.   (SWA81 [2018] ⟨4566⟩)
Calf leather, width 15mm, lining projects above the top (grain faces inwards). Centre-back seam with edge/grain stitches. Decorated by engraving and stamping.
Design elements:
    Front: lozenge and linear (engraved), dot and fleur-de-lys (stamped).
    Back: lozenge and linear (engraved), dot (stamped).
Four suspension slots on the side, hung vertically by a ring? Deliberate cut. Not for a knife. Cap missing?

394.   (TL74 [2467] ⟨2506⟩)
Calf leather, length 183mm, width 39mm. Side of back seam with flesh/grain and edge/grain stitches. Decorated by engraving and stamping.
Design elements:
    Front handle: linear (engraved), zoomorphic (stamped).
    Front blade: linear (engraved), zoomorphic (stamped).
    Back: linear (engraved), zoomorphic (stamped).
Four suspension slots on the back, hung vertically by a thong. Reused? See Plate 9 for detail of stamp.

395.   (SWA81 [2018] ⟨413⟩)
Calf leather, length 153mm, width 32mm. Side of back seam with edge/grain stitches. Decorated by engraving and stamping.
Design elements:
    Front handle: linear (engraved), fleur-de-lys (stamped).
    Front blade: linear (engraved), fleur-de-lys (stamped).
    Back: linear (engraved), fleur-de-lys (stamped).
Four suspension slots on the back. See Plate 10 for detail of stamp.

396.   (SWA81 [2050] ⟨534⟩)
Calf leather, width 36mm. Side of back seam with edge/grain stitches. Decorated by engraving and stamping.
Design elements:
    Front handle: linear (engraved), fleur-de-lys (stamped).
    Front blade: linear (engraved), fleur-de-lys (stamped).
    Back: linear (engraved), fleur-de-lys (stamped).
Four suspension slots on the back, hung vertically by a thong. Deliberate cut. Plate 11.

PLATE 9
Scabbard No.394:
detail showing lion
rampant sinister
stamps.

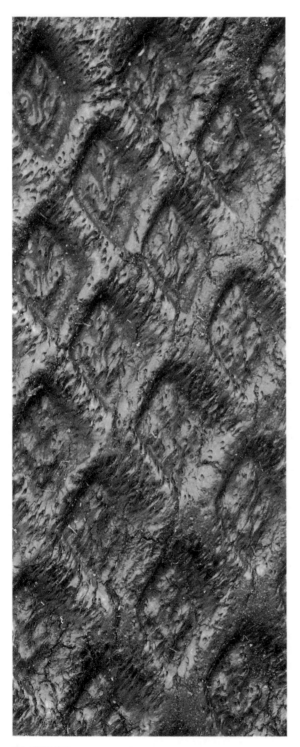

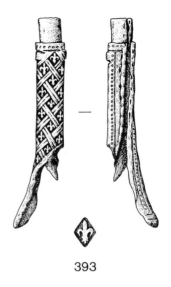

393

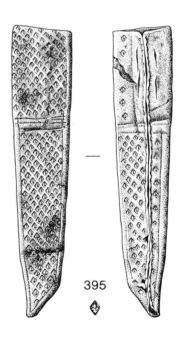

395

82   Scabbards, Nos. 393–396 (late 13th
     century) (393–4 SM; 395 JP). Scale 1:2;
     details of stamps 1:1.

PLATE 10
Scabbard No. 395: detail showing area of small
fleur-de-lys stamps.

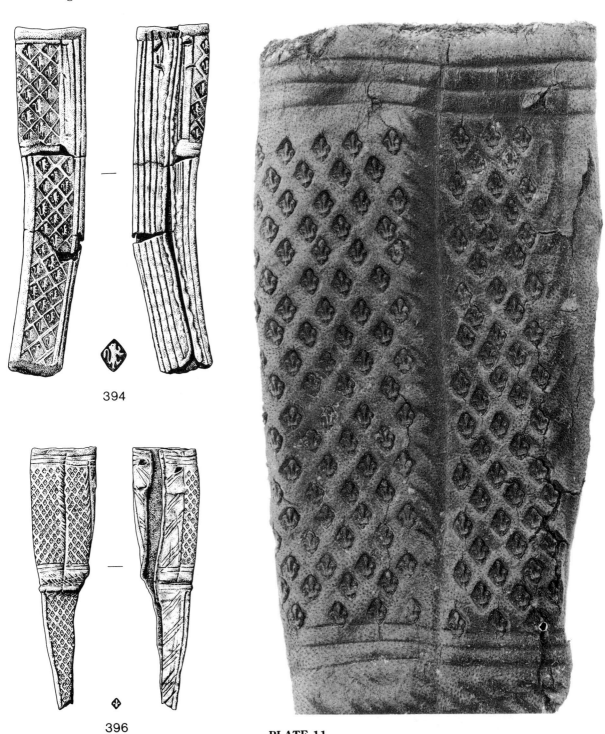

394

396

PLATE 11
Scabbard No. 396: detail of upper part of scabbard showing small
fleur-de-lys stamps and engraved decoration.

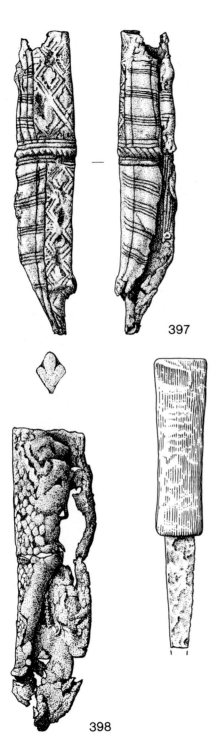

83 Scabbards, Nos.397–398 and knife 39 (late 13th century) (DS). Scale 1:2; details of stamps 1:1.

397. (SWA81 [2065] ⟨786/1⟩)
Calf leather, lined with No.398. Side of back seam with flesh/grain stitches. Decorated by engraving and stamping.
Design elements:
  Front handle: lattice (engraved), ?motif (stamped).
  Front blade: lattice (engraved), ?motif (stamped).
  Back: lattice (engraved), ?motif (stamped).
Four suspension slots on the back, hung vertically by a thong. Very worn, Knife found in scabbard (No.39). Plate 6.

398. (SWA81 [2065] ⟨786/2⟩)
Calf leather, length 161mm, width 26mm, lining. Side of back seam with flesh/grain stitches; stitched repair. Decorated by engraving and stamping.
Design elements:
  Front handle: lozenge and linear (engraved), dot and foliate (stamped).
  Front blade: lozenge and linear (engraved), dot and foliate (stamped).
  Back: lozenge and linear (engraved), dot and foliate (stamped).
The lining found in scabbard No.397. Knife found in scabbard (No.39).

399. (SWA81 [2134] ⟨4709⟩)
Calf leather, length 260mm. Side of back seam with edge/grain stitches. Decorated by engraving and stamping.
Design elements:
  Front handle: linear (engraved), rosette (stamped).
  Front blade: linear (engraved), rosette (stamped).
  Back: linear (engraved), rosette (stamped).
Two suspension slots on the back. Deliberate cut. Method of suspension cut free from scabbard. See Plate 12 for detail of stamp.

400. (SWA81 [2057] ⟨885⟩)
Calf leather, width 47mm. Centre-back seam with flesh/grain and edge/grain stitches. Decorated by engraving and stamping.
Design elements:
  Front handle: linear (engraved), rosette (stamped).
  Front blade: linear (engraved), rosette (stamped).
  Back: linear (engraved), rosette (stamped).
Four suspension slots on the back, hung vertically. See Plate 13 for detail of stamp.

401. SWA81 [2046] ⟨4921⟩)
Calf leather, length 79mm, width 31mm. Side seam with edge/grain stitches. Decorated by engraving and stamping.
Design elements:
  Front handle: linear (engraved), dots (stamped).
  Front blade: linear (engraved), dots (stamped).
  Back: linear (engraved), dots (stamped).
Four suspension slots on the side, hung diagonally by a thong.

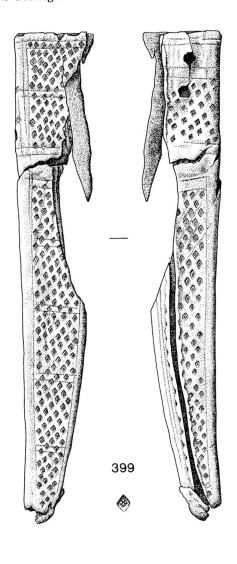

399

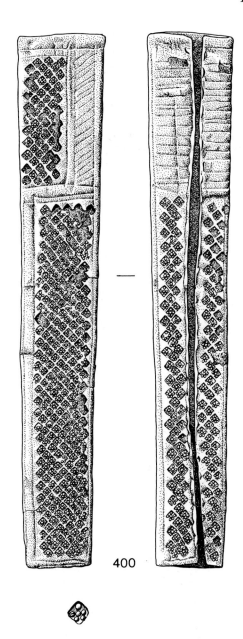

400

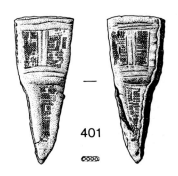

401

84   Scabbards, Nos. 399–401 (late 13th century)
(JP). Scale 1:2; details of stamps 1:1.

PLATE 12
Scabbard No.399:
detail showing stamps
(quatrefoils in
lozenges) overlain by
engraved lines.

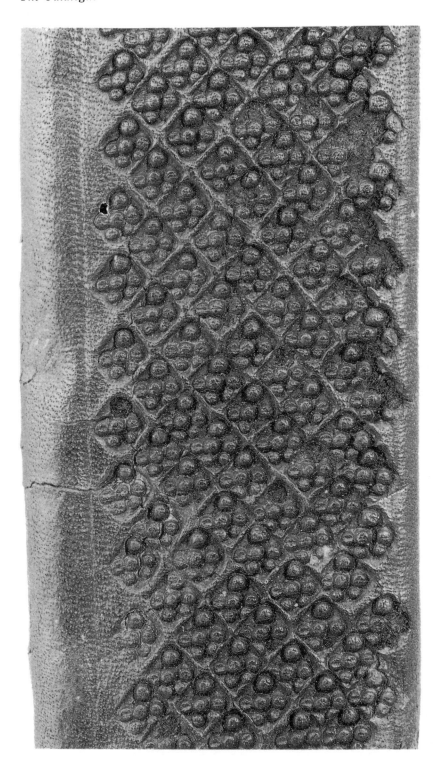

PLATE 13
Scabbard No. 400: detail
showing stamps, cinquefoils
in lozenges.

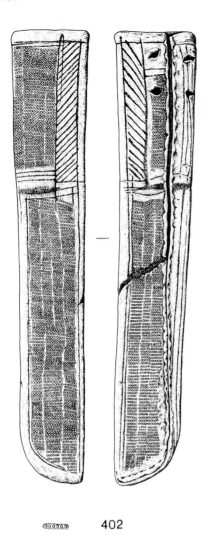

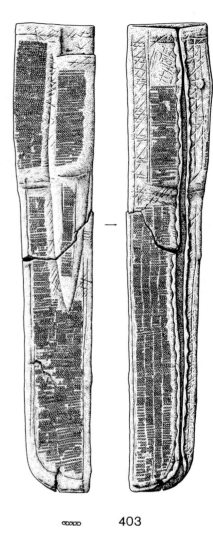

402

403

402. (SWA81 [2134] ⟨1027⟩ ⟨4521⟩)
Calf leather, length 239mm, width 43mm. Side of back
seam with edge/grain stitches. Decorated by
engraving and stamping.
Design elements:
   Front handle: linear (engraved), dots (stamped).
   Front blade: linear (engraved), dots (stamped).
   Back: linear (engraved), dots (stamped).
Four suspension slots on the back, hung vertically by
a thong.

403. (SWA81 [2055] ⟨1339⟩)
Calf leather, length 248mm, width 41mm, second
inner scabbard (grain faces out). Side of back seam
with edge/grain stitches. Decorated by engraving and
stamping.

Design elements:
   Front handle: linear (engraved), dots (stamped).
   Front blade: linear (engraved), dots (stamped).
   Back: linear (engraved), dots (stamped).
Three suspension slots on the back, hung by a thong.

404. (SWA81 [2078] ⟨4720⟩)
Calf leather. Side of back seam with flesh/grain and
edge/grain stitches. Decorated by engraving and
stamping.
Design elements:
   Front blade: linear (engraved), dots (stamped).
   Back: linear (engraved), dots (stamped).
See Plate 14 for detail of stamp.

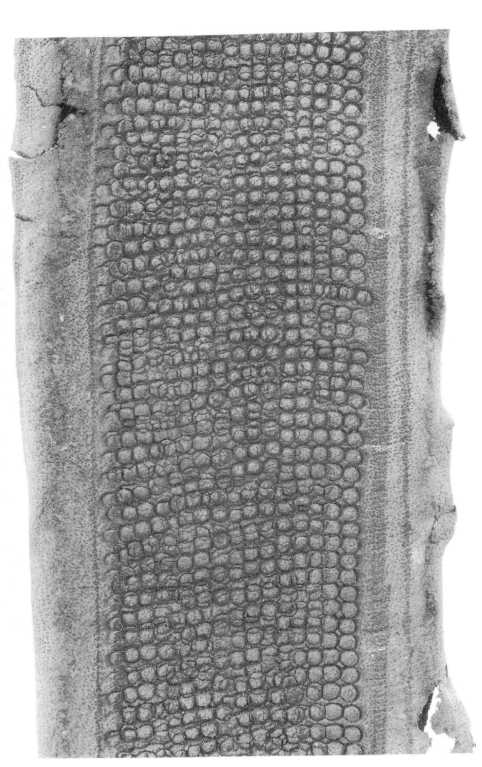

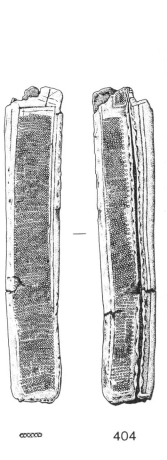

404

85 Scabbards, Nos. 402–
404 (late 13th
century) (402 SM;
403 JP). Scale 1:2;
details of stamps 1:1.

PLATE 14
Scabbard No. 404: detail
showing area of stamped
dots.

Early to mid 14th-century scabbards Nos. 405–451

The scabbards in this group generally conform to several fairly standard shapes. Linings and secondary internal sheaths seem to be more common than in the earlier periods. Several have 'false ferrules' at the tip (for example Nos. 407 and 409), perhaps imitating the grander dagger or sword scabbards. Engraving is the most common decorative technique but the use of stamps continues.

405. (BC72 [250] ⟨3522⟩)
Calf? leather, length 173mm, width 62mm. Split seam with edge/grain stitches. Decorated by engraving.
Design elements:
    Front handle: linear and plaits.
    Front blade: linear and plaits.
    Back: linear
Four suspension slots on the side, hung by a thong.

406. (CUS73 [VI 26] ⟨650⟩)
Calf leather, length 162, width 46mm. Split seam with edge/grain stitches. Decorated by engraving.
Design elements:
    Front handle: linear and plaits.
    Front blade: linear.
    Back: linear and plaits.
Two suspension slots on the front and back, hung diagonally by a thong. Ferrule missing?

407. (BC72 [250] ⟨3520⟩)
Calf leather, length 144mm, width 52mm. Split seam with flesh/grain and edge/grain stitches. Decorated by engraving.
Design elements:
    Front handle: linear and plaits.
    Front blade: linear and plaits.
    Back: linear and plaits.
Two suspension slots on the side, hung horizontally by a thong.

408. (BC72 [250] ⟨3286⟩)
Calf leather, length 158mm, width 33mm. Split seam with edge/grain stitches. Decorated by engraving.
Design elements:
    Front handle: linear and plaits.
    Front blade: linear and plaits.
    Back: linear.
Two suspension slots on the front and back, hung diagonally by a thong.

409. (LUD82 [1060] ⟨95⟩ ⟨96⟩)
Calf leather, length 289mm. Split seam with edge/flesh stitches. Decorated by engraving.
Design elements:
    Front handle: dot, linear and plaits.
    Front blade: linear and plaits.
    Back: linear and plaits.
Deliberate cut.

410. (BC72 [250] ⟨3645⟩)
Calf leather, length 153mm, width 39mm. Split seam with edge/grain stitches. Decorated by engraving and stamping.
Design elements:
    Front handle: linear and plaits (engraved), dots (stamped).
    Front blade: linear and plaits (engraved), dots (stamped).
    Back: linear (engraved).
Two suspension slots on the front and back, hung by a thong.

411. (CUS73 [III 10] ⟨226⟩)
Calf leather. Split back seam with edge/grain stitches. Decorated by engraving.
Design elements:
    Front handle: linear and plaits.
    Back: linear and plaits.
Deliberate cut.

412. (CUS73 [I 15] ⟨1221⟩)
Calf leather, length 98mm, width 28mm. Centre back seam with edge/grain stitches. Decorated by engraving.
Design elements:
    Front handle: linear.
    Front blade: linear.
    Back: linear.
Two suspension slots on the back, hung vertically by a thong.

413. (CUS73 [III 10] ⟨1220⟩)
Calf leather, width 34mm. Split seam with edge/grain stitches. Decorated by engraving.
Design elements:
    Front handle: linear and plaits.
    Front blade: linear and plaits.
    Back: linear and plaits.
Two suspension slots on the back, hung by a thong. Deliberate cut?

414. (BC72 [250] ⟨3427⟩)
Calf leather, length 173mm, width 37mm, second inner scabbard (grain faces inwards). Side of back seam with edge/grain stitches; stitched repair? Decorated by engraving.
Design elements:
    Front handle: foliate, linear and zoomorphic.
    Front blade: foliate, linear and zoomorphic.
    Back: linear and half quatrefoil.
Four suspension slots on the front and back, hung vertically by a thong. Rehung when the slot broke.

415. (BC72 [250] ⟨3287⟩)
Calf leather, width 28mm. Decorated by engraving.
Design elements:
    Front handle: fleur-de-lys and linear.
    Back: linear.
Deliberate cut.

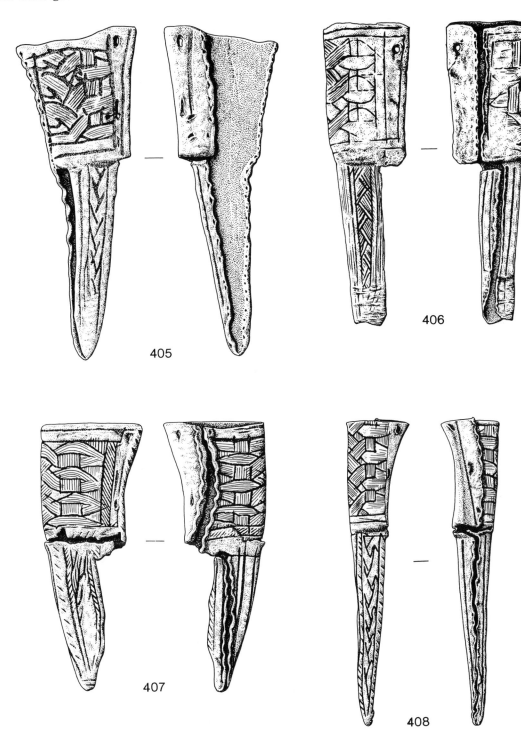

405

406

407

408

86 Scabbards, Nos. 405–408 (early to mid 14th century) (405, 407 SM). Scale 1:2.

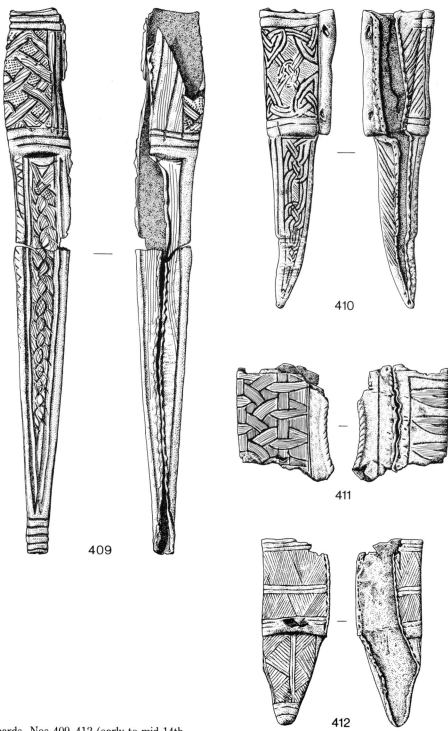

87 Scabbards, Nos.409–412 (early to mid 14th century) (409 CLR). Scale 1:2.

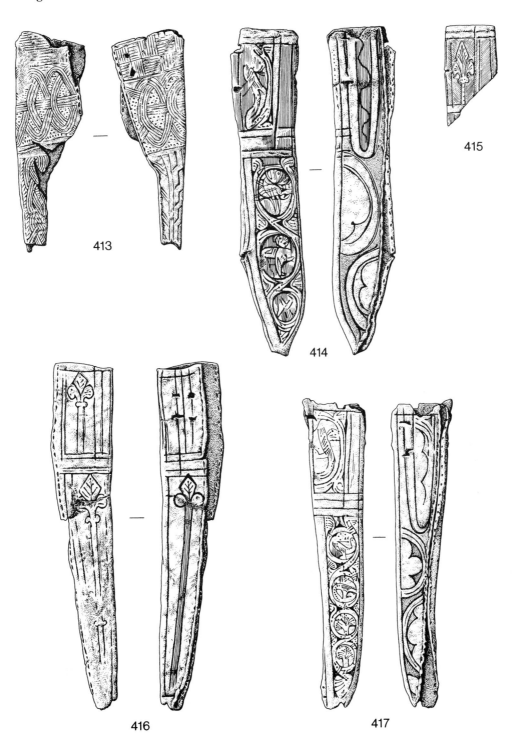

88 Scabbards, Nos. 413–417 (early to mid 14th century). Scale 1:2.

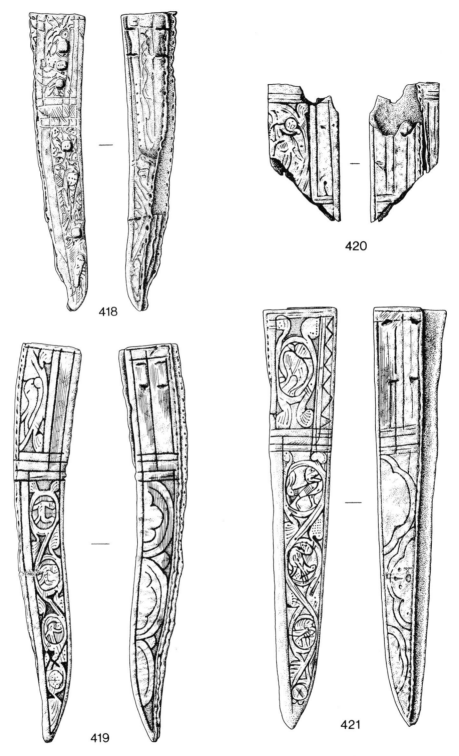

89 Scabbards, Nos. 418–421 (early to mid 14th century). Scale 1:2.

416. (BC72 [250] ⟨3411⟩)
Calf leather, length 183mm, width 38mm. Side seam
with flesh/grain stitches. Decorated by engraving.
Design elements:
    Front handle: fleur-de-lys and linear.
    Front blade: fleur-de-lys and linear.
    Back: fleur-de-lys and linear.
Four suspension slots on the back, hung vertically by
a thong. Deliberate cut.

417. (BC72 [250] ⟨3659⟩)
Calf leather, second inner scabbard (grain faces
inwards). Side of back seam with edge/grain stitches.
Decorated by engraving.
Design elements:
    Front handle: foliate, linear and zoomorphic.
    Front blade: foliate, linear and zoomorphic.
    Back: linear and half quatrefoil.
Four suspension slots on the front and back, hung by
a thong.

418. (PCD [ER518] ⟨7⟩)
Calf leather, length 158mm, width 30mm, lined (grain
faces inwards) and second inner scabbard. Side seam
with flesh/grain stitches. Decorated by embossing and
engraving.
Design elements:
    Front handle: foliate and zoomorphic (embossed),
      foliate, linear and zoomorphic (engraved).
    Front blade: foliate and zoomorphic (embossed),
      foliate, linear and zoomorphic (engraved).
    Back: linear and half quatrefoil (engraved).
Four suspension slots on the back, hung vertically.
Embossed areas supported with small cubes of
leather.

419. (BC72 [250] ⟨3412⟩)
Calf leather, length 208mm, width 33mm. Side seam
with edge/grain stitches. Decorated by engraving.
Design elements:
    Front handle: foliate, linear and zoomorphic.
    Front blade: foliate, linear and zoomorphic.
    Back: linear and half quatrefoil.
Four suspension slots on the back, hung vertically by
a thong. Deliberate cut.

420. (BC72 [250] ⟨3569⟩)
Calf leather. Side of back seam with edge/grain
stitches. Decorated by engraving.
Design elements:
    Front handle: linear, foliate and zoomorphic.
    Back: linear.

421. (BC72 [250] ⟨3632⟩)
Calf leather, length 220mm, width 39mm. Side of back
seam with edge/grain stitches. Decorated by
engraving.
Design elements:
    Front handle: foliate, linear and zoomorphic.
    Front blade: foliate, linear and zoomorphic.
    Back: linear and half quatrefoil.
Four suspension slots on the back, hung vertically by
a thong.

422. (BC72 [250] ⟨3630⟩)
Calf leather, length 150mm, width 42mm. Side of back
seam with edge/grain stitches. Decorated by engraving.
Design elements:
    Front handle: foliate, linear and zoomorphic.
    Front blade: foliate, linear and zoomorphic.
    Back: linear and half quatrefoil.
Four suspension slots on the back, hung by a thong.

423. (PCD [ER518] ⟨11⟩)
Leather, width 37mm. Side of back seam with edge/
grain stitches. Decorated by engraving.
Design elements:
    Front handle: foliate, linear and zoomorphic.
    Front blade: foliate, linear and zoomorphic.
    Back: heraldic and linear.
Four suspension slots on the back, hung vertically.
Deliberate cut. For discussion of heraldry see p.47.

424. (CUS73 [III 10] ⟨1210⟩)
Calf leather, length 122mm, width 21mm. Centre back
seam with edge/grain stitches. Decorated by engraving.
Design elements:
    Front handle: linear.
    Front blade: linear.
    Back: linear.
Four suspension slots on the back, hung by a thong.

425. (BC72 [250] ⟨3661⟩)
Calf leather, length 159mm, width 36mm, lined (grain
faces out). Centre-back seam with edge/grain stitches.
Decorated by engraving.
Design elements:
    Front handle: heraldic, foliate and linear.
    Front blade: heraldic, foliate and linear.
    Back: linear and half quatrefoil.
Four suspension slots on the back, hung vertically by
a thong which survives. For discussion of heraldry see
p.47.

426. (CUS73 [I 14] ⟨1219⟩)
Calf leather, width 36mm. Side of back seam with
flesh/grain and edge/grain stitches. Decorated by
engraving.
Design elements:
    Front handle: castle, fleur-de-lys, foliate, linear and
      lozenge.
    Front blade: castle, fleur-de-lys, linear, lozenge and
      half quatrefoil.
    Back: linear and half quatrefoil.
Five suspension slots on the back, hung by a thong.
Irregularly re-stitched.

427. (CUS73 [VI 25] ⟨299⟩)
Calf leather, length 142mm, width 31mm, lined.
Centre-back seam with edge/grain stitches; stitched
repair. Decorated by engraving.
Design elements:
    Front handle: castle, fleur-de-lys, linear, lozenge
      and half quatrefoil.
    Front blade: castle, fleur-de-lys, linear, lozenge and
      half quatrefoil.
    Back: linear.
Four suspension slots on the side, hung vertically by a
thong.

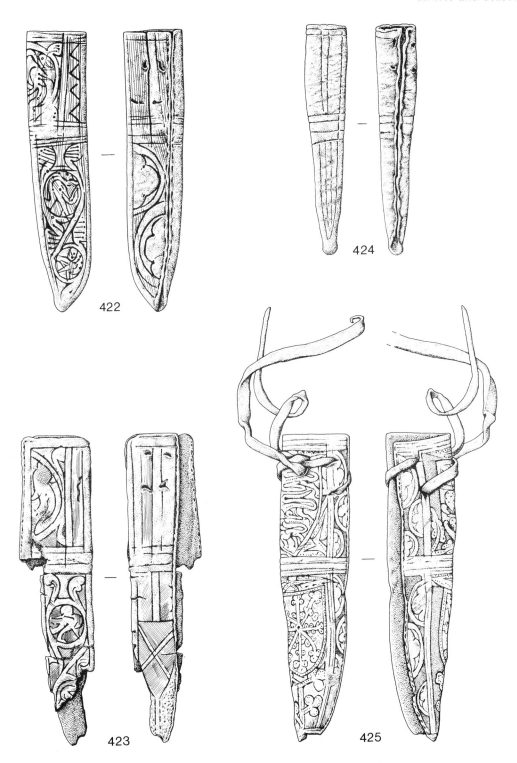

90   Scabbards, Nos.422–425 (early to mid 14th century). Scale 1:2.

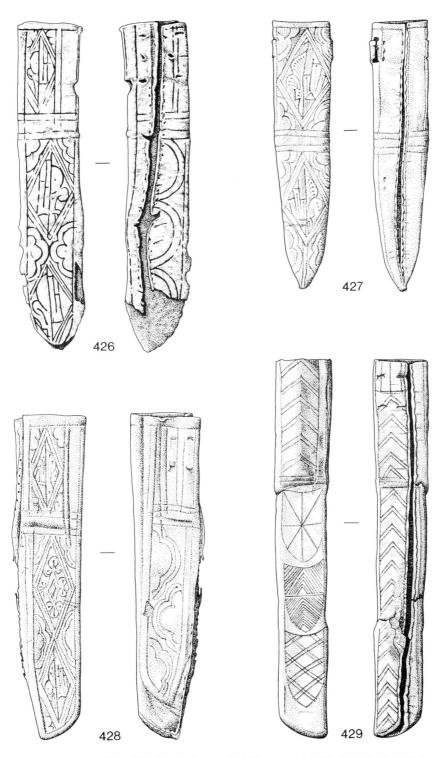

91 Scabbards, Nos. 426–429 (early to mid 14th century) (427–429 JP). Scale 1:2.

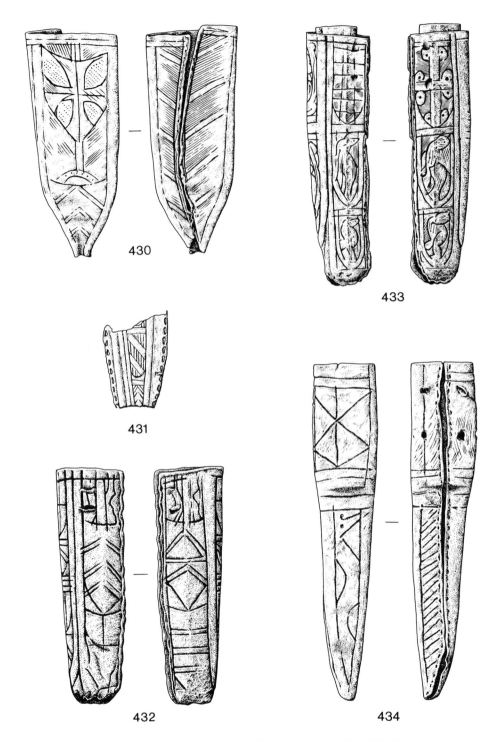

430

431

432

433

434

92 Scabbards, Nos. 430–434 (early to mid 14th century) (432 SM). Scale 1:2.

428. (CUS73 [I 12] ⟨649⟩)
Calf leather, length 172mm, width 35mm, second
inner scabbard. Side seam with edge/grain stitches.
Decorated by engraving.
Design elements:
   Front handle: castle, fleur-de-lys, linear, lozenge
     and half quatrefoil.
   Front blade: castle, fleur-de-lys, foliate, linear,
     lozenge and half quatrefoil.
   Back: linear and half quatrefoil.
Four suspension slots on the back, hung vertically by
a thong.

429. (LUD82 [1078] ⟨93⟩)
Calf leather, length 201mm, width 34mm. Side of back
seam with edge/grain stitches. Decorated by
engraving.
Design elements:
   Front handle: linear.
   Front blade: heraldic.
   Back: linear.
Four suspension slots on the back, hung vertically by
a thong. For discussion of heraldry see p.47.

430. (BC72 [250] ⟨3633⟩)
Calf leather, length 120mm, width 50mm. Centre-back
seam with edge/grain and flesh/grain stitches; stitched
repair. Decorated by engraving.
Design elements:
   Front blade: heraldic linear.
   Back: linear.
For discussion of heraldry see p.47. Deliberate cut.

431. (CUS73 [V 8] ⟨66I⟩)
Calf leather. Centre-back seam with edge/grain
stitches. Decorated by engraving.
Design elements:
   Front blade: heraldic and linear.
   Back: linear.
For discussion of heraldry see p.47.

432. (BC72 [250] ⟨3521⟩)
Calf leather, length 125mm, width 36mm, second
inner scabbard. Side seam with edge/grain stitches.
Decorated by engraving.
Design elements:
   Front: heraldic and linear.
   Back: heraldic and linear.
Four suspension slots, hung vertically by a thong.
Deliberate cut. Square in section with a side sheath
for a knife. Cap missing? For discussion of heraldry
see p.47.

433. (BC72 [250] ⟨3631⟩)
Calf leather, length 127mm, width 33mm, lining
projects above the top (grain faces out). Side seam
with flesh/grain stitches. Decorated by engraving.
Design elements:
   Front: heraldic, linear and zoomorphic.
   Back: heraldic and linear.
Four suspension slots, hung vertically by a thong.
Deliberate cut. Square in section with a side sheath
for a knife. Cap missing? For discussion of heraldry
see p.47.

434. (BC72 [250] ⟨3479⟩ ⟨3619⟩)
Calf leather, width 33mm. Centre-back seam with
flesh/grain stitches. Decorated by engraving.
Design elements:
   Front handle: heraldic and linear.
   Front blade: linear.
   Back: linear.
Four suspension slots on the back. For discussion of
heraldry see p.47.

435. (BC72 [250] ⟨3660⟩)
Calf leather, length 204mm, width 36mm. Centre-back
seam with edge/grain stitches. Decorated by
engraving.
Design elements:
   Front handle: heraldic and linear.
   Front blade: foliate and linear.
   Back: linear.
Four suspension slots on the back, hung by a thong.
For discussion of heraldry see p.47.

436. (BC72 [250] ⟨3523⟩)
Calf leather, length 168mm, width 50mm. Split seam
with edge/grain stitches. Decorated by engraving and
stamping.
Design elements:
   Front handle: heraldic and linear (engraved), dots
     (stamped).
   Front blade: foliate (engraved), dots (stamped).
   Back: linear (engraved).
Three suspension slots on the side, hung diagonally.
For discussion of heraldry see p.47.

437. (CUS73 [VI 26] ⟨829⟩)
Calf leather, width 48mm. Centre-back seam with
edge/grain stitches. Decorated by engraving.
Design elements:
   Front handle: heraldic and linear.
   Front blade: linear and zoomorphic.
   Back: linear.
Two suspension slots on the front and back. For
discussion of heraldry see p.47.

438. (LUD82 [1078] ⟨97⟩)
Calf leather, length 237mm. Centre-back seam with
flesh/grain and edge/grain stitches. Decorated by
engraving and stamping.
Design elements:
   Front handle: linear (engraved), other motif
     (stamped).
   Front blade: linear (engraved), foliate, heraldic and
     other motif (stamped).
   Back: linear (engraved).
For discussion of heraldry see p.47. See Plate 15 for
detail of stamps.

439. (BC72 [250] ⟨3518⟩)
Sheep/Goat leather. Flesh/grain stitches. Decorated
by engraving and stamping.
Design elements:
   Front blade: linear and ?zoomorphic (engraved),
     other motif (stamped).

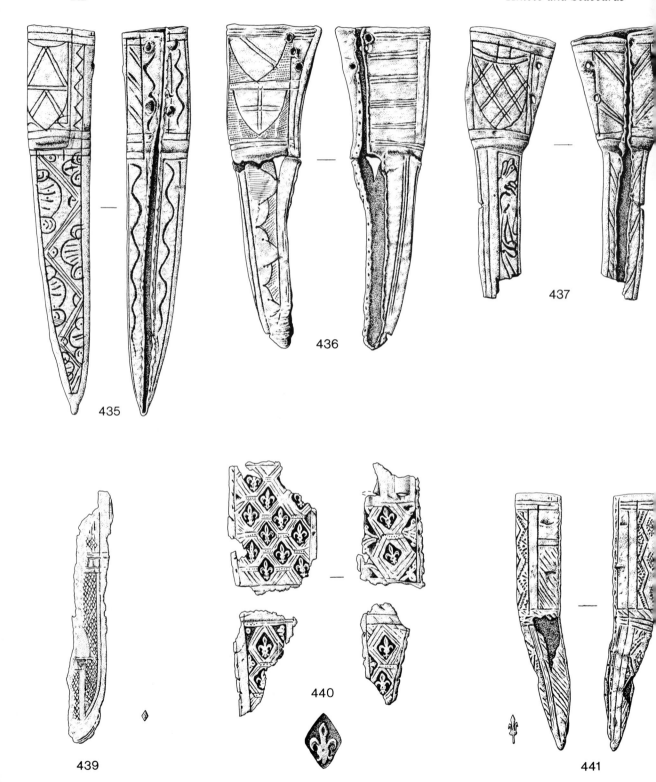

435

436

437

439

440

441

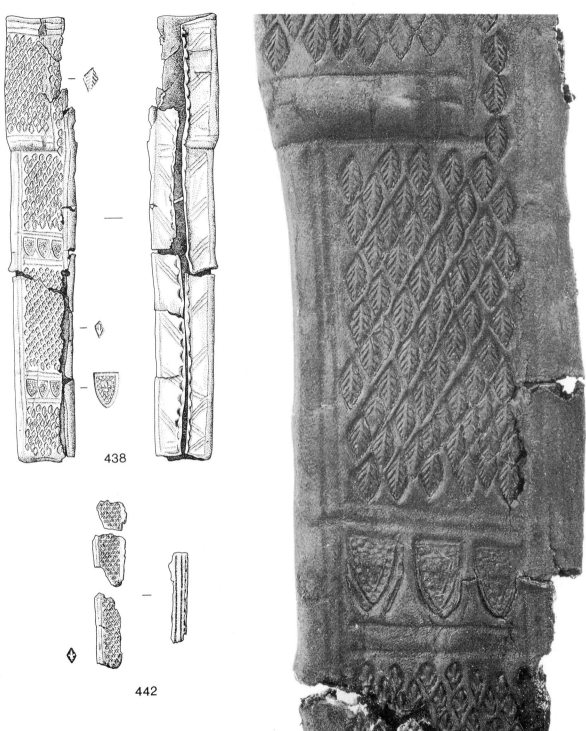

438

442

93 Scabbards, Nos. 435–437, 439 (early to mid 14th century). Scale 1:2; detail of stamp 1:1.

94 Scabbards, Nos. 438, 440–442 (early to mid 14th century) (438 JP). Scale 1:2; details of stamps 1:1.

PLATE 15
Scabbard No. 438: detail of central part of scabbard, showing leaf within lozenge, shield and fleur-de-lys within lozenge stamps. Note overstamping of shields.

PLATE 16
Scabbard No.440: detail showing fleur-de-lys within lozenge stamps, and engraved line and dot decoration.

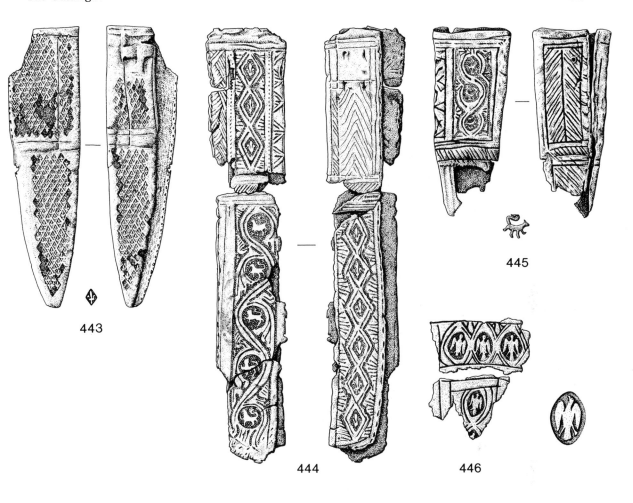

95 Scabbards, Nos. 443–446 (early to mid 14th century) (446 CLR). Scale 1:2, details of stamps 1:1.

440. (LUD82 [1060] ⟨330⟩)
Calf leather. Centre-back seam with edge/grain stitches; stitched repair? Decorated by engraving and stamping.
Design elements:
   Front handle: linear and lozenge (engraved), dots and fleur-de-lys (stamped).
   Front blade: linear and lozenge (engraved), dots and fleur-de-lys (stamped).
   Back: foliate, linear and lozenge (engraved), dots and fleur-de-lys (stamped).
Two suspension slots on the back, hung vertically by a thong. Side seam is probably a repair. See Plate 16 for detail of stamp.

441. (BC72 [250] ⟨3519⟩)
Calf leather, length 133mm, width 24mm. Centre-back seam with flesh/grain stitches. Decorated by engraving and stamping.
Design elements:
   Front handle: lines and lozenge (engraved), dots and fleur-de-lys (stamped).
   Front blade: lines and lozenge (engraved), dots and fleur-de-lys (stamped).
   Back: linear (engraved).
Four suspension slots on the back, hung vertically by a thong.

PLATE 17
Scabbard No.442: fragment showing
fleur-de-lys within lozenge stamps.

442. (CUS73 [VII 10] ⟨622⟩)
Calf leather. Edge/grain stitches. Decorated by
engraving and stamping.
Design elements:
 Front blade: linear (engraved), fleur-de-lys
 (stamped).
 Back: linear (engraved).
See Plate 17 for detail of stamp.

443. (PCD [ER518] ⟨10⟩)
Calf leather, length 150mm. Side seam with edge/grain
stitches. Decorated by engraving and stamping.
Design elements:
 Front handle: linear (engraved), fleur-de-lys
 (stamped).
 Front blade: linear (engraved), fleur-de-lys
 (stamped).
 Back: linear (engraved), fleur-de-lys (stamped).
Four suspension slots on the back, hung vertically.

444. (CUS [V 328] ⟨1223⟩ ⟨1224⟩ ⟨1225⟩)
Leather. Decorated by engraving and stamping.
Design elements:
 Front handle: linear and lozenge (engraved), dots
 and fleur-de-lys (stamped).
 Front blade: foliate and linear (engraved), dot and
 zoomorphic (stamped).
 Back: linear and lozenge (engraved), dots and fleur-
 de-lys (stamped).

445. (CUS [I 12] ⟨227⟩)
Calf leather, width 42mm. Side of back seam with
edge/grain stitches. Decorated by engraving and
stamping.
Design elements:
 Front handle: foliate and linear (engraved), dot and
 zoomorphic (stamped).
 Front blade: linear (engraved), dot (stamped).
 Back: linear (engraved).
One suspension slots on the back. Stitching around
the top edge.

446. (LUD82 [1060] ⟨329⟩)
Calf leather. Decorated by engraving and stamping.
Design elements:
 Front handle: linear and lozenge (engraved),
 zoomorphic (stamped).
 Front blade: linear and lozenge (engraved),
 zoomorphic (stamped).

447. (LUD82 [1047] ⟨331⟩)
Calf leather, length 124mm, width 24mm. Centre-back
seam with edge/grain stitches. Decorated by
engraving and stamping.
Design elements:
 Front handle: linear (engraved), dot and zoomorphic
 (stamped).
 Front blade: linear and lozenge (engraved), fleur-de-
 lys (stamped).
 Back: linear (engraved).
Two suspension slots on the back. See Plates 18 and
19 for details of stamps.

PLATE 18
Scabbard No. 447: detail of upper part
showing lion passant stamps and engraved
line decoration.

PLATE 19
Scabbard No.447: detail of lower part
showing fleur-de-lys within lozenge stamps,
and engraved line decoration.

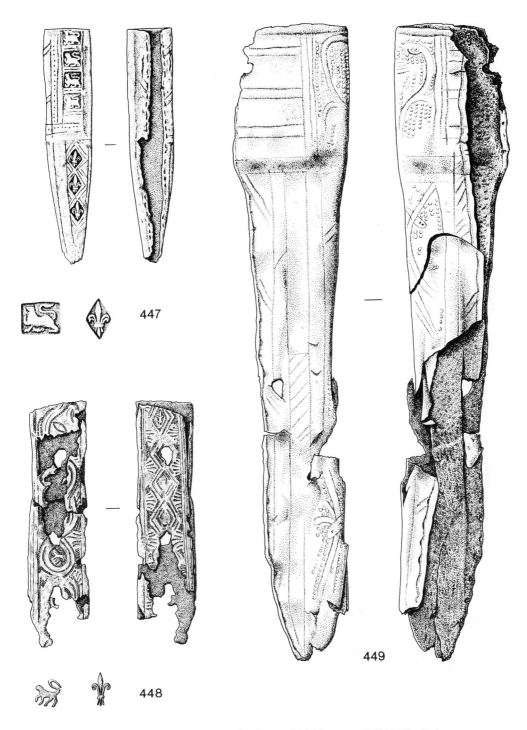

447

448

449

96 Scabbards, Nos. 447–449 (early to mid 14th century) (449 JP). Scale 1:2; details of stamps 1:1.

PLATE 20
Scabbard No.448: detail of lion passant and circle stamps, and engraved line decoration.

PLATE 21
Scabbard No.448: detail of fleur-de-lys and circle stamps, and engraved line decoration.

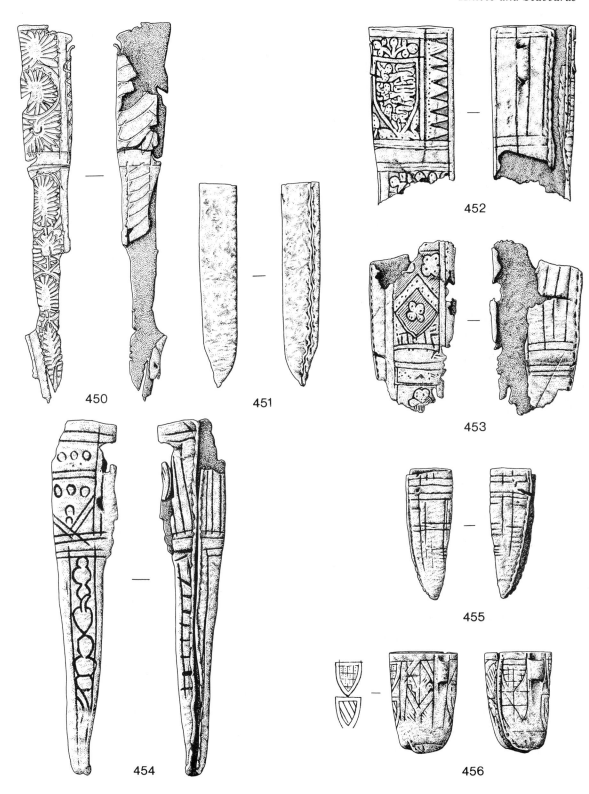

450

451

452

453

454

455

456

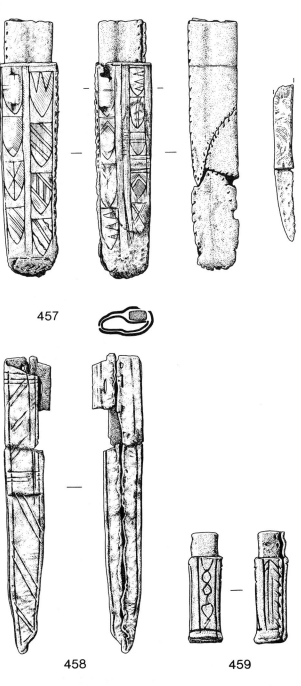

457

458   459

97 Scabbards, Nos. 450–451 (early to mid 14th century), Nos. 452–453, 455 (late 14th century) (450, 453 SM). Scale 1:2.

98 Scabbards, Nos. 454, 456–459, knife 96 with 457 (late 14th century) (454, 459 SM). Scale 1:2.

448. (LH74 [D 52 N] ⟨101⟩)
Calf leather. Side seam with edge/grain stitches.
Decorated by engraving and stamping.
Design elements:
    Front blade: foliate and linear (engraved), dots and zoomorphic (stamped).
    Back: foliate, linear and lozenge (engraved), dots and fleur-de-lys (stamped).
See Plates 20 and 21 for details of stamps.

449. (LUD82 [1078] ⟨367⟩)
Calf leather, length 328mm. Side of back seam with flesh/grain and edge/grain stitches. Decorated by engraving and stamping.
Design elements:
    Front handle: linear and other motif (engraved), dot (stamped).
    Front blade: linear and other motif (engraved), dot (stamped).
    Back: linear (engraved).
Four suspension slots on the back, hung vertically by a thong. Deliberate cut.

450. (TL74 [415] ⟨579⟩)
Calf leather. Side of back seam with flesh/grain stitches. Decorated by incising.
Design elements:
    Front handle: foliate and linear (incised).
    Front blade: foliate and linear (incised).
    Back: foliate and linear (incised).
Deliberate cut.

451. (BC72 [250] ⟨3570⟩)
Sheep/Goat leather, lining (grain faces inwards). Side of back seam with flesh/grain stitches.

Late 14th-century scabbards Nos. 452–463

This small group is similar to the previous group. Two scabbards have a simple stamped decoration.

452. (BWB83 [2] ⟨345⟩)
Leather, width 37mm, lined (grain faces inwards). Side of back seam with edge/grain stitches. Decorated by engraving.
Design elements:
    Front handle: foliate, heraldic and linear.
    Back: linear.
Four suspension slots on the back, hung vertically by a thong. For discussion of heraldry see p.47.

453. (TL74 [2684] ⟨2504⟩)
Calf leather. Side of back seam with edge/grain stitches. Decorated by engraving.
Design elements:
    Front handle: heraldic and linear.
    Back: linear.
For discussion of heraldry see p.47.

454. (TL74 [1651] ⟨2616⟩)
Calf leather, length 190mm. Centre-back seam with
edge/grain stitches. Decorated by engraving.
Design elements:
  Front handle: heraldic and linear.
  Front blade: linear and other motifs.
  Back: linear.
Four suspension slots on the front and back. For
discussion of heraldry see p.47. Deliberate cut. The
slots are damaged; perhaps to release the method of
suspension. Two additional slots which appear unused.

455. (CUS [IV 58] ⟨1217⟩)
Calf/Cattle leather, length 70mm, width 25mm. Side
seam with flesh/grain stitches. Decorated by
engraving.
Design elements:
  Front: linear.
  Back: linear.
Four suspension slots on the front and back, hung
vertically by a thong. Reused? Probably not for a
knife.

456. (CUS 73 [IV 60] ⟨1218⟩)
Calf leather, length 52mm, width 31mm. Centre-back
seam with edge/grain stitches. Decorated by
engraving.
Design elements:
  Front: fleur-de-lys, heraldic, lozenge, and linear.
  Back: fleur-de-lys, foliate, heraldic, lozenge and
    linear.
Four suspension slots, hung vertically by a ring? For
discussion of heraldry see p.47. Not for a knife.

457. (DUK77 [501] ⟨131⟩)
Calf leather, lining projects above top (grain faces
inwards). Side seam with edge/grain stitches.
Decorated by engraving.
Design elements:
  Front: heraldic and linear.
  Back: heraldic and linear.
Four suspension slots on the side, hung vertically by a
thong. For discussion of heraldry see p.47. Square in
section. Cap missing? Associated knife found between
lining and scabbard (No.96). Lining made from four
pieces of leather. See Plate 7 for detail of stamps.

458. (BC72 [88] ⟨2786⟩)
Calf leather, length 153mm, width 26mm. Centre-back
seam with flesh/grain stitches. Decorated by
engraving.
Design elements:
  Front handle: linear.
  Front blade: linear.
  Back: linear.

459. (TL74 [2332] ⟨1942⟩)
Calf leather, length 44mm, width 19mm, lining
projects above the top (grain faces inwards). Side
seam with flesh/grain and edge/grain stitches.
Decorated by engraving.
Design elements:
  Front blade: linear and other motifs.
  Back: linear.
Two suspension slots on the side, hung vertically. Cap
missing? Not for a knife, possibly a needlecase.

460. (BC72 [88] ⟨2948⟩)
Calf leather. Centre-back seam with flesh/grain
stitches. Decorated by engraving and stamping.
Design elements:
  Front blade: linear (engraved), other motif
    (stamping).
  Back: linear (engraved).
Deliberate cut.

461. (CUS73 [II 14] ⟨651⟩)
Calf leather, width 22mm. Side of back seam with
edge/grain stitches. Decorated by engraving.
Design elements:
  Front handle: heraldic and linear.
  Front blade: linear.
  Back: linear.
Four suspension slots on the back. For discussion of
heraldry see p.47.

462. (BC72 [83] ⟨2576⟩)
Calf leather, length 175mm, width 33mm. Side of back
seam with flesh/grain stitches. Decorated by engraving
and stamping.
Design elements:
  Front handle: foliate and linear (engraved), dots and
    zoomorphic (stamped).
  Front blade: foliate, linear and lozenge (engraved),
    dots and fleur-de-lys (stamped).
  Back: linear (engraved).
Four suspension slots on the back, hung vertically.

463. (BC72 [79] ⟨2341⟩)
Calf leather, lining (grain faces inwards). Centre-back
seam with flesh/grain stitches. Two suspension slots
on the back, hung diagonally. Deliberate cut.

Early to mid 15th-century scabbards No.464

The only scabbard from this date range is very similar
to others of early to mid 14th-century date (Nos.414,
417 and 418). It has an additional internal sheath and
small cubes of leather supporting the embossed areas.

464. (TL74 [368] ⟨2612⟩)
Calf leather, length 170mm, width 30mm, lined (grain
faces inwards), second inner scabbard (grain faces
inwards). Side of back seam with flesh/grain stitches;
stitched repair. Decorated by embossing and
engraving.
Design elements:
  Front handle: zoomorphic (embossed), linear and
    zoomorphic (engraved).
  Front blade: zoomorphic (embossed), linear and
    zoomorphic (engraved).
  Back: foliate (embossed), foliate and linear
(engraved).
Embossed areas supported with small cubes of
leather.

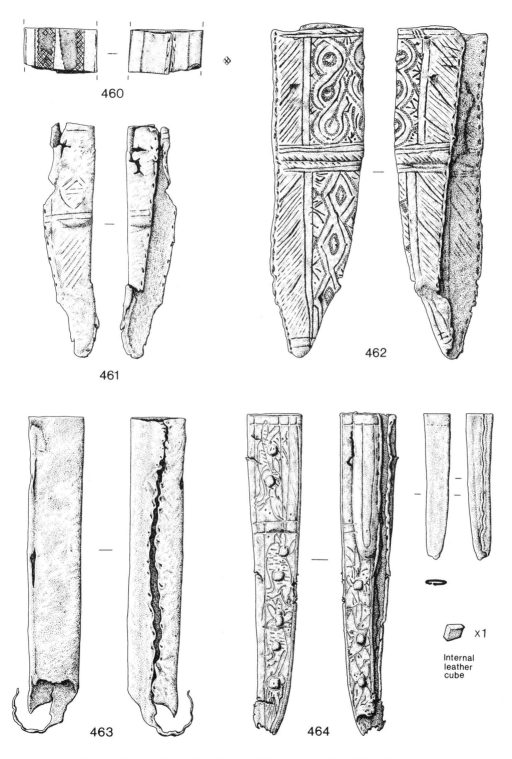

460

461

462

463

464

×1

Internal
leather
cube

99 Scabbards, Nos.460–463 (late 14th century), No.464 (early to mid
15th century). Scale 1:2; detail of stamp 1:1.

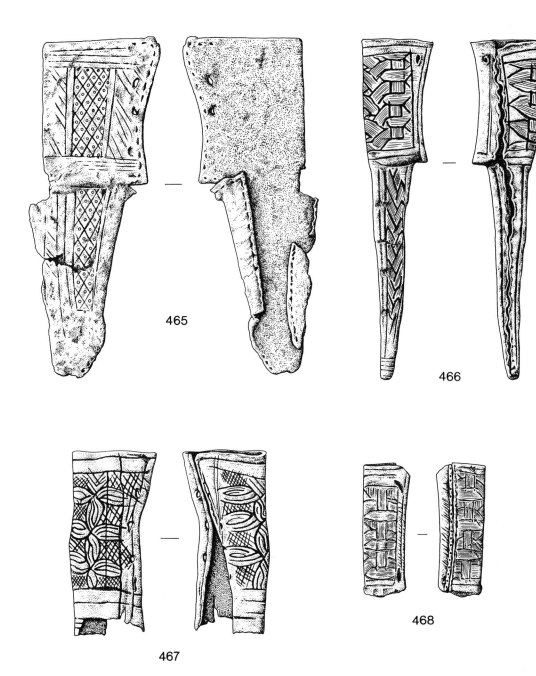

465

466

467

468

100 Scabbards, Nos. 465–468 (unstratified) (467
CLR). Scale 1:2.

UNSTRATIFIED SCABBARDS Nos. 465–491

Twenty-seven unstratified scabbards are included in the catalogue; all are illustrated, including five from the Museum's collections (Nos. 487–491). These include a rondel dagger scabbard and a short sword scabbard for comparison.

465. (SWA81 [+] ⟨4215⟩)
Calf leather. Split seam with flesh/grain and edge/grain stitches. Decorated by engraving and stamping.
Design elements:
Front handle: lattice and linear (engraved), dot stamped).
Front blade: lattice and linear (engraved), dot (stamped).
Back: linear (engraved).
Deliberate cut.

466. (BC72 [+] ⟨46⟩)
Calf leather, length 183mm, width 36mm. Centre-back seam with edge/grain stitches. Decorated by engraving.
Design elements:
Front handle: linear and plaits.
Front blade: linear and plaits.
Back: linear.
One suspension slot on the front and back, hung by a thong.

467. (BIG82 [3134] ⟨2394⟩)
Calf leather, width 45mm. Edge/grain and edge/flesh stitches. Decorated by engraving.
Design elements:
Front handle: plaits and linear.
Back: plaits and linear.
Three suspension slots on the front and back, hung by a thong.

468. (BC72 [+] ⟨2785⟩)
Calf leather, width 26mm.
Side of back seam with edge/grain stitches. Decorated by engraving.
Design elements:
Front handle: linear and plaits.
Back: linear and plaits.
Two suspension slots on the front and back, hung by a thong. Deliberate cut.

469. (CUS73 [+] ⟨835⟩)
Leather, length 196mm, width 57mm. Split seam with edge/grain stitches. Decorated by engraving.
Design elements:
Front handle: linear and plaits.
Front blade: linear and plaits.
Back: linear and plaits.
Four suspension slots on the front and back, hung diagonally by a thong.

470. (BIG82 [2595] ⟨2296⟩)
Calf leather. Side seam with edge/grain stitches. Decorated by engraving and stamping.
Design elements:
Front blade: foliate, linear and zoomorphic (engraved), dot (stamped).
Back: foliate, lozenge and zoomorphic (engraved), dot (stamped).
Deliberate cut.

471. (BIG82 [4177] ⟨2964⟩)
Calf leather. Centre-back seam, edge/grain stitches. Decorated by engraving and stamping.
Design elements:
Front handle: linear and plaits (engraved).
Front blade: linear and other motif (engraved), dot (stamped).
Deliberate cut. Reused. Copper alloy stud near tip associated with reuse.

472. (BC72 [+] ⟨2127⟩)
Calf leather, length 238mm, width 40mm. Side of back seam with edge/grain stitches. Decorated by engraving.
Design elements:
Front handle: foliate, linear and zoomorphic.
Front blade: foliate, linear and zoomorphic.
Back: linear and half quatrefoil.
Four suspension slots on the back, hung by a thong.

473. (BWB83 [+] ⟨157⟩)
Calf leather, length 165mm, width 27mm. Side of back seam with edge/grain stitches. Decorated by embossing and engraving.
Design elements:
Front handle: zoomorphic (embossed), foliate, linear and zoomorphic (engraved).
Front blade: zoomorphic (embossed), foliate, linear and zoomorphic (engraved).
Back: zoomorphic (embossed), linear and zoomorphic (engraved).
Four suspension slots on the back, hung by a thong.

474. (BIG82 [2854] ⟨2376⟩)
Calf leather. Side seam with flesh/grain stitches. Decorated by engraving and stamping.
Design elements:
Front blade: linear (engraved), dots (stamped).
Back: linear (engraved), dots (stamped).
Two suspension slots. Reused?

475. (BWB83 [+] ⟨93⟩)
Calf leather, length 323mm, width 60mm. Centre-back seam with flesh/grain stitches, stitched repair. Decorated by engraving and stamping.
Design elements:
Front handle: linear and zoomorphic (engraved), dot (stamped).
Front blade: linear and zoomorphic (engraved), dot (stamped).
Back: linear (engraved).
Three suspension slots on the back.

476. (SWA81 [+] ⟨4923⟩)
Calf leather, lining? Side of back seam with edge/grain stitches. Deliberate cut.

477. (BC72 [+] ⟨1881⟩)
Sheep/Goat leather, width 38mm, lining (grain faces out). Centre-back seam with flesh/grain stitches.

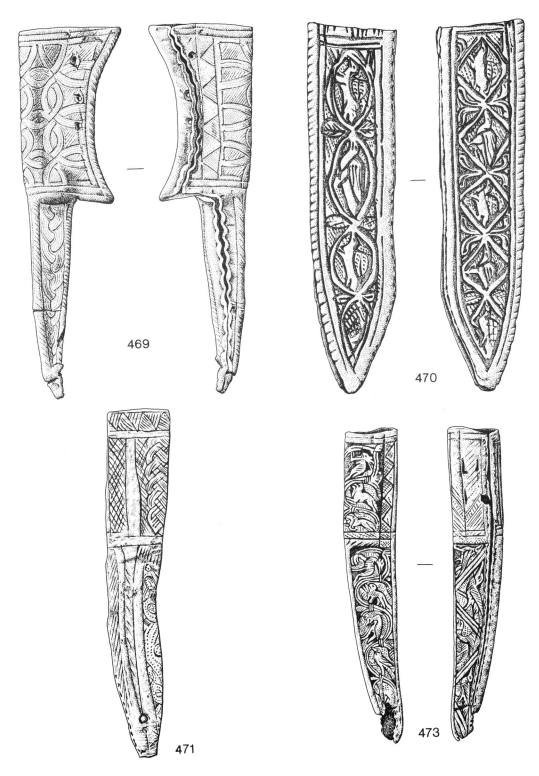

101   Scabbards, Nos. 469–471, 473 (unstratified) (469 JP, 470 CLR). Scale 1:2.

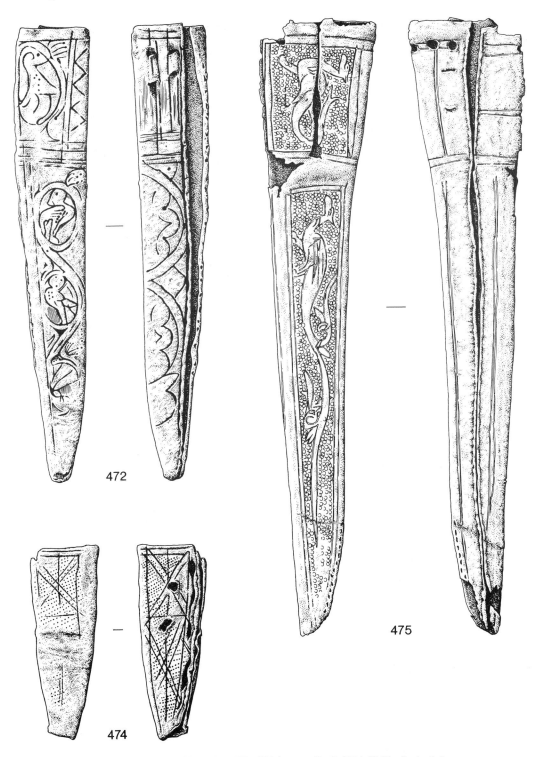

102 Scabbards, Nos. 472, 474–475 (unstratified) (474 CLR). Scale 1:2.

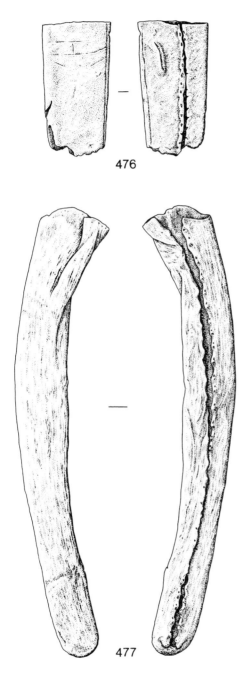

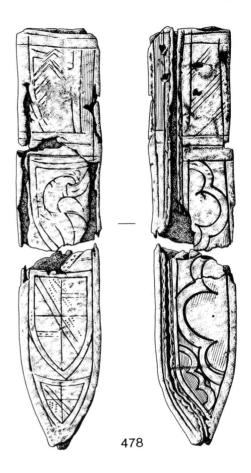

478

103 Scabbards, Nos.476–478 (unstratified). Scale 1:2.

478. (TUD78 [+] ⟨24⟩)
Calf leather, length 282mm. Side of back seam with edge/grain stitches. Decorated by engraving.
Design elements:
    Front handle: heraldic and linear.
    Front blade: heraldic and linear.
    Back: linear and half quatrefoil.
Four suspension slots on the back, hung vertically by a thong. For discussion of heraldry see p.47.

479. (BWB83 [112] ⟨3⟩)
Calf leather, length 218mm, width 45mm. Side seam with edge/grain stitches. Decorating by incising.
Design elements:
    Front handle: foliate and linear.
    Front blade: foliate and linear.
    Back: foliate and linear.
Four suspension slots on the front and back, hung vertically by a thong. Patches of red pigment survive.

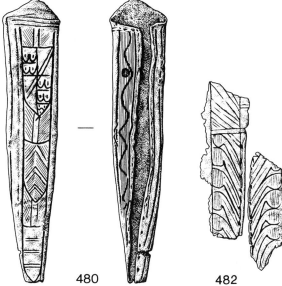

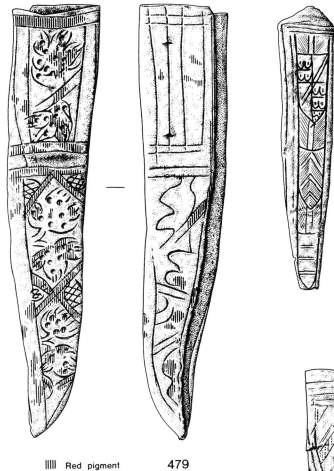

|||| Red pigment   **479**

480 **482**

480. (BC72 [+] ⟨2126⟩)
Calf leather, lined. Centre-back seam with edge/grain stitches. Decorated by engraving.
Design elements:
Front handle: heraldic linear.
Back: linear.
For discussion of heraldry see p.47.
Deliberate cut.

481. (SH74 [436] ⟨137⟩)
Calf leather, length 170mm, width 35mm. Side seam with flesh/grain stitches. Decorated by engraving.
Design elements:
Front handle: heraldic and linear.
Front blade: heraldic and linear.
Back: linear.
Two suspension slots on the front and back, hung by a thong. For discussion of heraldry see p.47.
Reused.

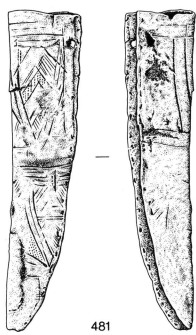

481

104 Scabbards, Nos.479–482 (unstratified). Scale 1:2.

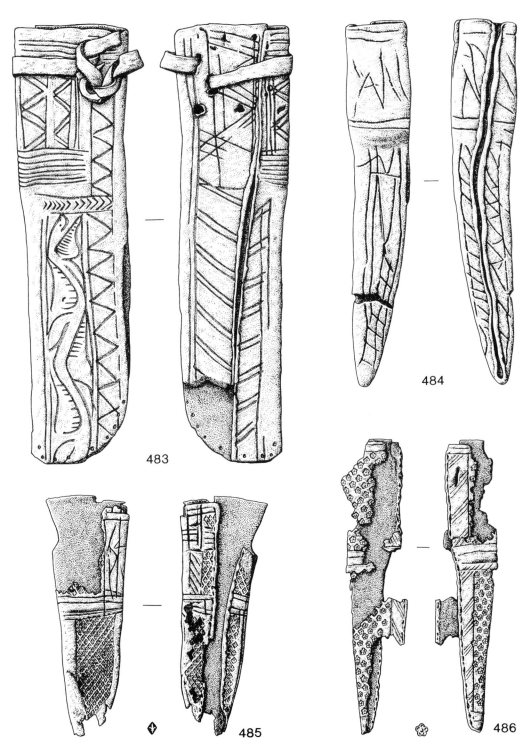

105 Scabbards, Nos. 483–486 (unstratified) (483–4 CLR, 485 SM). Scale
1:2; details of stamps 1:1.

PLATE 22
Scabbard No.486: detail of cinquefoil within lozenge stamps, and engraved line decoration overlying stamps.

487

488

489

490

||||| Red pigment

106 Scabbards, Nos. 487–490 (Museum of London Reserve Collection). Scale 1:2.

482. (LH74 [F 66] ⟨74⟩)
Calf leather. Centre-back seam with flesh/grain stitches. Decorated by engraving..
Design elements:
Back: foliate and linear.

483. (BIG82 [2595] ⟨2335⟩)
Calf leather, length 210mm, width 53mm. Centre-back seam with flesh/grain and edge/grain stitches. Decorated by engraving.
Design elements:
Front handle: linear.
Front blade: foliate and linear.
Back: linear.
Six suspension slots on the front and back, hung by a thong. Reused. The thong is threaded through only four of the six slots.

484. (BIG82 [1914] ⟨2046⟩)
Calf leather, length 185mm, width 31mm. Centre-back seam with edge/grain stitches. Decorated by engraving.
Design elements:
Front handle: linear.
Front blade: linear.
Back: linear.
Four suspension slots on the back, hung vertically by a thong.

485. (TL74 [2466] ⟨3292⟩)
Calf leather. Centre-back seam with edge/grain stitches. Decorated by engraving and stamping.
Design elements:
Front handle: linear (engraved), fleur-de-lys (stamped).
Front blade: linear (engraved), fleur-de-lys (stamped).
Back: linear (engraved), fleur-de-lys (stamped).
Four suspension slots on the back, hung vertically by a thong?

486. (CUS73 [III 17] ⟨513⟩)
    Calf leather, length 157mm. Side of back seam with
    edge/grain stitches. Decorated by engraving and
    stamping.
    Design elements:
        Front handle: linear (engraved), rosette (stamped).
        Front blade: linear (engraved), rosette (stamped).
        Back: linear (engraved), rosette (stamped).
    See Plate 22 for detail of stamp and engraved line
    decoration.

487. (MOL L30–13457)
    Side of back seam with edge/grain stitches. Decorated
    by incising.
    Design elements:
        Front blade: linear and foliate.
        Back: linear and foliate.
    Four suspension slots at the side, hung vertically by a
    thong. Red pigment visible. Deliberate cut.

488. (MOL 4658)
    Centre-back seam with edge/grain stitches. Decorated
    by engraving.
    Design elements:
        Front handle: lozenge and fleur-de-lys.
        Front blade: lozenge, heraldic, fleur-de-lys and
            castles.
    Scabbard for rondel dagger.

489. (MOL 4643)
    Centre-back seam with edge/grain stitches. Decorated
    by engraving, stamping and embossing.
    Design elements:
        Front handle: zoomorphic (engraved and
            embossed); linear (engraved); dots (stamped).
        Front blade: zoomorphic (engraved and embossed);
            linear (engraved); dots (stamped).
    Pricked background decoration.

490. (MOL 4662)
    Centre-back seam with edge/grain stitches. Decorated
    by engraving and stamping.
    Design elements:
        Front handle: heraldic and dots (stamped); linear
            and lozenges (engraved).
        Front blade: heraldic and dots (stamped); lozenges
            and foliate (engraved).
    See Plates 23–25 for details of decoration.

491. (MOL 38.319)
    Decorating by engraving.
    Design elements:
        Front blade: linear.
    Two internal scabbards. Sword scabbard.

PLATE 23
Scabbard No.490: detail of upper part
showing eagle displayed within a lozenge
stamps, and circle and line decoration.

PLATE 24
Scabbard No.490: detail of central part, showing two addorsed birds and tree in lozenge motif stamps, and circle and line decoration.

PLATE 25
Scabbard No. 490: detail of lower part
showing lion passant stamps within scrolls,
and circle and line decoration.

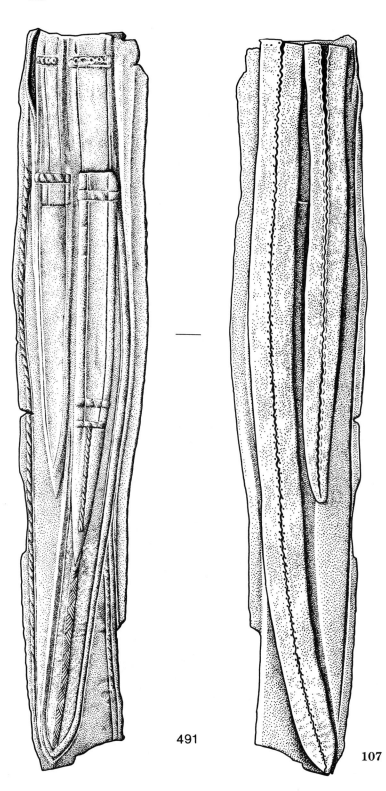

491

107 Scabbard, No. 491 (Museum of London
Reserve Collection). Scale 1:2.

Addenda

Post-excavation work on the finds and stratigraphy of the waterfront excavations is still continuing, indeed as new classes of artefact are studied in depth they may yield further information on the relative or absolute date of the deposits in which they were found. Consequently, in the interval between preparation of this report and its final publication there have been several modifications to the dating of individual artefacts. These arise through two processes. Firstly, archaeological contexts which initially could not be related to datable structures have now been assigned to their proper place in the sequence. Secondly, re-examination of the information relating to individual layers has in a few cases lead to their supposed position in the excavated sequence being changed. In total these changes affect 55 out of the 491 artefacts catalogued here. These revisions do not affect the conclusions drawn from the finds but are presented here in order to provide the most accurate information available. The complete excavation archive is available for study at the Museum of London.

Late 12th century
2 – early 13th
7 – early 13th
9 – early 13th
10 – early 13th
311 – early 13th
372 – early 13th

Early to mid 14th century
54 – late 13th
68 – late 14th
369 – late 14th

Late 14th century
72 – early 15th
87 – late 13th to early 14th
97 – late 13th to early 14th
112 – early 15th
116 – early 15th
145 – early 15th
152 – late 13th to early 14th
154 – early 15th
158 – late 13th to early 14th
160 – early 15th
174 – early 15th
182 – late 13th to early 14th
183 – early 15th
186 – early 15th

216 – early 15th
217 – early 15th
218 – early 15th
223 – late 13th to early 14th
231–37 – early 15th
240 – late 13th to early 14th
310 – late 13th to early 14th
327 – early 15th
338 – late 13th to early 14th
343 – late 13th to early 14th
354 – early 15th
355 – early 15th

Early to mid 15th century
253–55 – late 14th
277 – late 14th
279 – late 14th

Unstratified
281 – late 14th
284 – mid 13th
289 – early 13th
290 – early 15th
303 – late 14th
362 – mid 14th
371 – late 13th to early 14th
467 – early 13th
471 – late 12th